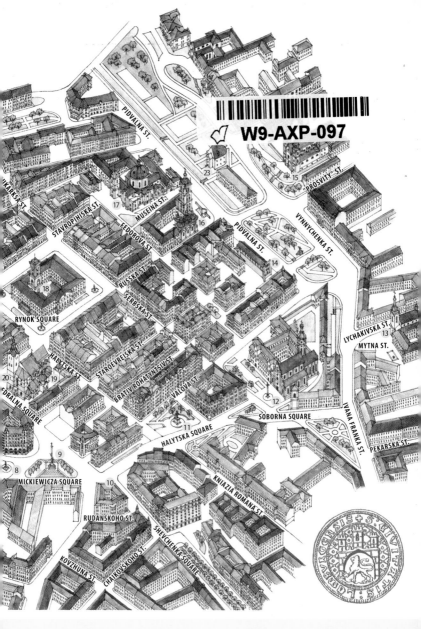

W9-AXP-097

GUIDE BOOK

TOURING
LVIV

BALTIJA DRUK

Kiev 2005

Guide Book "Touring Lviv" TM

ISBN 966-8137-08-6

Authors:
Ihor Liljo, Zoriana Liljo-Otkovych
Translated into English
by Katherine Kobushkina

Published by **"Baltija Druk"**
Director General
Ruta Malikenaite
Editor-in Chief
Virginijus Strolya

Executive Editor
Alisa Hryhoruk
Art work by
Olena Zhelezniak

Photography by **Viktor Khmara**,
Serhij Tarasov, **Olena Zhelezniak**,
Volodymyr Petrynenko
Axonometry by **Yaroslav Martynyuk**

Design by
Stanislav Stepanovych
Layout by
Volodymyr Sulzhenko

Proof-read by **Myrov Kapral**

Maps by the State Scientific-Production
Enterprise "Kartografiya" ("Cartography")

© **"Baltija Druk", 2005**

Published with the support
of the Ukrainian State Tourist Board

"Baltija Druk"
51/2, Barbusa Street, Kiev, Ukraine, 03150
tel. +380 44 502 1047, 502 1048
e-mail: baltija@ukr.net
www.baltija.com.ua

State Register of Publishers; certificate No
DK 643 issued 10.23.2001 by the Ukrainian
State Committee for Information Policy,
Television and Broadcasting

The authors and the publisher made
every effort to ensure that the information
given in this guidebook is accurate as of
May 2005. However, telephone numbers,
prices and oopening and closing hours are
subject to change.

CONTENTS

TIPS FOR THE TOURIST

Once upon a time, a Paris train and a Moscow train stopped at a railway station in a large and ancient town in the center of Europe. Two travelers were enjoying the view of the town they were passing by. "I am in the East at last", - the French traveler thought. "Here I am, in the West", - the Russian traveler exclaimed. This old tale is about Lviv, the city where the ardors of the mysterious East and the sounds of the romantic West intertwine with the expressiveness of the South and tranquility of the North.

When the Ukrainian King Danylo presented the city to his son Lev, nobody could have imagined how powerful the city would be in the future. During its 750 year-long "official" history Lviv has undergone numerous adventures. Ukrainian, Polish, Austrian, German and Soviet rulers changed the city's appearance, adjusting it to their own needs. Each new governor would give the city a new name: Lviv, Leopolis, Lwow, Lemberg, Lvov. However, the local population always treasured the history of their native town and, regardless of its turbulent past, Lviv managed to preserve its unique identity.

May be it was for St. George's intercession, who had been chosen the city guardian angel, that Lviv escaped many hardships. Today Lviv is one of the most important political, economic and cultural centers of Ukraine and Central-Eastern Europe. In 1999 UNESCO proclaimed Lviv part of the world cultural heritage.

The history of the ancient and at the same time modern Lviv abounds in legends. Each day, each minute it is waiting for an eager listener to open up its mysteries. Having visited the city once, you will always want to visit it again and again, to stay there just for one day, to plunge into the streams of a spring or autumn rain, to marvel at the whirlwind of falling leaves in Stryisky park, or to find oneself in a winter fairy-tale in the High Castle Mountain.

Once again the clock on the City Hall tower would chime for you only. For more than 150 years it has been guarding the peace and quiet of the city. Having learned yet another of its legends, you may try and lose your way in the narrow intertwining streets of the old town. Stop by one of the numerous cozy coffee shops and have a cup of their famous coffee. Enjoy the aromatic drink and listen to the soft sounds of the city by night.

About half of all the architectural sights in Ukraine are concentrated in Lviv. Only here the Armenian quarter neighbors the Catholic district, and the Ukrainian quarter streets interlace with Jewish locality. Strolling leisurely along the underground river of Poltva you will reach the famous Opera House, and from the Opera House you will climb the top of Visoky Zamok (High Castle) Mountain. And there, enjoying the panoramic view of the city, you will understand why its numerous guests compare it to Paris and Rome, and the locals call it the Great Lviv.

Haven't you ever heard about the giant lion, which lived in a cave in Sviatoyurska (St. George) Mountain? And you don't know anything about the white vampire that terrified the local chimneysweepers? You have never been told the romantic and at the same time tragic story of Galshka from Ostrih? Then a trip to Lviv is a must. It is a unique city and its inhabitants will cordially welcome you.

History
in facts and figures

It seems that sledges of the north
and ocean liners bring all the
treasures of the world to this
border town

Sebastian Klonowicz

A view of Lviv. A. Pasarotti

Lviv was founded on the dry bare Podillia bank and the marshy valley of the Poltva River. It is believed that the founder of the city was Russian King Danylo Romanovych, who named the town after his son Lev (Lviv in Ukrainian means belonging to Lev) and gave it to him as a present. It is surmised that ancient Lviv consisted of three parts: the fortification, the upper and lower districts. The fortress was located on the top of the mountain, which in the 15th century was called Horay, but in the chronicles of 17th century it was already known as Lysa (Bald). The mountain was separated from Visoky Zamok Mountain by a deep ravine that was filled up in 1830-1840. The fortress was fortified by ramparts, barricades of felled trees and paling. However, the strong winds made Prince Lev move his castle to a different location. The town, built on the trade route between the Baltic and the Black seas, continued to thrive. The Halych-Lviv-Kholm route passed by the Old Market. Numerous churches and monasteries decorated the ancient town; some of them, though reshaped and redesigned, have survived till the present. The old town was densely populated – there were German, Armenian and Tartar communities, each easily recognized by the unique architecture of houses and chapels, by gardens and orchards. Fields and hayfields were on the other bank of the Poltva. The ancient town covered about 50 hectares and bordered the village of Znesinnia in the East.

THE CITY OF LEV

The first written evidence about Lviv dates back to the year 1256. The chronicler recalls a major conflagration that could be seen "from Lviv". Lviv was an important political and economic center of the Halychyna and Volhyn Principality. King Danylo was a wise ruler. Regardless of the difficult political circumstances he still managed to reach agreement with his enemies - the Tartars in the

Monument to
King Danylo

East and restless neighbors in the West – and if need be he would not linger to resort to force. His son, Lev, moved his capital from Przemysl to Lviv and fortified the city. He maintained the tradition established by his father to invite to Lviv people of all nationalities, especially Germans and "people from the East", thus giving the boost to handicraft and trade. It should be mentioned here, that during its long history the city has often suffered from natural disasters. Many times Lviv was destroyed by fire, and each time it rose from the ashes like Phoenix to once again reveal itself in all its glory.

Much water has flowed under the bridges since the city's foundation. And it is the water that poses the most fascinating of the town's mysteries. Partly, it is attributed to the fact that the only river in Lviv, the Poltva, like the mythical Styx, flows in the darkness of underground crypts under the city's main street. People say that when it rains, one can find a mysterious house somewhere by the railway station. The water that drips from the right side of its roof runs into the Baltic Sea, and from the left side – into the Black Sea. The legend could be explained by the fact that the city is situated right in the middle of the main watershed in Europe.

The city's very geographical position destined it to be the meeting place for East and West, North and South. In the old days only two towns, Halych and Przemysl, could rival Lviv. In 1274 Lviv became the capital of the Halychyna and Volhyn Principality. The contender to the Byzantine throne, Andronikos, sought shelter in Halychyna. In 1240 on their

King Lev

1256
the first written evidence of Lviv.

1340
the death of the last Halychyna Prince and the beginning of Polish reign in Lviv.

1363
the establishment of the Armenian Metropolia.

1379
Lviv was granted the "storehouse" right.

1527
a conflagration devastated the downtown area.

1572
the construction of the church of the Dormition of the Holy Virgin (also known as Russka or Voloska church).

January 5, 1585
the establishment of the Lviv Orthodox Fraternity.

March 4, 1629
the Lviv merchant Bandinelli was granted a permit to conduct mail-delivering services.

October 22, 1648
Cossacks under the command of Bohdan Khmelnytsky assaulted and conquered the Vysoky Zamok fortress.

April 1, 1656
King Jan Kazimierz made a pledge to protect the city.

1658
Lviv's nobilitation.

1661
the foundation of Lviv University.

September 26, 1672
the Turkish army besieged Lviv.

September 4, 1704
the troops of King Karl XII assaulted and plundered the city.

1761
St. Yura's (George's) church was completed.

way to Western Europe the tartar troops burned the largest cities of the Halychyna Principality to ashes. In 1261 Khan Burundai ordered King Lev to demolish the fortification walls around Lviv, and King Lev had no other choice but to perform the order. However, in 1283 the newly erected fortifications protected the city from another assault by the Golden Horde.

THE HIGH CASTLE

In 1360 King Kazimierz the Great built the High Castle on the mountain right next to the place where the Princes' castle once stood. It was there behind the strong wooden paling where the treasury, the arsenal and the archives with the most important documents were kept.

The mould commemorating the Lublin Union

Detail of a grotto on Vysoky Zamok (High Castle) Mountain

The subsequent owners of the castle reshaped it and faced it with stone. Some premises of the High Castle were used as a prison for the disobedient gentry. In 1410 the knights of the Teutonic order, that had been captured prisoners in the Grunwald battle, were kept in its vaults. The Polish poet S.Klonowicz, in his verses about the High Castle, wrote that its towers support Heaven and its vaults reach Hell. Yet, despite its favorable location the Castle suffered bad luck. After the 1648 assault by the Cossacks commanded by M. Kryvonis, and the 1704 attack by the Swedish army the building was badly damaged and in 1772

Franciszek Smolka

the Austrian government ordered its remains demolished. Nowadays, only a small part of the fortification on Visoky Zamok (High Castle) Mountain (413 meters above sea level) reminds us about the turbulent past. By the debris of the walls there is a mound commemorating the 1569 Lublin Union (the agreement under which Poland and the Great Principality of Lithuania united and formed the Rech Pospolita State), which nowadays also serves as a viewing area. The mound was constructed in 1869-1900. One of the initiators of the project was the famous Polish public figure Franciszek Smolka (1810-1899). The soil and stones for the

The High Castle.
Anonymous artist

monument were brought from the adjacent Prince's mountain. In the mound Polish patriots installed a capsule containing the soil from the battlefield at Rac-lawicami as well as bits of A. Mickiewicz's and J. Slow-ack's coffins.

ROYAL PRESENT

Few edifices survived since the times when princes ruled the land. Leg-ends say that the Church of

The Church of John the Baptist

St. John the Baptist on Stary Rynok (Old Market) Square was built especially for King Lev's wife Constance, a Hungarian Princess. Some burial remains dating back to the Prince's times were discovered during the restoration works of the church's foundation. In 1886 the architect Yu. Zakharevych reconstructed the church in pseudo Romanesque style that intertwines with the architectural fragments of the 17th century. In 1989 the church was turned into the museum of ancient Lviv and is now a branch of the Lviv picture gallery. In the soviet days, if a rare foreign tourist happened to come to the "closed" city of Lviv (under the Soviet rule some cities were closed for tourists for safety purposes; one could visit them only if he had permission issued by military authori-ties), it was recommended he saw, among few other sacral edifices in town, the church of St. John.

THE CHURCH OF ST. NICHOLAS

The Church of St. Nicholas is yet another relic of the times of the Principality. The church is the oldest in town. Its foundation dates back to the 13th century. Thick walls and tiny narrow windows evince that it could have been used as a fortress. The church was built in the form of a Greek cross with a round apse. It was richly decorated inside, but unfortunately, none of the ancient fresco survived. The paintings, which adorn the church today, were

September 19, 1772
Austrian troops conquered Lviv. Halychyna became part of the Austrian Empire.

1773
publication of the first issue of "Gazette de Leopoli", the first newspaper in Lviv.

1777
the Austrian authorities ordered the old city fortifica-tions pulled down.

January 21, 1786
the first burial in Lychakivske cemetery.

July 11, 1792
the first hot-air balloon with a person on board was launched in Lviv.

April 11, 1811
publication of the first issue of the "Gazeta Lwowska" newspaper.

June 4, 1817
the establishment of the Ossolinskys Foundation (Stefanik Library).

July 14, 1826
the City Hall collapsed for the second time.

St. Nicholas's Church

executed in 1955-1957. According to some sources, the church was built as a burial vault for Halychyna princes. For an extended period of time it was the main spiritual sanctuary for Russins in Lviv. The church was under the auspices of Prince Lev. It had a favorable location in the old town. The church is situated on Bohdana Khmelnytskoho Street (former Zhovkivska Street), which has always been one of the central streets in Lviv.

DMYTRO DEDKO

Dmytro Dedko

Princes were not only fighting outside enemies, but also trying to reach understanding with the local gentry. Unlike boyars in Kiev, the Halychyna gentry remained independent, and some of them even owned salt-mines in the Carpathians. Salt-mine ownership could be compared to owning an oil well nowadays. In some cases boyars could even choose a bride for the Prince. However, in hard times some of the boyars, setting aside their personal interests, would step in and take action. Such was boyar Dmytro Dedko, who, after the last prince Yuri II Troidenowych had been poisoned, assumed power in 1340 and headed the almost independent boyars' government of the Halychyna and Volhyn Princedom. The boyars' government ruled the town till 1349, when Lviv fell under the administration of King Kazimierz III the Great.

Kazimierz III the Great

The Boims' chapel.
A. Kamenobrodzki

LVIV UNDER THE RULE OF POLAND

On April 7, 1340, Kazimierz the Great, one of the most prominent Polish kings, assaulted and seized the town, confiscated the treasury, and thus determined Lviv's fate to be a part of the Polish Kingdom for several centuries ahead. A few years later, after the old town was completely decimated by the attack conducted by the Lithuanian Prince Lubart, King Kazimierz moved the city closer to the bank of the Poltva River. It was King Kazimierz who reinforced the privileges of Magdeburg Law given to the Lviv's German community.

To facilitate the development of the city, the King encouraged merchants and craftspeople to settle in Lviv. In the 15th century Lviv was called "the Eastern Gate" of the Polish

State, while Krakow was considered "the Western Gate". During the period when Lviv belonged to Poland and Lithuania, the city saw rapid economic growth. The vast majority of the population of Northern Rome (as Lviv was called at that time) were engaged in trade with the East. In the fierce struggle for power, Lviv won the right to be a "storehouse",

The remains of old stone-pavement on one of the Lviv lanes

i.e. all the merchants traveling through the city had to stop in Lviv for two weeks selling their goods to the locals. The City Council had their own weights and the police to help them supervise the trade. All the Lviv's most important privileges were written down in "the Golden Book", that is now stored in the city archives.

The Lviv's market looked very animated in those days. The local chemist Johan Alnpeck stated in his "Chronicles", that on the Market Place one could see a crowd of merchants, flocking to the city from all over Europe and Asia. Most of the vendors were Greeks, Turks, Armenians, Tartars, Hungarians, Germans and Italians. A Lviv saying goes that when a Greek merchant was trading, two Jewish vendors were crying, but when an Armenian merchant came to the market, two Greeks would burst into tears. It was the fierce competition and national diversity that formed Lviv's unique character.

In 1527 the city was completely destroyed by fire and was later rebuilt in the Renaissance style. Only one building survived in the flames and the

Water-pipes in Lviv

1848
Lviv University library and City Hall were burnt down during street fights.

January 4, 1849
the first professional fire brigades were organized.

May 3, 1851
the new clock was installed on the City Hall tower. This day was proclaimed the City Hall visiting day for the bourgeois.

July 14, 1853
the discovery of the gas lamp by the pharmaceutical chemists Ihnaty Lukasesych and Johan Zekh.

1861
the completion of Lviv-Kharkiv railway line.

February 1, 1879
the agreement was reached to start horse-drawen tram system.

August 1, 1894
General Halychyna Exhibition.

September 13, 1896
the first presentation of "moving pictures" in the Hartman's arcade.

1897
first cars appear on Lviv streets.

1900
the inauguration of Lviv Opera House.

January 13, 1901
the curtain by Semiradsky first dropped over the Opera House stage.

March 26, 1904
the inauguration of the Lviv Railway Station.

December 13, 1905
Metropolitan Andriy Sheptytsky handed over the Lviv National Museum to the city community.

1906
the introduction of traffic regulations, drivers' licenses and car registration numbers

The interior of the
Armenian Cathedral

Armenian crosses,
the khachkars

inhabitants of Lviv attributed this fact to the protection of Holy Mary. According to approximate estimates the population of Lviv in those days was about twenty-five to thirty thousand people, which made it one of the largest cities in Central Eastern Europe. The main institution of local government – the Rada – gained much popularity. The elections to the Rada took place each year, and the government was obliged to report annually to the merchants. Lviv was one of the first towns in Europe equipped with water and sewage systems. The present-day tradition of paving streets with stone goes back to the 15th century. Soon professional associations, otherwise known as guilds, increased their significance in the life of the town. In the 16th-17th centuries Lviv inhabitants were involved in about 133 different trades and formed more than 30 guilds. Jewelers, hatters and smiths were famous far beyond the city's borders.

The very history of Lviv determined it to be the city of three Christian Churches: Latin (the head of the local Catholic Church moved from Halych in 1412), Orthodox and Armenian. In addition to this, since the 15th century more Jews were settling in the city and by the 16th century the Jewish population averaged 25 % of Lviv's total population.

Despite the declared democratic and transparent city development there were times

An old watchmaker's shop

when non Lviv-born families ruled the city, some of them coming from as far as Poland. The families of Boim, Campiani, Scholtz-Wolfovych set up their own rules, built family vaults, increased their wealth and… gradually disappeared among the newcomers from Scotland, Italy, France, Germany and the Balkan Peninsular.

EAST-WEST

Armenians came to Halychyna long before the first written evidence of Lviv appeared. Having settled in Lviv, they

created an influential community that enjoyed one of the most important rights of the Middle Ages – the right to legal autonomy. The community built a church and a school. In 1616 Ovanes Karmataniants published "The Book of Psalms". Armenian merchants were one of the richest people in Lviv and because of their knowledge of oriental languages and innate hatred toward the Turks they were as-

An Armenian courtyard.
A. Kamenobrodzki

signed to diplomatic missions as secret agents. In wartimes the Armenian youth bravely defended the city, as the elderly Armenians claimed "they got used to danger and handling weapons from their early childhood". The Armenians always valued their right to remain independent. Once having resided in Lviv, they soon established their own district, with the main street being Virmentska (Armenian) Street.

"THERE ARE FEW RUSSINS, BUT TOO MUCH OF RUSS"

With the change of the ruling power, the Ukrainians (Russins) lost their right to practice some professions, especially trading and certain crafts. Despite frequent religious disagreements, which often entailed serious conflicts, the Orthodox community flocked around the Stavropogiali Orthodox Fraternity and the Church of the Dormition of the Holy Virgin and never ceased to be engaged in all sorts of social activities. Like any other ethnic community, the Ukrainians owned a school, a hospital and a publishing house. The

1914-1915
Russian occupation.

August 2, 1922
the first Warsaw-Lviv flight on "Junkers F-13".

February 2, 1930
Kristina Gotlinger from Lviv won the "Miss Poland" competition.

1930
the launch of broadcasting in Lviv.

October 22, 1933
the member of the Ukrainian Nationalists Organization M. Lemik assassinated the USSR diplomat Mailov, thus protesting against the man-made famine of 1932-1933.

October 29, 1939
following the declaration of the Western Ukraine representatives' meeting in the Opera House, the Western Ukraine joined the USSR.

The Church of the Dormition of the Holy Virgin

A stone statue of a monk
of the Bernardine order decorating the pediment of the former Bernardine church

congregation received considerable moral and financial assistance from the Moldovan and Muscovite States. In 1586 Patriarch Joachim of Antioch ratified the Fraternity's Charter and empowered them to guard other Orthodox communities. The Ukrainians made their presence in town known by means of the "Cyril" bell, placed on an elegant Renaissance belfry that had been erected by the Greek architect Cyril Korniakt. It was the loudest bell in town and the monks of the Dominican order often complained to the City Rada that the chime impeded them while conducting their services. It was in Lviv that the Russian emigrant Ivan Fedorovych (Fedorov) printed the Book of the Apostles in 1574.

UNIVERSITY

The 15th century saw the mass arrival of representatives of different monastic orders. They built their churches in the old part of the city and in the neighboring districts. When monks of the Heart of Jesus Order (better known as the Jesuit Order) arrived in the town, they were literally broke, but personal contacts and successful administration helped them gather wealth, and some hundred years later they were already known to be giving loans to the City Treasury. In 1661 they founded the first University in Lviv, where students mastered the five liberal arts. One of the most prominent alumni of Lviv Jesuit University was Bohdan Khmelnytsky.

ENTERTAINMENT IN LVIV

"The Apostles", early printed edition by Ivan Fedorov

Lviv was famous all over Europe for the entertainment it offered. 1622 was marked by one long week of celebrations on Rynok (Market) Square. Once dusk fell over the town, the representatives of all gilds, dressed in festive attires, poured out onto the Square carrying flags to nominate the most beautiful women, the beauty queens. Then, the merry god Bacchus invited the bravest to test their strength and drain a huge goblet of wine without dropping drunk. After that, the astonished audience marveled at the moving stars, nailed to rotating circles. Then, a band of laughing dancers, musicians and athletes burst into the crowd. This was followed by huge trays and salvers brought from the City Hall, and boned gammons, frankfurters and pork sausages tossed to the public. Giant Mahomet, Calvin, Luther and Arius walked on stilts along the streets, sending meaningful glances at young ladies, who, feeling spring in the air, flung opened their windows. By the end of the performance people gathered by the City Hall and, encouraged by loud applauses and cheerful shouts, dragged down a basket with confetti off the City Hall tower and burned it. And finally, when the clock struck midnight and an orchestra struck the first chords of some beautiful music, the City Hall Tower glittered with bright festive lights. Fireballs, lights and "Volcano pots" were thrown up in the air. At the same time dozens of people were watching the performance from the roofs, holding

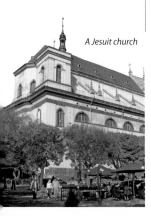

A Jesuit church

buckets of water, ready to prevent a fire. Everybody was having a good time and not just those with thick wallets or at the helm.

LVIV'S MYSTICISM

The 17th century was a turbulent time for Lviv. Cossacks' and peasants' wars against the Poles and tartars, tartars' frequent attacks, epidemics, Polish gentry's riots, all this exhausted Lviv. In addition to all the mishaps, a large Turkish army with their ally Cossack troops led by Hetman (General) Doroshenko, made an attempt to storm the town in 1672. After the Turks had seized Kamianets-Podilsky, the Sultan boastfully pronounced that one eye of the Polish Kingdom had been pricked out and Lviv's defeat would open up the way to Warsaw. The battle at Lviv was to settle the fate of the Polish Crown. During one of the assaults a cannon ball flew over the city-walls, broke a stained-glass window in the Catholic cathedral, landed by the altar, but never exploded. People viewed this as a miracle. Soon the cannon ball was hung on one of the cathedral walls and a plaque, certifying the veracity of the event, was put next to it. Lviv thanked those who had assaulted them by naming one of its streets after Hetman Doroshenko.

A cannon ball in a Cathedral's wall

THE SWEDES IN LVIV

The Lviv fortification withstood twenty-four sieges and not even once was the town taken by storm. It managed to preserve its treasures and mysteries. It was only in 1704 that the Swedish King Karl XII conquered Lviv and plundered the City Treasury. As the legend goes, during the assault one of the city defenders hiding on the Korniakta tower shoot an arrow and knocked the King's hat off his head. Either this little incident, or money shortage made the King order his soldiers to ravage the town. On the Lviv gates the Swedes hanged several rabbis and made other Jews fill baskets, placed by those hanged, with gold. In a couple of hours the demands of the Swedes were granted. The Swedes did not hesitate to raid the famous collection of Oriental carpets and arms from the City Hall. It had taken several centuries to gather the unique exhibits. To make a little more money, the

June 30, 1941
  the declaration of the
  Ukrainian State reconstruction.

1941
  German occupation.

1943
  the extermination
  of the Jewish ghetto.

March 6, 1946
  the pseudo-synod of the
  Russian Orthodox Church
  declared the Greek Catholic
  Church illegal.

November 27, 1952
  the launch of the first trolley
  bus line in Lviv.

1955
  the inauguration of the new
  airport in Lviv.

February 7, 1956
  the production of the first "Lviv"
  bus at the Lviv bus factory.

December 24, 1957
  the first broadcasting of Lviv
  local television channel.

Swedish King Karl XII

ABOUT THE CITY
EXECUTOR THE UNKIND

The 18th century marked one of the most tumultuous periods in the town's history. Feudal lords made an attempt to deprive the town inhabitants of their most precious possession – the autonomy of their town. Many feudal lords, granted with land estates within the town boundaries, refused to pay taxes; yet, they did not hesitate to use the city communications, build new enterprises and move their vassals into town. The locals tried to resist the lords. The servants of the King's governor aroused the

The emphyteusis emblem notifying the general tenancy right on a house down Staroevreiska Street

most virulent hatred among Lviv inhabitants. Once, during another of the governor's unscheduled tax collection raids, the guardians of one of the Lviv city-gates bang-closed the gate behind the governor's suite and broke legs of several of his servants. A long string of lawsuits drained the City Treasury and emptied the pockets of city inhabitants. Nobody bothered any longer to sweep the streets. For centuries the head janitor had been responsible for keeping the town clean and tidy. However, with time he was replaced by the city executor, better known among the locals as the "Unkind". He didn't wear any special uniform, unlike other civil agents, but anyone could tell when the Unkind was approaching their quarters, as a distinguished stench would precede his arrival. It is hard to say how the history of Lviv would have developed, if the neighboring states had not torn apart the falling Kingdom of Poland. In 1772 Lviv fell under rule of the Empire of Austria. The Austrians called it Lemberg.

soldiers resorted to various tricks, like charging fees for crossing streets. The Swedes decimated Lviv and when they finally left, the epidemic of cholera was raging through the town.

GOOD OLD AUSTRIA

On September 19, 1772, Austrian troops marched into Lviv. People say, that when

The defense of Lviv against the Swede's assault

the Austrian ruler Maria Teresa was signing the decree of Poland's division, she was crying. The Prussian King Frederick II made an apt observation about her behavior: "She was crying, yet taking". Promptly after the new governors assumed office they formed the main state institutions. The old Magdeburg laws were repealed. Lviv became the capital of Royal territory of Halychyna and Volodymerii. In the 19th century a palace for the Governor was built; and in the same century, in 1861 the Halychyna Seym was constucted. Austrian administrative officials sought appointments to Lviv. In 1777 a decree was issued to demolish the remains of the old fortification walls and the general city development plan was approved. The local cultural centers reached a new, European level. Young people received an oppor-

Austrian Empress Maria Teresa

tunity to acquire education in the best universities in the country. At the same time, fortune hunters and adventurers flocked to Lviv in hope of finding new ways to demonstrate their talents. Anyone fluent in German was sure to make a brilliant career and make a handsome fortune even in the poorest province of the Empire. Legend goes that it was then when the following funny story occurred. A local noble lady, accompanied by her friend, an Austrian official, was approached by two beggars. One was local, the other

– German. The first tramp got a copper, the latter – a silver coin. As she explained it to her astonished friend, "tomorrow the German beggar might become a high official" and she wanted to make sure he remembered her.

FIRST TIME IN LVIV

The first Lviv newspaper, the "Gazette de Leopoli" was published on Lychakivska Street in 1773, and the first edition of the famous "Gazeta Lwowska" was presented to the world in 1811. Austrian authorities were building new roads,

A city police department in Lviv. Ya. Bauer, 1814

banks, and enterprises. The first gas lamp, the invention of two pharmacists Ignatsi Lukasevych and Johan Zeh, was lit in the "By the Golden Star" drugstore in 1853. The opening of the railway line between Lviv and Krakow in 1861, became a landmark event in Lviv's history. The railway station itself was inaugurated in 1904. The Austrian and Hungarian Empire became the third largest in the world based on the amount of oil pumped in two towns close to Lviv, Drohobych and Boryslav.

In 1897 city authorities took a loan of several millions to construct some important civic buildings. Thus, in 1900 they completed the construction of the Opera House. In 1894 the first electric tram traveled down the city streets in celebration of the opening of the General Halychyna Exhibition. In 1881 the professor of Lviv and Krakow universities, Ludwik Rydygier, performed the first successful operation on a stomach ulcer. The first operation by the gas lamp was also performed in Lviv.

January 18, 1963
the "Carpaty" Lviv football team, the former "Silmash", was set up.

August 17, 1969
the "Carpaty" Lviv football team won the USSR Football Cup.

1980
the completion of the first building in the Sykhiv district.

January 22, 1990
the "Wave of Unification" project between Kiev and Lviv.

1990
the first post-war transparent elections for the City Rada.

May 14-16, 1999
the summit of Central-Eastern Europe.

December 12, 1998
UNESCO declared Lviv's historical center a world cultural heritage.

June 25, 2001
Pope John Paul II visited Lviv.

May, 2004
the Lviv singer Ruslana won the Eurovision competition.

November-December, 2004
the city supported the Orange Revolution

An old tram depot

The first issue of a newspaper with an attachment

COFFEE

It was during Austrian rule that the tradition of drinking coffee firmly rooted itself in Lviv. For Lviv inhabitants it was a sign of good taste and an opportunity to once again prove their European ties. To reaffirm the tradition, Carl Hartman, at the agreement of the City Council, built the famous "Vienna Café" (coffee-shop) on the Governors' Rampart. There in the relaxed atmosphere of the coffee shop the local officials and bourgeois enjoyed the beverage. Travelers, impressed by the quality of Lviv coffee and the amount of courtesans and cheery people on the streets, enjoyed these public places of recreation. It was in one of these numerous recreation places in Lviv, that one of the first manifestations of women's emancipations was noted: a lady was seen walking down a street smoking a cigarette. The incident evoked a whirl of astonishment and indignation.

BABY BOOM

The end of the 19th century was marked by a population explosion in Lviv. In 1890-1914 the population increased by 75 per cent and reached a level of 90 thousand people. In the beginning of the last century the population of Lviv was twice as large as in Krakow. People arrived in Lviv hoping to find a job, and the construction boom provided opportunities for them to settle in. A historian from Krakow wrote that the Halych poor lived penned up together. A whole family would be sharing one room with the baby sleeping on the floor, her sister – on a box with coal, their parents – on a couch, and the only bed in the house was rented to a tenant, whose "sister" would often come and stay overnight. However, despite all the difficulties, the most important thing was that they all had jobs and thus could afford the necessities. The majority of laborers lived in the fringe districts of Krakiwske and Halytske, where they developed their own unique subculture. Each year the city was becoming more and more beautiful, and its inhabitants – more and more prosperous. Why do we wonder then that the people of Lviv talk about the period between the 19th century and the beginning of the First World War with such feeling of nostalgia for Great Europe?

A poster of the 1894 General Regional Exhibition, by P. Stakhevych

OSSOLINEUM

The beginning of the 19th century was marked by the boost of activities in Lviv's cultural institutions. The Ossolinsky National Foundation was established on June 4, 1817. The city authorities granted Jozef Maksymilian Ossolinsky permission to set up the chair of Polish Language and Literature in Lviv University. To facilitate future students in their studies a library was opened on the premises of the former

ⓘ*Important! If you are invited for a cup of coffee, you should remember that drinking coffee has always been regarded as a sacred ritual, which should take at least 40 minutes and be accompanied by a slow and pleasant chat. A cup of coffee drunk hastily burns not only lips but also the soul of your companion.*

Carmelite convent. However, the building itself was in a shabby state and it took much time to repair it. Many prominent figures, among them Jozef Bem, took an active part in fixing the edifice. The closest assistant of the prince, Samuel Bogumil Linde, collected books for more than ten years. Visiting the neighboring estates he bought, begged for, and sometimes even stole books from private collec-

Joseph Ossolinsky

tions. At the end of his life Ossolinsky presented the library to the Lviv community. Today, the former Foundation, now the Stefanik Library of the Ukraine's National Academy of Science, is still at the service of Lvivites.

HEAD RUS RADA (COUNCIL)

The Ossolinskys's emblem

The Head Rus Rada (Council), the first Ukrainian political organization in Halychyna designated to safeguard the rights of the Ukrainian population in the region, was established on May 2, 1848, right after the revolution in Austro-Hungary. At the onset of its existence Rada proclaimed the unification of Ukrainians, that numbered up to fifteen million, into one nation. The organization demanded that the Austrian government divided Halychyna into two separate administrative territories – East-Ukrainian region and West-Polish region. Rada consisting of thirty members (mainly the priests of the Greek-Catholic Church and well-educated citizens) insisted on introducing the Ukrainian language as the language of instruction in schools. Although Rada operated during a short period of time (till 1851), it managed to establish a cultural and educational organization, opened the People's House in Lviv and published the first Ukrainian newspaper in Halychyna, the Zora Halytska ("The Dawn of Halychyna").

LVIV'S LAST BUGLER

In 1826 the old building of Lviv City Hall collapsed. Previously, a committee had assessed the conditions of the edifice and reached the conclusion that the building was in a good state and all it needed was some insignificant redecoration. However, while the venerable city authorities were discussing the costs for the redecoration, a local official rushed into the room and informed the assembly that the City Hall had collapsed. In the incident several people died, including the Lviv's last bugler. This governor of the City Hall tower was very popular among city dwellers. He was a welcomed visitor at all solemn ceremonies. He spent days and nights on the tower peering into the distance and guarding the town from enemies that came mainly from the East. He also kept vigilant watch for fires and immediately sent signals in the direction

The collapse of the Lviv's City Hall. An old engraving

from where the calamity might be expected. He was responsible for the city-watch maintenance. And, of course, it was he who every hour sent signals to Lviv dwellers that their peace was closely guarded. Unfortunately, his successor has not yet been appointed.

Thus, Rada was the first to affirm that the Ukrainians in Halychyna are not only "priests and serfs".

THE BELOVED CAESAR

Halychyna peasants loved and deeply respected King Franz Joseph I (1848-1916). In some regions of Eastern Halychyna, Franz became the most popular name. Serfs regarded their beloved King as the embodiment of justice; they knew that anyone could write him a letter complaining about their lords. In Vienna, Tuesdays and Thursdays were set as visiting days for petitioners. The procedure of lodging complaints was fairly easy. Prior to appointing a state official, the King himself meticulously studied the candidate's file. With the abrogation of serfdom in 1836 the public's admiration with their beloved King increased sharply. In 1859, after Austria lost the war against France, thousands of people armed with pitchforks and scythes volunteered to protect their King. The people's deep-rooted devotion to this protector of all the abused and aggrieved made the King a character of folk tales. Maybe it was because of his wise and kind government, that King Franz Joseph reigned over the country for sixty-eight years.

King Franz Joseph I

The King accepting a petition, by V. Kossak

BETWEEN THE TWO WORLD WARS

World War I turned the city into a battlefield, where the Austria-Hungarian and Russian armies in their fierce fights tried to settle their differences. 1918 saw the beginning of a raging armed conflict between Ukrainians and Poles. In 1920 the Bolshevik cavalry, in their headlong pursuit to introduce the Socialist revolution in Western Europe, made an abortive attempt to break Lviv's defense. Starvation, epidemic diseases, social conflicts, all these hardships badly hit the Lviv population. It was only with the Riga peace agreement, under which Lviv became part of the Second Polish Republic, that the city managed to retrieve its potential and soon became one of the most important cultural, scientific, economic and religious centers. In that time celebrated Poles, Ukrainians and Jews lived and worked in Lviv.

A poster of the exhibition dedicated to the Lviv's defense in 1918-1919

An anti-Bolshevik poster

THE RUSSIAN INVASION

The beginning of World War I was unsuccessful for Austria. Following a surprise attack, launched on September 3, 1914, the Russian Army occupied Lviv. Russian troops stayed in Lviv for nine months, and it was then that the city was visited by Russian Emperor Nikolay II. The occupation had grave consequences for the city: Greek Catholic clergy and local political leaders were subjected to mass repressions; Metropolitan Andrey Sheptytsky was exiled to Russia; the city governor Count Bobrynsky, Russian by origin, guarded by imperial ideas of Pan-Slavism, openly ignored national interests of the Polish and Ukrainian populations. During its retreat the Russian Army confiscated a large amount of cultural and

Metropolitan Andrey Sheptysky

material values. Upon their return to Lviv, the Austrians resorted to repressive measures against the Ukrainian Russophile intelligentsia, suspecting them in the collaboration with the Russians. These political prisoners were kept in the ill-famed concentration camp of "Thelerhof".

THE UKRAINIAN-POLISH BATTLE FOR LVIV

Taking advantage of Austria's tenuous grip over Lviv and to avert a possible coup of the Polish patriotic forces, especially of the Polish Committee for Liquidation, a group of Austrian officers of Ukrainian origin took the city under their control. At 4 a.m. on November 1, 1918, the troops, consisting of sixty officers and one thousand five hundred soldiers, occupied the City Hall, the Central Post Office, the railway station and the bank and hoisted the Ukrainian national flag over the buildings. The Halychyna Governor, General Guina, and the town major, General Porsfer, were imprisoned. In the morning, officer Dmytro Vitovsky reported to the future head of the Western Ukrainian People's Republic, Kost Levytsky, that the Ukrainians were controlling the city. The same day, after the Poles recovered from the surprise attack, they resorted to skirmishes, which later developed into a full-scale street war. Both armies mostly consisted of young men of 17-19 years of age. The Lviv "batiars" (tramps), who were perfectly familiar with the city communications, took the Poles' side, helping them deliver ammunition and disseminate information. With the arrival of Polish troops from Przemyzl, the Ukrainian troops surrendered and left the city

The "Lviv orliats (eaglets)" Polish military memorial at the Lychakivske cemetery

THE "HAPPY" DAYS

In the 1920s-1930s the city became a transit point for the emigrants fleeing from the Bolsheviks. One of the fugitives was the Russian entrepreneur Smironov, famous for the vodka, which he first produced in Lviv. The Lviv market was bursting with gold and works of art. The black market, where one could buy or sell any currency, was openly

Advertisements of Lviv firms from the early 20th century

operating right in the downtown area. To reduce the fast-growing amount of smugglers, profiteers and political adventurers, the city authorities had to take immediate measures, which sometimes acquired ridiculous forms. Thus, in 1929 the City Rada made a feeble endeavor to bring order to the city streets and issued a decree, equaling beggars to prostitutes and determining their "work place".

"MERRY LVIV WAVE"

"Merry Lviv Wave" was first broadcasted in the pre-war Poland on June 16, 1933. It was a entertaining, cabaret-like pro-

Tantsio and Sheptsio,
from a Polish Radio poster

gram directed by Victor Budzinsky, starring Kazimierz Waida (Scheptsjo) and Henrik Wogelvanger (Tontsjo). Presenting in their radio programs and films the lifestyle a-la-Lviv, the actors became the embodiment of veracious Lviv "batiars" (tramps). The program enjoyed unprecedented in Poland popularity and soon attracted more than six million listeners. Despite the vigilant censorship and constant threat of being closed down, "Merry Lviv Wave" withstood all the hardships and following a short break was about to resume broadcasting on September 15, 1939. More often then not, the actors and guest-actors performed live. Unfortunately, most of the records, that had been stored in Lviv, were destroyed during World War II or in the post-war period.

on November 21, 1918. The armed conflict took more than 1000 young lives. In 1921, on the Lychakivske cemetery, the Polish community built a pantheon for 439 Polish kids, the youngest being only nine years old, who died in the conflict.

THE SOCIAL CRÈME-DE-LA- CRÈME

The social life of ethnic communities concentrated around cultural and scientific centers of each respective community. After its reorganization in 1918 the Franz I University was named after King Jan Kazimierz. Such prominent scientists as S. Bamach, J. Ptasnik, F. Bujak, J. Czekanowski and L. Rydygier taught at the University. Because of the prohibitions to study and teach at Polish Universities, the Ukrainian community founded Lviv (Underground) Ukrainian University in July 1921. Among the professors were M. Levytsky, R. Kovshevych and V. Starosolsky. Established in 1873 the Shevchenko Scientific Society was engaged in conducting research in different fields of sci-

A portrait of Professor Ludwig Rydygier

ence. Metropolitan Andrey Sheptytsky, who in 1913 handed over the Lviv National Museum to the Ukrainian community, gathered an active cultural society.

Yet, there was something else that made Lviv attractive. That was the bohemian atmosphere of artistic coffee shops, elitist restaurants and sinister semi-basements of snack bars, known as "mordovnya". It was here, in the "Pekelko" ("Hell"), "Atlas", "Oseledets na lantsuhu" ("A Herring on a Chain"), that brilliant poems and prose saw the world, fickle muses were sought and found, and young and aging talents drowned in the oceans of alcohol.

THE FIRST SOVIET RULE

At the beginning of the Second World War, Lviv found itself in an awkward political situation. German troops were pressing hard on the western boarder, and Soviet troops crossed the eastern border at the Zbrootch River

Lviv National Museum

on September 17, 1939. Yet, Lviv's fate was set in August of 1939, when the Ministers of Foreign Affairs of Germany and the USSR signed the ignominious secret protocol, known in modern history as the protocol of Molotov-Ribbentrop. Europe was divided between two almost identical political regimes. On September 22 General Wladislaw Langer gave Lviv to the Bolsheviks, who, in their turn promised not to persecute the civilians and to release the military. The Soviets failed to fulfill the commitments. Lviv to the full extent experienced the "kindness" of tovarisch (comrade) Stalin, the "father of all nations".

A memorial plaque to M. Lemyk on the former USSR consulate in Lviv

THE RED TERROR

During the short period of their first rule, the Bolsheviks engaged themselves in their pet activities: persecution and repression. The former military, police and civil servants, whose families were removed to the most remote corners of the USSR, were the first to experience the Red Terror. Until the outbreak of World War II the "capitalists'" property was being shipped from the city far inland. Executions, arrests, forced collectivization, and compulsory studying of the Russian language soon alienated the Soviets from even their most ardent advocates. All this gave an impetus to the Polish and Ukrainian resistance movements. From the first day of the war until the first troops entered the city, more than eight thousand political prisoners were executed by the People's Commissariat of Internal Affairs. The Lviv population greeted the first German squadron with flowers. Once again, the vicious circle of History locked.

THE SECOND SOVIET RULE

In 1944 the Soviets restored their power. Unlike 1939 nobody greeted them with flowers. The conse-

Monument to the victim of communists' reprisals,
by sculptor P. Staier, 1997

FOR GERMANS ONLY

The successive occupants made it clear that they did not have the slightest intention to share the power. On June 30, 1941, the attempt of the Ukrainian Organization of Nationalists to proclaim the restoration of the Ukrainian State was cruelly suppressed, with most participants being imprisoned and exterminated.

Before the war, a large Jewish community inhabited Lviv. Right

A Nazi commandant's appeal to Lviv inhabitants during the Nazis invasion

at the onset of their invasion, the Germans blew up all the synagogues and decimated some of the Europe's oldest Jewish cemeteries. They set up a ghetto and embarked on a systematic extermination of Jews. Despite all the hardships, Lviv struggled for its right to live. Some of the occupant's actions provoked an ironic smirk on the part of the locals. Before the war there was a luxurious café, "De la Paix", for Jewish customers called by the locals, "De la Peis". The new owners put a new doorplate at the entrance – "For Germans Only".

quences of their rule were embedded in the memory of the Lviv inhabitants all too well. The "new old" government traditionally commenced its reign with renaming the streets, setting up monuments to communist leaders and repressions. The majority of the Poles were compulsorily displaced. The Resistance Movement constantly aggravated the precarious position of the Soviets, until the Movement was quelled in 1950. Stalin's death slightly changed the situation, and Khrushchev's policy melted Moscow's attitude to already "Bandera's" Lviv. (Bandera was one of the Resistance Movement leaders). The large amount of newly built defense factories gave rise to the city's population. Despite the swift changes and relative stability, Lviv inhabitants never ceased struggling with the regime. The trials over dissidents, which increased after 1972, manifested the strength of the people's mind. Such names as V. Chornovol, the Horyniv brothers, V. Stoos, and the Kalyntsy's are known to the world as symbols of the struggle against the totalitarian regime. It was the demonstrations in Lviv that marked the beginning of Ukraine's Independence in the 1990s.

MODERN LVIV

Today, Lviv covers more than 155 square kilometers. Its population consists of about 820 thousand people, with yet another several thousands commuting to Lviv from the neighboring towns and villages. More than one hundred thousand young people attend Lviv educational establishments. The industrial past of the city is continued by the enterprises, whose trademarks are famous outside Ukraine: Lviv brewery, the "Svitoch" confectionary, Lviv distillery, and bus factory.

A view on the present-day Shevchenka Prospect

All this constitutes Lviv's glory. Annually, thousands of tourists – sentimental travelers, children, adventurers in their pursuit of authenticity and originality – flock to the city to marvel at its beauty. In the evening numerous Lviv coffee shops are filled with the hustling multi-colored crowds merrily chattering in different tongues. The border with Poland, a member of the EU, is only eighty kilometers away from Lviv. The rash statements, made by some Ukrainian politicians, that Europe is a distant land evoke nothing by ironic smirks from Lviv inhabitants. Lviv has always been part of Europe, regardless of all the borders. It is only in Lviv a beggar will address you in several languages. Where else do the hucksters know not only the price for their goods but also their own (the hucksters') value? Here by the "flower-bed", the favorite meeting place of Lviv inhabitants, one has a unique opportunity to discuss politics or gossip about their neighbors. Or, if politics are not your thing, delve into the cozy atmosphere of old and at the same time always young Lviv.

The pearls
of architecture

I wandered to You
From the far-away land
Where the River Slavoota
Streams down the steppes.
And I am praying to You
To strengthen my heart
With thy powerful heart
of a Lion.

V. Simonenko

The western side of Rynok Square

A relief on the "Seasons" mansion at 23, Virmenska Street

Virmenska Syreet

A view on the Latin Catholic Cathedral from the City Hall

A sculpture of Madonna decorating the fence around the Armenian Cathedral

A view on the Dominican Cathedral

A relief on the Black Mansion façade at 4, Rynok Square

DRUKARSKA ST.

STAVROPIHISKA ST.

MUSEINA ST.

FEDOROVA ST.

RUSSKA ST.

...SKA ST.

...SKA ST.

SERBSKA ST.

RYNOK-SQUARE

HALYTSKA ST.

CATHEDRALNA SQUARE

STAROEVREISKA ST.

A relief on the Armenian cathedral facade

When crossing the Rynok Square, you might be surprised to see two superimposed tram rails. This is one of the narrowest streets in the Old Town, so when two trams meet one should make way for the other to pass.

THE MAGIC OF RYNOK SQUARE

You can get to the Square from the train station by trams № 1, 9
It is a pedestrian area but authorities may grant permits to enter the Square by car.

■ Rynok (Market) Square is the heart of Lviv. It forms an almost equilateral rectangle 142 and 129 meters on the sides. The present-day Square is framed by 44 richly decorated mansions. Till the early 18th century, houses surrounded the old City Hall in the middle of the Square. However, with time they were all demolished. When a Lviv inhabitant wants to play a trick on an unsuspecting visitor, he makes an appointment to meet at № 1, Rynok Square. After some roaming around the Square, the visitor realizes that the meeting place is by the City Hall, the main edifice in Lviv. The City Hall has been re-erected three times. The City Hall made of wood burnt down in 1527. Its "successor" collapsed in 1825. Having carefully examined the state of the build-

ing, the city committee concluded that it was strong enough to survive another hundred years and it only needed some minor redecoration. While the authorities were approving the resolution and the estimated costs for the repair, a local official rushed into the room and informed the committee that the City Hall had collapsed . Right after the construction of the present-day City Hall was completed, the locals nicknamed it a "huge and hideous chimney". The new City Hall (by architects Yu. Marklya and F. Tresher), which consists of 156 rooms and 9 halls, was designed to meet the needs of the authorities. Yet, today's Lviv officials find the building too small and keep rebuilding the upper floor.

THE BANDINELLI PALACE

2, Rynok Square

After more that a decade of restoration works, the Bandinelli Palace (17th century, reconstructed in 1737-1739) is gradually acquiring its original look. In 1629 R. Bandinelli received a license to conduct mail-delivering services. His couriers covered by horse the distance between Lviv and the north of Italy at the tremendous speed, for those days, of two weeks. For a short period, known in the history of Poland as "Flood", the palace was turned into a mint. In the near future, it will house the Museum of the History of Postal Services in Lviv. The portal of the palace, supported by stone columns and decorated with two dolphins, which symbolize the successful trading, attracts the attention of curious tourists.

THE BLACK MANSION

4, Rynok Square
Branch of the Lviv History Museum
📞 72-0671

The Black Mansion is considered the visiting card of the city. The main part of the building, designed by the famous Italian architects Peter Barbon and Paul Rymlianyn, was decorated in the Renaissance style (1573-1596, with the second floor being built in 1884). In the late 14th century Jan Lorenzovych opened in the mansion the first pharmacy in the city. The composition of St. Martin sharing his cloak with a beggar, placed by another owner of the mansion, Martin Anchevsky, among the figures of St. Florian and the Virgin against the background of the beautiful bossage, produces a profound impression on the viewer. The sandstone bricks of the man-

ⓘ *Those who want to have a look at the city from the top of the City Hall Tower should be ready to climb 350 steps. The majestic view that opens up to the eyes of the amazed tourist will compensate for the costs and lost calories. The tickets to the City Hall (2 UAH) can be purchased in the ticket office, located in the semi-basement to the left of the main entrance.*

Neptune Fountain

sion, exposed to the rain and wind, have gradually acquired a darker tint. However, the mansion has never been of black color, but rather of dark-gray. Yet, recently, guarded by some mysterious rationale, the authorities have painted it black. If you want to try yourself in the role of a mansion security guard, sit on the bench on the right side to the entrance. Today, the edifice houses a branch of the Lviv History Museum.

Italian courtyard

ROYAL MANSION

6, Rynok Square

The coffee-shop is in the Italian patio "Royal Chambers" exposition of the History Museum

📞 *74-9061*

🕙 *10.00-18.00, daily except Wednesdays*

🎫 *entrance fee – 3UAH*

This richly decorated edifice consists of two buildings (architects P. Barbon and P. Rymlianyn) that were re-planned and combined into one large mansion. The buildings were purchased by a Greek merchant, Konstantin Korniakt, who arrived in Lviv from Crete. Being engaged in wine trading and serving as a customs official of the Rus land, he soon became rich and was conferred a gentry's title. After his death his family sold the house, which later became the property of Jacob Sobieski, the father of the future Polish King Jan III. Since then the house has been named the Royal Mansion. In 1634 Wladislaw IV stayed in the building. In 1908 it was turned into a museum. Having paid a nominal entrance fee, you enter the famous Italian courtyard, where, under the supervision of the Lviv pillory and at the soft sounds of classical music, you can plunge into the bohemian life of modern Lviv. A few steps up the stairs, and the traveler is roaming the "Royal Chambers" – one of the

The eastern side of Rynok Square

best expositions of the History Museum. Even these meager fragments of the city's long lost glory produce a profound impression on the visitor.

ARCHBISHOP'S PALACE
9, Rynok Square

In the 17th century this 68-room mansion (architect Ja. Prokopovych) belonged to Lviv archbishops. Some of the gold decorations for the Golden Hall were brought from Gdansk. Unfortunately, only small parts of the embellishment survived. Zygmunt III Waza and Wladislaw IV stayed in this palace while visiting Lviv. It was here that King Michael Corbut Vishnevetsky died in 1673. However, the building became famous after the wedding of Sofia Seniavska, the daughter of Lviv elder Adam Seniavsky. The wedding was organized by her fiancé S. Denhorf. Because of the fear of epidemics, the palace was allowed to accommodate and entertain only 18 guests and serve four dishes. The elder could not break the law, but he could easily "improve" it. Musicians cheered the numerous relatives and friends, who gathered in front of the house, and the window-sills on the top floor were groaning with huge beer-barrels. The beer was then poured down the rain sewers and anyone was free to dive into this merry stream. One of the guests even lay down on his back and gulped the beer till he was drawn aside dead drunk. Six hundred candles and four hundred lanterns lighted the celebration. In 1909-1914 the palace housed the English Club for the English who lived in Lviv. Now it is the City Children's Library.

LIUBOMYRSKYS' PALACE
10, Rynok Square
**Museum
of Ancient European
Furniture and Chinaware**
📞 74-3388
🕐 *10.00–17.00,
Wednesday through Monday*

*Liubomyrkys' Palace in Lviv.
A. Kamenobrodzki*

This large, for Lviv Rynok Square, mansion has undergone numerous reconstructions. It was designed at the request of Count Sapiga by the famous Bernard Meretin in 1744. However, the best part of the present-day decor was executed in 1763 by the architect Jan de Vitte. At that time the palace belonged to the

MASSARI'S MANSION
24, Rynok Square
**Branch of the
History Museum**

On the western side of the square there is the mansion once known as Gibliov's or Massari's. In the 16th century it belonged to the celebrated family of Scholtz. Later, it was carried over to Antonio Massari as part of his wife's dowry. To commemorate this event a winged lion was placed at the stairs to the palace. Later, the house was owned by Lviv adviser Gordon, a Scot by origin. In the 18th century the walls of the edi-

fice witnessed the conversations between the Russian Tsar Peter I and the local Russins and Polish gentry. The bas-relief as well as the third floor were added only during the reconstruction works carried out in 1920. After the latest restoration the antique god Mercury surrounded by little putti looks exceptionally attractive. In 1946 the palace was turned into the History Museum. Nowadays, among other interesting exhibits, it displays one of Lviv's oldest relics – the famous vane made in the form of a little lion, which in the old days used to catch winds on the City Hall roof. Every time danger loomed over the town, the vane fell off the steeple. When the City Hall collapsed it was the last nasty fall of the "little lion". To avert possible evil prophecies, the vane was locked in the museum and firmly attached to a wall.

A vane in the form of a little lion

Liubomyrskys. Anyone, who is turning round the corner into Russka Street, is bound to take one step aside so as not to bounce into the ornamental abutment that props up the building. For some time the palace belonged to the Governor of Halychyna; in the 1850s it was bought by the "Prosvita" (Education) Ukrainian Association. On June 30, 1941 a group of Ukrainian activists headed by Ya. Stetsko gathered in the palace and singed "The Decree of the Renovation of Ukraine". Nowadays the palace is the Museum of Ancient European Furniture and Chinaware.

VENICE MANSION
14, Rynok Square

The polychromatic nature of the mansion (architect Pavlo Schaslyvy) bears evidence of the numerous reconstructions that Lviv edifices have undergone. The building was designed by the architects P. Rymlianyn and P. Schaslyvy. The grand entrance of the palace is guarded by a winged lion holding an open book. This sculptural composition might have been taken as a proof, that the edifice once housed the diplomatic mission of Venice in Lviv. Although there is no convincing evidence that the Republic of St. Mark granted the "consul" A. Massari any real authority, one could most certainly affirm that due to the consul's energetic nature the interests of the citizens of Signoria were well protected.

WENING'S MANSION
17, Rynok Square
**In the basement -
the "Zoloty Vepr"**
restaurant

🕐 *12.00–21.00, daily*
📞 *72-6794*

The interior of the "Zoloty Vepr (Golden Wild Boar)" restaurant

If you are looking for a building that reflects the polyphony of modern Lviv, then you should visit the former Wening's mansion. During the last decades it accommodated the Society of Polish Culture in Lviv, the German House, the "Czech Talk" Society, the Hutsulschyna, Nadsiannya and Lemkivschyna Societies. Today, on the porch of the house there is a souvenir-shop and the former beer basement is now under the restaurant "Zoloty Vepr" ("The Golden Boar").

HAPPNER'S MANSION
28, Rynok Square

Built in 1610, it is one of the few edifices of the Renaissance period that remains almost intact. The house was owned by Pavlo Happner, a city advisor and a doctor. Its façade is richly decorated with various Latin inscriptions of moralistic character and a passer-by can count up to 20 images of lion cubs. Special attention should be paid to the décor of the entrance door portal. It was in this building that the Cossack's leader Ivan Pidkova spent his last days before execution. For the interference in the political activities conducted by the Turkish vassal in Moldova, the Turkish Sultan had the Polish King arrested and condemned Pidkova to death. The public's interest prevailed and Pidkova was executed on June 16, 1578. Under the weight of the people who gathered on Rynok Square to watch the execution, the attachment to the City Hall collapsed, which was taken as an evil sign.

Take a few steps off the northeast corner of the square down Krakiwska Street and listen to a legend about the famous lady Abrekova. In the late 16th century people used the walls and the windows of her mansion (**1, Krakiwska Street**) as an

The western side of Rynok Square

Punishment of a bungler baker

A PILLORY

Walking around the western part of Rynok Square the tourist should always bear in mind that somewhere in the middle of the square there once stood a pillory, which served as a place for executions. Criminals, merchants that traded poor quality goods, political criminals, and unfaithful wives were "taken care of" by the pillory. Strange to relate, but his place also bears the memory of some "funny" incidents. For example, in the 18th century, they beheaded a portrait of the Austrian official Rudolf Strasoldo, who together with his mistress ran away to Constantinople, but not after having grabbed a large sum from the treasury "to cover travel expenses".

THE ALL-CONQUERING LOVE
30, Rynok Square

Built in the 16th century, this mansion was first called by the name of its first owner Jacob Regul, the Regul's palace. In the second quarter of the 17th century it belonged to the merchant Lushkovsky, who lived here together with his beautiful daughter Jadviga. During one of King Wladislaw IV Waza's visits to Lviv, she was standing at the window greeting the monarch. One glance at the young beauty and the King was head over heels in love with her. Later, he took Jadviga to Warsaw and made her his mistress. Their son got the surname of Waza. However, kings rarely marry those they love and in 1637 under constraint from a papal nuncio and the most powerful people in the state, Wladislaw married Austrian princess Cecile Renata. Jadviga married Jan Vypysky, who was rewarded

with a huge estate by Trakai, Lithuania, to compensate for the "inconveniences" of the marriage. Yet, the King did not betray his true love, and often visited her in her estate. He died in her presence in Merech in April 1648. His death aggravated the already strained relations between the Polish State and Ukrainian Cossacks.

improvised rostrum. Greeting each other in the morning citizens shared the latest news from lady Abrekova. People were free to voice their views on authorities, judges and enemies. The flow of anonymous opinions got out of control, and in 1601 the Magistrate issued a decree prohibiting such actions. However, people continued to break the law, and only with the interference of the Church the situation was brought back in control.

Decorative motives on the façade
at 6, Shevska Street

At the start of the 20th century building **№ 12** on **Shevska Street**, which begins on the same corner of the square, housed a restaurant owned by Naftul Tempfer. Among the gifted and, in most cases, yet infamous youth, Naftul's restaurant was known under the name of "Pekelko" ("Little Hell"). The establishment was distinguished by its unique atmosphere. Naftul's son made his fortune by acquiring pictures and other works of art from poor artists and selling them after the artist's death of "artistic life".

The northern part of the Rynok suffered more than any other part of the square. Till the mid-18th century some of the buildings remained abandoned. Among the houses, that survived the difficult times, № 33, 41 and 45 still attract tourists' attention.

In 1637 **№ 33** was acquired by Lviv pharmaceutical chemist Jan Kalianista. In the first half of the 18th century the building underwent a reconstruction under the supervision of one of the most famous Lviv architects B. Meretin. In the Soviet times, the "Na Rynku" ("On the Market") coffee-shop, located on the ground floor, was nicknamed "Za Plechyma

The northern side of Rynok Square

Decorative motives of the "Olmar" restaurant interior

Radianskoi Vlady" ("Behind the Soviet Authorities"). Nowadays, it houses the "Olmar" restaurant, famous for its richly decorated interior and top-notch chef. (2, Krakiwska, tel. 798542).

Since Lviv fell under Austrian rule the house at **№41, Rynok Square**, was known under different numbers and names: M 160, WH 138, Grenzowsky's (Grentsivsky's) mansion or Kernytovsky's (Karvivsky's) mansion. In the 17-18th centuries it was occupied by a jewelry guild. In 1664 it was owned by Stanislav Karvovsky and Anna Gavinska. The further fate of the house is unclear; we can only presume that since 1704 it was abandoned like many other buildings on the northern part of the square. There is some evidence that in 1792 it belonged to Marianna Sheptytska (nee Yablonovska). In 1793 the famous

architect Clement Fesinger stayed in the house. According to some official documents, in 1889 the mansion was owned by Samuel and Anna Bronch. In this very house the well-known Lviv sculptor T. Bronch lived.

On the "modern", compared to other buildings on Rynok Square, façade of **№ 45** (1803) one still can trace fragments of the Gothic style. Yet the building's history is more interesting than its appearance. At the start of the 20th century it housed the only candle and waxwork factory in Halychyna. This was a profitable enterprise, which since 1851 had been supplying the city with the means of illumination and had been making fortunes by trading exotic "colonial" goods, such as tea, coffee and cocoa. Yet, the major attraction of the

A balcony console at 36, Rynok Square

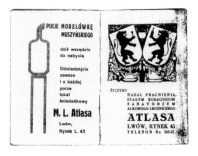

An advertisement of the "Atlias" restaurant

building was the "Atlias" restaurant, named after its owner M. L. Atlas and located on the ground-floor. It was frequented by the crème-de-la-crème of artistic circles. The atmosphere of the establishment could be compared to that of the well-known restaurant in Krakow, "Yama Ya. Mikhalika." The restaurant walls were decorated with works of art and humorous poems.

PHARMACY-MUSEUM

2, Drukarska Street
📞 *72-0041*
🕐 *Monday through Friday 9.00–19.00, Saturday-Sunday 10.00–17.00*
🎫 *entrance fee – 1UAH*

The tour around Rynok Square is worth finishing in the pharmacy-museum. This is the only place in Lviv where you can buy "Iron Wine" (3,50 UAH), which increases the content of hemoglobin in blood, as well as "Vigor" (8UAH), a popular with tourists herb tincture (alcohol content is 36%) and is believed to improve sexual potency. The museum is an operating pharmacy. Having looked around the main hall, ask the assistant for permission to see other rooms, where you can examine pharmaceutical instruments for producing pills, various vials for medicines that are more than 100 years old, a cabinet for drugs and poisons, as well

A medical cabinet with different medications

as a reconstruction of a pharmaceutical chemist's apartment. In the damp and somewhat sinister basement you will see the remains of an alchemical laboratory. The lucky ones might even bump into the alchemist himself. At the exit from the basement a female sculptor, which in Lviv is considered to be a monument to a sorceress, will whisper you a "good bye".

THE WORLD
OF DOWNTOWN LVIV

■ *There are many towns that consist of a gaudy patchwork of different nations, religions and customs, which for centuries have been interweaving with one another, thus producing interesting social and territorial formations. Yet, the uniqueness of Lviv lies in the fact that just a couple of dozen steps, down the old worn-out cobblestone streets, separate different cultural environments.*

The belfry of the Armenian Cathedral

ARMENIAN QUARTER

The Armenians, who had large colonies in Kiev, Kamianets-Podilsky and the Crimea, were one of the first peoples to settle in Lviv. Forced by the Turks to leave their historical homeland, some of the Armenians moved to Lviv and were granted by Prince Danylo of Halychyna a residential permit. Krakiwska, Lesy Ukrainky and Virmenska Streets circumscribe the present-day Armenian Quarter. Successful merchants and skillful craftsmen, the Armenians soon formed a strong influential community. The Armenians opened the first bank, "Hora Myloserdia" ("The Mountain of Charity"- "Mons Pius"). They made the best translators and goldsmiths. In the 16th-17th centuries their innate hatred towards the Turks made them spies at the service of Polish Kings. Almost every merchant coming back home from the East had some valuable information to share. The community owned a school, a publication and a nursing home for elderly people. The Armenian Church in Lviv was headed by a Metropolitan. Such Lviv's celebrities as burgomaster Bartholomew

Zimovych, historian Sadok Bronch, the discoverer of spa springs in Trouskavets and Drohobych Theodore Torosevych were all Armenians by origin. The Armenian Cathedral has always been the cultural and religious center for the Lviv Armenians.

ARMENIAN CATHEDRAL ENSEMBLE

To get to the Armenian Cathedral take Drukarska Street on Rynok Square and then turn into Virmenska (Armenian) Street. If you want to have a better view of the Cathedral, start with the "Armenian courtyard", which connects Virmenska and Lesy Ukrainky Streets. Have a seat on the stairs under the St. Christopher's column (by Christopher Augustynovych, 1726) and feel the relaxed atmosphere of the place. The heart of "the Armenian world in Lviv" consists of the Cathedral, Archbishop's

The cathedral's courtyard with the carved composition of Calvary

Palace, belfry and the premises of the former convent. The foundation of the Cathedral was laid in 1363. Jacob from Kaffa and Phanos from Gaisarants were the first benefactors of the project. Historians surmise the Cathedral was designed by an Armenian architect named Dorhi (better known as Doring), who actually copied the cathedral in Ani, the ancient capital of Armenia. The edifice has undergone several reconstructions, yet the most significant changes were introduced in 1723 when it was adorned with the decorations in the Late Baroque style. The belfry, located close to the Cathedral, was erected in 1571 according to the designs of the architect A. Krasovsky. The Cathedral's interior is richly embellished with mosaics by J. Mehoffer (1912). Special

After 1939 the Lviv Armenians suffered a tragic fate. Some of them left Lviv and fled to the West, the others perished during the Nazi occupation. Nowadays, the most numerous Lviv Armenian's communities are in Krakow and War-

The belfry of the Armenian Cathedral in Lviv.
V. Hrabovsky, 19th century

saw. Several years after World War II the Soviets closed down the cathedral and later turned it into a Lviv National Museum icon storage. It was only in 2003 that the cathedral was returned to the community. Ukrainian and Armenian politicians of the highest ranks, the Armenian Catholicos as well as the famous French songwriter of Armenian origin, Charles Aznavoure, were present at the ceremony of inauguration.

The Armenian Cathedral

Entrance to the Armenian Cathedral from Krakiwska Street

attention is drawn by the Trinity, a mosaic composition on the inside of the dome, and the modernist frescos by Jan Rozen, executed in 1925-1929 at the request of Ju. Teodorovych. In the altar part the Armenian crosses, the khachkars (XIV-XV), can still be observed. The last restoration of 1908 revealed the frescos that are considered the oldest in Lviv. In the altar fresco, the Last Supper, Judas is allegorically represented in the form of a shade. The cathedral's courtyard is covered with tombstones – the remains of a cemetery. The interior and exterior of the walls are decorated with epitaphs, one of them stating that the Patriarch of Armenia Stephan V died in Lviv in 1551. Of a special interest might be the carved composition of Calvary

Sculptural composition of "Doubting Thomas" placed in the courtyard of the former Armenian convent

(mid-17th century). Pope John Paul II visited the Armenian Cathedral during his pilgrimage to Lviv. **(Liturgy is held on Sundays and on religious holidays at 11.00, evening service – at 17.00 daily).**

A church dome

CHURCH OF TRANSFIGURATION
26, Krakiwska Street

A few steps away from the Armenian Cathedral is the majestic edifice of the Church of Transfiguration .Until 1848, this site was occupied by a monastery and the St. Trinity Cathedral of the Trinity order. The order was involved in ransoming Christians held prisoners by the Turks. After King Joseph II commanded

the order closed, the monastery premises were turned into a University library. However, during the riots, known as "Peoples' Spring", the University burnt down, which was a great loss for the city. At the cost of much effort, the University library was finally opened in different premises. The vestiges of the monastery were handed to the Ukrainian community. The construction of the church of Transfiguration started in 1875 and was completed in 1898 (architect S. Havryshkevych). The church was consecrated in 1906. The delay was caused by the high costs of the construction. The interior decoration of the church is one the most exquisite in the city. To light the buildings the architects resorted to the technique applied in St. Sophia's Cathedral in Constantinople by placing numerous windows in the dome. The church was decorated by K. Ustyianovych, M. Osinchuk, A. Pylykhovsky, and A. Koverko. In 1919 a memorial capsule was placed in the exterior wall of the church, which faces K. Korniakta Street. In the contemporary history of Lviv the church is famous for being the first place of worship that was returned to the Greek Catholic Church.

ROYAL ARSENAL
13, Pidvalna Street

*Walking down to the Russins Quarter it is not hard to notice the monument to the **Russian emigrant and publisher Ivan Fedorov** at 13, Pidvalna Street. The location of the monument slightly mars the impression of the Royal Arsenal premises (1639-1646, by architect P. Grodzitsky). Due to its strategically fortunate position and exceptional importance to the state, Lviv was under the Royal auspices and had two arsenals – the city arsenal and the royal arsenal. Anyone granted city citizenship was obliged to present or acquire some weapon. Kings strengthened the city's defensive capacity at their own expense. The arsenal's open courtyard was a deadly trap for the enemy, who would be driven back by point-blank fire. Today, the arsenal houses the State archives of the Lviv region (tel. 720030, open: 10.00-18.00, Monday through Friday).*

View on the Royal Arsenal and the monument to Ivan Fedorov

View on the Dominican church in Lviv. K. Auer, 19th century

The façade of the Dominican church

DOMINICAN CATHEDRAL

1, Muzeina Square
Museum of the History of Religion
Basement of Dominican Cathedral
📞 *72-0032*
🕐 *10.00-17.00, daily except Mondays*
🎫 *1 UAH, 0.50 UAH for student*

Having walked down Virmenska Street up to Muzeina (Museum) Square you will find yourself in front of one the largest and the most impressive edifices in the Baroque style, the Dominican Cathedral. Built in the 15th century in the Gothic style, it preserved its appearance until 1745, when it was redecorated by the architect and Governor of the Kamianets-Podilsky fortress, Jan de Vitte. The walls of the church remember Russian Emperor Peter I signing the 1707 agreement with Poland to create the alliance against Sweden. The facade was decorated in 1792-1798 by Clement Fesinger. The cathedral resembles St. Carl Bartholomew's church in Vienna. The interior is decorated with sculptures by S. Fesinger. The altar part was designed by M. Poleyovsky. It is hard not to notice the tombstone of Yu. Dunin-Borkovska by B. Torwaldsen (1816), as well as the monument to Halychyna Governor F. Gauger, by A. Schimzer, and the monument to A. Grotger, by V. Hadomsky (1880). The Soviet authorities found another, more "innovative" use for the Dominican cathedral and monastery by turning it into the Museum of Atheism and Religion. Children from Lviv and its outskirts were brought to the Museum to be shown the "frightening" side of religion, thus implanting in their minds the ideas of atheism. For

many years the Foucault's pendulum was hanging down from the church's dome. Yet, since the Museum contained a collection of the best examples of the sacral art, it helped to preserve the masterpieces from being sold or destroyed. Today, tourists can see the exhibition of items of worship displayed in the vaults of the Dominican cathedral and listen to a concert of organ music.

THE RUSSINS QUARTER

The Russins Quarter is located between the eastern fortification wall and Rynok Square. The Church of the Dormition of the Virgin is considered the center of the district and is situated at №7, Russka Street.

For centuries Russka Street and the church have been the focal point of Ukrainian culture in Lviv. After the city fell under Polish rule, the Russins were allocated the most dangerous district to settle in. In 1525 Seym (Polish government) issued a decree allowing the Russins to buy property only in this part of town. Polish rulers imposed certain restrictions on the Orthodox Lviv inhabitants, for example, prohibiting them from conducting trading and plying some crafts. The community had to fight for their right to practice their belief and preserve their ethnical character. Yet,

Russka street

despite the persecutions, the Russins together with the Greeks, Moldavians and other nations of the Orthodox Creed managed to create this unique and peculiar part of the city. In the 16th century an Orthodox fraternity was organized in the district to fight obstruction from the Catholic religion. Among the fraternity members were Stefan and Lavrenty Zizaniy, Pamvo Berynda, and Job Boretsky. The fraternity had its own school. Polish Kings, Russian Emperor Peter I and Swedish King Karl XII visited the district. During his pilgrimage to Lviv, Pope John Paul II passed down Russka Street. Each building in the district reveals its own fascinating mystery.

THE UNFORTUNATE ARCHANGEL

Every city should have a guardian angel to protect city-dwellers in time of pain and sorrow. Lviv was not an exception. Sculptures of saints decorated all the city administration buildings; some districts and even houses had their own divine protectors. The statue of Archangel Michael with gilded wings was first set up on top of the Royal Arsenal. He then became the city guardian. During the 1672 Turkish assault the statue was dropped by a cannon ball. Later the statue was returned on its pedestal, yet soon a fitful gust of wind shook the heavy metallic sculpture to the ground. Regardless of the evil sign, the city refused to break the bonds with the Archangel. Soon they found another appropriate place for the statue, an area that was always bustling with people. Yet… One night several criminals sawed off the gilded wings. Fortunately, it did not take long for the Lviv police to find the vandals. This time it was clear that the statue didn't bring good luck. Thus, to avert danger, the statue was taken to the City Museum and later moved to the Museum of Weaponry. The statue is still there at the end of the exposition with St. Michael trying to kill the devil. In the early 1990s several armed burglars broke into the museum and opened fire. Luckily, the statue of Archangel Michael escaped damage.

THE CHURCH OF THE DORMITION OF THE HOLY VIRGIN

7 Russka Street

🚋 № 1, 2, 5, 7, 9

The chapel of Three Bishops

The construction works of the Church of the Dormition (also known as Russka or Voloska church) began in the 14th century. First wooden, later made of stone, the church was burnt and rebuilt several times. The construction of the building that survives till today started in 1591 by architect Pavlo Rymlianyn. The works were completed in 1629 by architect A. Prykhylny. The width of its walls and the windows, that are made high above the ground, confirm that the church could have been used as a fortification. The building was designed in the best traditions of the Ukrainian wooden church architecture. The crypts still hide the tombs of such prominent fraternity members as K. Korniakt and I. Pidkova, as well as that of the relatives of Moldavian rulers. The church is made of white squared stone, which adds to the aesthetic perfection of the building. The central dome is decorated with the emblems of the benefactors, Moldavian rulers and Russian State. To the left of the altar are the relics of St. Mercury, presented to the church by Hetman M. Khanenko. The iconostas and the altar were made in 1773 by M. Filevych and F. Olendzky. The stained-glass windows by P. Kholodny (late 1920s) impress one with their elegance and perfection.

The **Chapel of Three Bishops** was attached to the church in 1578-1590 at the request of K. Korniakta. After the fire in 1671, it was renovated by the Greek merchant A. Balaban. The chapel is considered one of the best examples of Lviv Renaissance architecture. It still impresses visitors with their exquisite interior and exterior decorations, especially the mosaics and the cupola lantern.

Among other buildings in the district, the most interesting is **№ 20**, embellished with Ukrainian ornament and ceramic patches. It was designed in 1905 by I. Levynsky, O. Lopushansky and T. Obminsky at the request of the "Dnister" Society. In 1914 the first floor was turned into a gym of the "Ukraine" Student Society. Memorial plaques remind us that in this house the famous director and actor Les Kurbas began his artistic career.

THE TOWER OF KORNIAKT
Beginning of Russka street

The tower of Korniakt (by architect P. Barbon), attached to the church of the Dormition of the Holy Virgin in 1572-1578, is the tallest building in the Old Town. During its long history the tower has suffered numerous hazards. The monks of the Dominican order could not stand the chimes of the tower-bells that muffled the toll from other belfries. During the 1672 assault a cannon ball struck the roof and made the tower "shed tin tears". In 1779

lightning hit the belfry and set it on fire. The 65.8-meter tower has not been renovated for three hundred years and now is in bad need of repair.

Let's walk down Russka Street to the intersection with Ivana Fedorova Street. **Building № 11** once housed the school and publishers that belonged to the Orthodox fraternity. Here on July 27, 1599, the fraternity members reached agreement to defend their rights in court. The trials, which lasted many strenuous years and consumed large sums of money, finally ended in 1745, when the court ruled in favor of the Russins. However, they couldn't enjoy the victory to the full extent – the Austrian authorities repealed the regulations of the Magdeburg Law. In 1893, Isidor Sharanevych opened the Museum of the Orthodox Fraternity in the premises. The museum displayed a collection of Russin art, which now is exhibited in different Lviv Museums.

THE JEWISH QUARTER

The Arsenal Museum
5, Pidvalna Street

☎ 72-1901

🕐 *10.00-17.45, daily except Wednesdays*

Let's return to Pidvalna Street and take a few steps to the City Arsenal, turn the corner, and here we are in the Jewish Quarter. The evidence of the Jewish community in Lviv is found in the oldest of the city documents. The scarcity of living space made the fast growing community split in the 14th century when part of the Jews moved into the "city in the fortress", while the rest stayed in the Krakiwske outskirts. The "old" and "new" Jews did not get on too well. Trading, finance and some crafts were the predominant occupations of the local Jews. The community, controlled by the head of Kahal, lived by their own laws, sometimes different from the city legislation. Such religious and ethnical alienation evoked suspicion and caused pogroms. On Koliivschyna Square (a weird name for the Jewish Quarter) there are the remains of the well, which once was used by the Jewish community. Water was strategically important in wartime, and a convincing argument of any economic policy. Many Jews were involved in bootlegging home-brewed

Exhibits of the "Arsenal"

*Cannon Powder Tower.
A Kamenobrodzki*

*Having left the Russin Church courtyard, you will notice the ruins of old fortifications. The name of the street itself, **Pidvalna** (Basement), indicates that it was once part of the fortress. Under the present-day street's traffic area, there was a water gang. Here on the remains of the fortification rampart, crowned by the only well-preserved part of the fortress, the **Cannon Powder Tower**, one should listen to the story of the **Carmelite Church** (22, Vynnychenka Street) and observe the tall walls which can be seen from Rynok Square. Built in 1634 by the architect Ya. Pokorovych, it was decorated in 1731-1732 by K. Pedretti and B. Mazurkevych. History blames the monks of the Carmelite order for letting Swedish King Karl XII in Lviv. They had persuaded the city authorities to let them use a crack in the walls by the Royal Arsenal, the crack through which the Swedish army managed to get into the city.*

The city arsenal

THE GOLDEN ROSE

The synagogue, known as the "Golden Rose", constitutes the main attraction of the Jewish Quarter. According to some sources, its floor was decorated with a mosaic rose, thus giving the name to the whole edifice. In 1580 the wealthy merchant Isaac Na-khmanovych acquired a plot of land to construct a house (27, Fedorova Street) and a chapel, built in 1582 by architect P. Schaslyvy. First, it was named the Turhei Zakhav (The Golden Gate). Yet, monks of the Jesuit order dug out a document confirming that the plot once had belonged to the catholic priest D. Seniavsky and the synagogue was confiscated. "All the Lviv Jews were weeping in grief…" A popular (though not necessarily veritable) Lviv legend goes that the monks couldn't get into the synagogue, as they first had to cross the I. Nakhmanovych's yard. That was private property, which means - no trespassing… Meanwhile, the Nakhmanovych's daughter-in-law, named Rosa, was delegated to negotiate the matter with the King. She returned home with a document certifying that the synagogue belonged to the family. After Rosa's death, an inscription was placed on her tombstone, saying that here lies the most venerable woman in the city. In 1604 the synagogue became the main Jewish house of worship, which was also used as an archive for their most important documents. Unfortunately, during World War II, the Nazis destroyed almost all the synagogues, and those sacral edifices that survived the invasion, together with Jewish cemeteries, were shut down by the Soviets. Nothing remained of the Great Synagogue, which had occupied part of the present-day building at Nº54, Staroevreiska Street, it was wiped away by the Nazis. Today only the reconstruction of the old foundations gives a rough idea of the grandeur of the Quarter.

A Jewish boy the beggar from an old postcard

beer and vodka. Knowing that the Jews' financial possibilities were unlimited, the city plumber would turn off the water and demand extra taxes. Such an ultimatum resulted in fierce conflagrations. In addition to this, the illegal production of spirits in wooden premises led to fires, which sometimes burnt down large parts of the city.

The life of the Lviv's Jewish community concentrated around **Staroevreiska** (Old Jewish) **Street**. Divided into three parts in the old days, it was finally united into one street in 1871. The amount of currency exchange offices gave the street a new name, Veksliarska (Bill) Street. Due to the lack of land and the swiftly growing Jewish population, it became harder to find a living space in the ghetto. Even today one notices the difference in the ceiling height of floors in the Jewish buildings, with the upper floors being considerably smaller. Even if you make yourself enter one of the courtyards in the district, you won't stay there long.

The "Golden Rose" synagogue.
A. Kamenobrodzki

Among other residential buildings down Staroevreiska Street **Nº 36** is notable for the architectural décor of its facade. Commencing 1784 the ground floor of the building was occupied by a non-ferrous metals warehouse that belonged to Jacob Rokhmis. The decoration and arrangement of the windows and entrance doors give an idea of economic development of the Quarter. In the 18th century one of the neighboring buildings (**NºNº 30, 32, 34**) housed a stable and a wax factory. The latter was under the close surveillance of city authorities. Wax was considered a strategically important good, thus any counterfeiting was punished severely. Sometimes counterfeiters were sentenced to death. The most widely spread way of counterfeiting wax was by adding ground peas.

THE BOIMS' CHAPEL

Beginning of Halytska Street
Branch of Lviv Art Gallery
⏲ 11.00-18.00

The interior of the Boims' chapel

Walking down Staroevreiska Street to the West, we leave the Jewish Quarter and get to Halytska Street. A few steps to the right and we are in a small yard in front of the Boims' Chapel. The chapel was built in 1611-1615 by the architect A. Bremer and was then part of the cemetery that surrounded the Latin Catholic Cathedral. Most historians agree that the chapel constitutes the best example of the Mannerism style in Central East Europe. In the late 16th century King Stefan Batoria invited Yuri Boim, who lived on the boarder between Hungary and Germany, to settle in Lviv. According to his will only three Boim generations could be buried in the chapel. The luxuriant façade and interior were decorated by H. Sholtz and J. Pfister. The façade is notable for the Passion scenes and the statue of Mourning Christ, located on the cupola. However majestic the exterior is, the interior part of the chapel surprises one with its splendor. Strange to relate, yet, it looks taller from the inside than the outside. The cupola, which visually widens the space, is decorated with the images

Yuri Boim

of Apostles, Prophets, prominent Church figures and Polish Kings, who are all represented as commoners. The entrance door is crowned with the portraits of Yuri Boim and his grandson Pavlo. Pavlo became a doctor, traveled to China, where he studied Oriental cultural and medicine traditions, and wrote a manuscript about the country. The altar is decorated with polychromy and scenes from the Old and New Testaments. The fresco of the Last Supper is distinguished by the figure of Judas, who has already received the 30 coins and thus is represented sitting on a chair with the devil grinning angrily from under his seat. Because of the fresco of the devil the archbishop D. Solikovsky refused to consecrate the chapel. The portrait of Yuri Boim and his wife Jadviga, surrounded by the three generations of the Boims, is depicted on the southern wall of the chapel. The sculptural composition of "Mourning" in the central part of the wall is cut out of the alabaster of honey tint, produced in Zhuravno. A disguised door to the right of the altar fuelled the rumors about a secret passage under the chapel and the Boim's house. The recent excavations confirmed the legend. Among the remains of old civilizations, archeologists and restorers found empty bottles of "Soviet Champaign" – the trace of contemporary "explorers". Even Yuri Boim himself could not have foreseen such twist of fate.

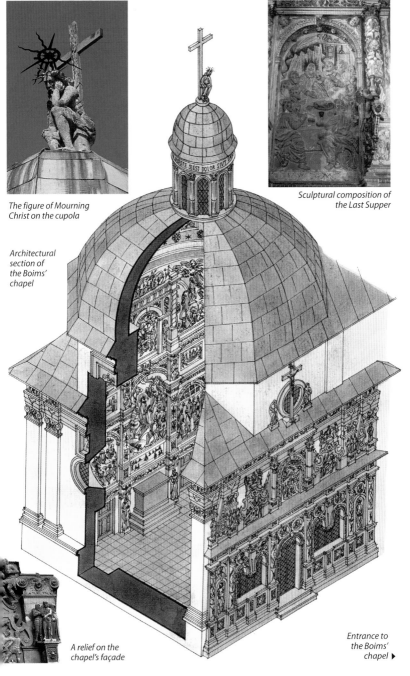

The figure of Mourning Christ on the cupola

Sculptural composition of the Last Supper

Architectural section of the Boims' chapel

A relief on the chapel's façade

Entrance to the Boims' chapel ▶

LATIN (CATHOLIC) CATHEDRAL

Cathedralna Square

📞 *72-5682*

🚌 *№ 1, 2, 9*

Mass is held daily at 7.30 and 18.00

Interior of the Latin Cathedral

On Cathedral Square, not far from Rynok Square, there is a majestic edifice of the Latin Catholic Cathedral. It was erected in 1360-1493 by the order of King Kazimierz the Great. The initial project by Peter Stecher was implemented by Michael Gensecke and Hanus Blecher. Yet, it was Peter Poleiovsky who executed most of the decoration works. On April 1, 1656, King Jan Kazimierz made a pledge to protect Poland at the icon of the Virgin, called "The Most Affectionate", in the Catholic Cathedral. The original of the icon is now in the Royal Castle in

Memorial plaque commemorating the visit of Pope John Paul II

Krakow. There is a beautiful main organ in the Cathedral (1839), and another smaller organ is to the left of the altar. The exquisite stained-glass windows by Yu. Mehoffer and J. Mateika, as well as the stained-glass window in the gallery by T. Aksenovych,

The façade of the Campiani's chapel and the "God's Tomb" chapel

produce a profound impression on the viewer. To the right of the central altar there is the magnificent monument to K. Yablonovska in the Empire style (by sculptor H. Vitver, 1806). The chapels, attached to the cathedral in different periods, constitute a single harmonic entity with the church. Situated to the left of the main entrance, the chapel of the famous family of Campiani attracts tourists' attention. The chapel, that underwent numerous reconstructions, with the most significant changes being introduced in 1619-1629 and 1660, is famous for the sculptures of Apostles Peter and Paul by Henry Horst and for the sculptures of the Evangelists by Jan Pfister. The Cathedral has always been the center of Polish culture in Lviv. In the Soviet era not only the Catholics but also the Greek Catholics, whose religion was then prohibited, conducted their masses in the Cathedral. One can get inside the Cathedral only through the side entrances. Some sources confirm that by shutting down the main entrance the authorities thus expressed their protest against the 1772 Austrian invasion. Numerous epitaphs and memorial plagues, which cover the cathedral walls, reflect the city's complicated history. On the façade wall which faces Halytska Street there are plagues commemorating the events of 1672 when Turks and Cossacks assaulted the city, as well as the results of the 1918 war between Ukraine

Nativity scene in the Cathedral

and Poland. This very wall is also decorated with the fresco of the Holy Virgin holding Christ. It is a copy of the icon, which was ordered in 1598 by Joseph Volf in the memory of his deceased granddaughter.

A stained-glass window in the Cathedral

Interior

Pope John Paul II

Architectural section of the Latin Cathedral

View on the Cathedral's belfry

ALONG
THE UNDERGROUND RIVER

BERNARDINES MONASTERY

■ *Lviv, like any other city in Europe, has its own river. The river Poltva divides the old town in two epochs: constructions of the 15th-18th centuries on the east bank, and constructions of the 19th-20th centuries on the west bank. Unfortunately, those who want to enjoy the sound of river's lapping waters first have to put on a rubber suit and a gas mask and only after that they may brave the descent down into the sewage collector, where the Plotva has been flowing for more than 150 years. But do not despair, the excursion down the riverbed above the ground will also prove to be interesting. The best starting point is Soborna (Cathedral) Square.*

3a, Soborna Square

🚋 *to get to the monastery take trams № 3 and 5, or one of the minibuses going to the Center*

Let's linger at the square and enjoy the monumental look of St. Andrew's Cathedral. The first thing that catches your eye is the white eagle, the state emblem of the Polish Republic, and the Lithuanian emblem of the "Pogon". The first written evidence about the wooden church, built on this spot by a monk named Bernard Avelides, goes back to 1460. In 1600-1630 the architects Pavlo Rymlianyn and Ambrosi Prykhylny reconstructed the sanctuary. It was in this cathedral that Hryshka Otrepiev, notoriously known in Russian history as the traitor Psuedo-Dmitri I, was wedded to Maria Mnishek. After the wedding Otrepiev led the Polish Army to Moscow. Although the cathedral was outside the fort town, it constituted an integral part of the city's

fortifications. The monks of the Bernardine order were crowned with fame after the 1648 Cossacks' siege. In 1736 a rostral column was placed in front of the cathedral to commemorate the victory. Once, the column was topped with the statue of St. Jan of Duklya, but in 1944 the statue "mysteriously" vanished. Today, a statue of a Bernardine monk decorates the crest of the rotunda over a well, which is to the right of the cathedral. The cathedral's interior is known for the 17 wooden altars (by architects Tom Gudder and Conrad Kutschenreiter), as well as for the murals by Benedict Mazurkevych. Today,

Figures of monks of the Bernardine order decorating the cathedral's pediment

Interior of St. Andrew's church, that formerly belonged to the Bernardine order

St. Andrew's cathedral belongs to the Greek Catholic Church. Under the edifice and along Valova (Rampart) Street there is a branched network of the main sewage collector, which gave shelter to Jews during the Nazi invasion. Some of their belongings were found during the recent remedial maintenance. In Austrian times the monastery premises were used as an archive. Today, the storages of the Lviv branch of the State Historical Archive contain the richest in Europe collection of documents of the 13th- 19th centuries.

Between Soborna and Halytska Squares stands a **house in the Modern style** (1, Soborna Square). In 1773 a pharmacy "Under the Hungarian Crown" was opened on the ground floor of the building. Forge iron decorations complemented the exquisite stained-glass window with the image of St. Stefan's crown. It cost 300 crowns to make the "Crown" (a tidy sum for the time), yet, it did not stop hooligans from breaking the pane.

On the corner of the street there is now a public call office (8, Halytska Square, open: 9.00-18.00, Monday through Saturday, tel. 723573). In the early 20th century

OLD WATCH'S PRESENT

Poor are those who do not wake up in the morning at the sound of an old clock on a clock-tower. Today, soothing chimes are replaced by the metallic scraping sound of an electronic mutant, which is programmed to flip on a radio or play music. Permanent stress, sullen mood and depression are all the result of the nagging sound of an alarm-clock. Our civilization pays for this so-called comfort. The irresistible fear of being late for work or classes makes us endure the torture. However, Lviv used to offer other more pleasant ways of ensuring that its dwellers would always be on time. The tower-clock on the belfry of the Benedictine monastery definitely stands out among its numerous "counterparts". Once, the monks, standing guard on the belfry, noticed the approaching enemy and notified the city dwellers. The city was saved. To commemorate the incident, the tower-clock was set five minutes fast. Anybody who heard its aged hourly tinkling knew that they were given another five minutes. They didn't have to rush at breakneck speed, or burn lips with still boiling coffee or shorten the pleasant kiss with their beloved. Sometimes the extra five minutes could be an eternity.

A memorial column in front of the church

PRICE DANYLO'S CROWN

In 2001 the monument to Prince Danylo of Halychyna, the founder of the city, was unveiled on Halytska Square (sculptors V. Yarych, R. Romanovych, architect Ja. Churylyk). The rumors circulated that Kiev City administration, gnawed by political envy, forbade putting the crown, conferred to Danylo by the Pope, on the prince's head. Yet, in the search for a compromise, they finally placed it on a pedestal. Like any other monument in Lviv it aroused animated discussions among the locals. Apparently, time will reveal its artistic value. On the opposite side of the square, right by the underground crossing

is the Halychyna Cinematography Center (15, Halytska Square). At the time when the Plotva was not yet fettered by underground pipes, there was a bridge with the statue of St. Jan Nepomuk. Till the end of the 19th century, close by the place, there was the famous "Pid Tygrom" ("Under the Tiger") hotel. Cheap prices and the convenient location made the hotel popular with the visiting clergy. In 1937 on the ground floor of the building was opened the first-class cinema "Europe", that featured newly released Polish and foreign movies. "Europe" was the biggest cinema-hall in town. During the Nazis invasion a police station operated in the premises.

the building housed the "Central" coffee-shop, which was second best after the "Videnska" (Vienna) coffee-house. One could enjoy the pleasant atmosphere of the restaurant, which had its own library and a Lady Saloon, till 3 a.m. It was a proud domain for the Ukrainian Bohemia, where, according to memoirs, the composer Stanislaw Liudkevych wrote his music.

THE "GEORGE" HOTEL
½ Mickiewicz Square
📞 72-2925

Allegorical statue of America decorating the façade of the "George" hotel

One of the most elegant edifices on Mickiewicz Square is the "George" hotel, completed in 1793 by its owner George Hoffman. Yet, the present appearance of the hotel came after the reconstruction of 1900-1901 (architects H. Helmet and F. Fellner). The statue of St. George on the pediment and four allegorical statues of Asia, Europe, America and Africa on each corner of the roof (architect A. Popel) complement the architectural integrity of the edifice. Honoré de Balzac, Ferdinand Liszt, Maurice Ravel and Jean-Paul Sartre are only a few among other celebrities, who stayed in this hotel. The famous Russian writer A. Tolstoy, who visited the city to promote the advantages of the Soviet Proletarian Art, left interesting memoirs about the hotel. He recalled that every room was equipped with installed buttons, and one could even call

"George" hotel

"a female companion" by pressing one of them. The writer probably misread the word "kurtyna", a "Venetian blind" in Polish, and took it for "courtesan". In Soviet times the hotel enjoyed the status of "Intourist" (abbreviation for "international tourist", a five-star hotel a-la-Soviets) and was immensely popular among the Poles. In those days, a dinner in this restaurant spoke volumes about the diner's social status and his pocket. Today, a smiling porter will invite you to have a look at the restaurant's pre-war interior.

Let's linger at the monument of the famous Ukrainian poet Taras Shevchenko (sculptors V. and A. Sukhorskys, 1992-1995). From November 1898 up till 1939, when the

Western Ukraine was joined to the Soviet Union, close to this place there was the monument of the Polish King Jan III Sobieski (sculptor T. Bronch). In 1950 the monument was moved to Poland and since then it has been decorating one of the squares in Gdansk. In the Soviet era the place where the monument once stood was turned into a flowerbed, which since the 1980s has become Lviv's Hyde Park. Here, by the bronze statue of Taras Shevchenko surrounded by the most prominent historical figures, were held the first political meetings that involved thousand of participants. There were heated political discussions and for the first time the national yellow-blue flag was flown.

The Holy Virgin's statue placed on Mariinska Square

To the monument's right there is the **"Vienna Kaviarnia"** coffee-shop. On the left side of the monument towers the college and St. Paul's and St. Peter's Church of the Jesuit order (by architects S. Lamkhius and D. Briano), one of the earliest examples of the Baroque style in Lviv architecture. (12, Teatralna (Theatre) Street). The church is closed for services, as at the moment it is being used for periodical editions storage of the Stefanik library of the Ukrainian National Academy of Science. Yet, the church's fate has already been settled and after the editions have been moved elsewhere for storage the church will become one of the most majestic sacred places in Lviv.

One of the busiest highways in the Old Town, Svobody Prospect, takes its beginning right off Marijska Square. In the numerous books about Lviv it appears under different names, for example, Hetman's Ramparts. (Hetman, a general in the Cossack army). The avenue has always been popular with the Lviv inhabitants for the shady promenade it offered. It is the place where the latest trends in the world and Lviv fashion are demonstrated. Here one can join the choir and sing patriotic songs, or forget the politics and find a "companion" to spend a wild night in one of Lviv's restaurants. Walking down the avenue, pay attention to landmark edifices on both sides of the street.

View on the Jesuit church and the monument to Taras Shevchenko

THE BEST OF THE BEST

On November 30, 1904 the monument to the Polish poet Adam Mickiewicz was placed on the square bearing his name. The contest for the best monument draft, called by the city authorities, was won by the sculptor Antony Popel. The composition "The Inspiration" represents an allegorical winged Genius handing a lyre to Mickiewicz. The twenty-five meter column is made of Italian granite, and the bronze figures are cast by the Czech firm "Serpeka from

Vienna". Numerous political and patriotic demonstrations have marched past the monument. In his book about Lviv Ju. Witllin recollects, that the advertisement of the "Baika" cinema, lighting on and off to the rhythm of the chanted political slogans, enhanced the impression, produced by the manifestations. Right after the monument had been unveiled, it was nicknamed "a candlestick" or "a pencil". Despite these critical remarks, it is considered the world's best monument to Adam Mickiewicz. Unfortunately, it has been spoilt by the "masterpieces" of modern architecture, accurately called "night-pots".

Grand Hotel

Across Svobody Prospect stands a building decorated with multicolored flags. It is the Grand Hotel – the most expensive and fashionable hotel in the city (13, Svobody Avenue, tel. 724042). The hotel was completed in 1898 in accordance with the projects by E. Hermatnik and decorated with atlantes by the sculptor L. Marconi. The interior was completely changed during the restoration works of 1990-1992.

Next to the hotel there is the **Museum of Ethnography and Crafts** (tel. 727012, open: 10.00-17.00, Tuesday through Sunday). The building was constructed by the architect Yu. Zakharevych in 1891 and initially belonged to the Halychyna Saving Bank. The edifice's rich decorations of polychrome loam, majolica and smith embellishments attract attention of passers-by. The allegorical composition with a statue representing Economy tops the cooper and tiled cupola and

The "Fortune" statue by Ju. Markovsky

attic. The statue bears a striking resemblance to the Statue of Liberty in the United States, and sometimes is introduced as such to tourists. The building is in a shabby state, which prompted the decision to close the museum and move the exposition elsewhere. Despite the ragged look of the façade, do enter the museum to see the imposing statue of "Fortune" by Yu. Markovsky, a coach of the 18th century, a beautiful staircase with Innsbruck stained-glass decorations, and the luxurious conference hall with its decorative oak dado.

NATIONAL MUSEUM

20, Svobody Prospect

📞 *74-2280*

🕐 *10.00-18.00, daily, except Fridays*

National Museum

This late Neo-Renaissance edifice was built in 1898-1903 by the architects L. Marconi and Yu. Yanovsky as the Museum of Fine Arts and Crafts. Its façade and richly ornamented interior, reconstructed in 1999, produce a lasting impression. In Soviet times the building housed the Museum of Lenin, but since 1990 part of the Lviv National Museum exhibits have been displayed. The Lviv National Museum itself was created by the Greek Catholic metropolitan Andrey Sheptytsky on December 13, 1905. Apart from masterpieces by foreign artists, there is a permanent exhibition of works by Ukrainian masters of the 12th-17th centuries. The Museum's icon collection is considered one of the richest in Central Eastern Europe.

Museum of Ethnography and Crafts and the "Promivestbank" premises

THE BRAINCHILD OF COUNT SKARBEK

1, Lesy Ukrainky
take trams № 6, 7

To the right of the Opera House there is another theater that has always been called "La Scala of Halychyna". The theater holds 1460 seats. Commissioned by Stanislaw Skarbek, the architects A. Pihl and J. Zaltsman constructed a multifunctional building in 1837-1842, with the largest part of it being under the theatre. To strengthen the foundation, 16,000 oak piles were driven into the marshy soil under the theatre. One of the first performances staged was the "Girls' vows" by A. Fredro. Count Skarbek's wife, the beautiful actress Sofia Yablonovska, deserted her husband for the playwright Fredro. This theater, where N. Paganini and F. Liszt performed concerts, had been the city theatre hall until the construction of the Opera House. During World War II the theatre was open for the Germans only. They started the restoration works of the interior. Now the edifice is home to the Zankovetska National Drama Theater.

OPERA HOUSE

28, Svobody Prospect
📞 *72-8672*
🚋 *№ 7, 6, 5, 4*

The Krushelnytska Opera House is justly regarded the pearl of city architecture. By the way, it is the only edifice in Lviv printed on the national currency (20 UAH bill). In 1896 the city administration made the decision

Details of sculptural decorations of the Opera House

to build several public establishments, with the Opera House being at the top of the list. The construction started in 1897 on the site where the palace of the Holukhovkys once stood. The works conducted under the supervision of the architect Z. Horholevsky were completed in three years. In those days the theatre was a real accomplishment from the architectural and construction

points of view. In 1900 the Poltva made a breach in the pipe and flooded the theatre's basement and machinery hall. This constituted a serious threat for the building could have sunk to one side, yet, the theatre survived. The restoration works were last carried out in the Soviet times. Several kilograms of gold leaf were used for the interior decorations and tons of copper – to cover the roof.

The façade is adorned with the image of Genius, holding a golden olive branch, with the statue of Drama to the left and the

Architectural section of the Opera House

Opera House.
An old postcard

An allegorical statue of Comedy on the façade of the Opera House

Opera House lobby

"Mirror Hall"

The recent reconstructions gave the square its present look. In the Soviet times on the spot, where now is the flowerbed, there was a monument to Lenin. The hideous construction of a "bearded old man climbing out of the chimney", made it difficult to take pictures of the Opera House. It was the second dismantled monument in the USSR to Lenin, after the one in Vilnius. When the monument was being disassembled, it turned out that the pedestal contained concreted crosses and tombstones from a Lviv cemetery.

statue of Music to the right. Beneath the sculptures, there is the composition of "The Joys and Sorrows of Life" placed in a triangular tympanum. The principal cornice is crowned with the statues of eight muses (architects A. Popel, Yu. Markovsky, T, Vyshnovetsky, Yu. Beltovsky). On the both sides of the loggia are placed the statues of Tragedy (A. Popel) and Comedy (T. Bronch). Even more refined is the decoration of the interior. Above the entrance to the stalls there are the statues of Comedy and Tragedy by the sculptor P. Vijtovych. The plafond in the lobby is embellished with 12 lockets that in the allegorical form symbolize the art seasons (A. Popel). Above the entrance door to the circles, there is a painting by I. Rybkovsky representing different types of Lviv bourgeoisie and nobility. Yet the most gorgeous place in the theatre is probably the Mirror Hall on the first floor with the Four Seasons by M. Herasymovych and allegories of Europe, Asia, Africa and America, which together with the allegories of Love, Envy, Pride and Maternity (S. Debicki), form a single ensemble. The ceiling is adorned with plafonds with the allegories of Poetry, Dance, Music, Love, Hatred, Justice and Wisdom, as well as with a scene from the ballad by Ju. Slowacki. The sculpture of the prima donna S. Krushelnytska, whose name was given to the theatre, was placed in the hall in 2000. The circles were decorated by M. Herasymovych, P. Vijtovych, E. Pidhorsky and D. Giovanetti. S. Reihan painted the ceiling. In the center is the image of Genius and an angel holding the Lviv's emblem.

Waist-length sculpture of S. Krushelnytska, by sculptor Ya. Skakun

The plafond above the stage represents Poland in its glory. The ceiling is decorated with allegorical female figures symbolizing Grace, Music, Truth, Dance, Hatred and Illusion, as well as with portraits of leading actors and actresses. Made in the shape of a lyre, the theatre holds 1000 viewers.

THE MOST BEAUTIFUL STREET IN LVIV

■ *The present-day Shevchenko Prospect is considered the most elegant adornment of the city. The first recollections of the street date back to the 16th century, which then was a Lviv's fringe quarter with a pond and two streams – the Soroka and Pasika. The people who inhabited the district were predominantly involved in different kinds of craft. In 1871 the street was reorganized and given the name of Akademichna (Academician), as at the end of the street there were several University buildings. Despite the new name (Shevchenko Prospect), the majority of Lviv's population still call it Akademichna. Since the 19th century it has been one of the favorite promenade places in town. It used to be lined with twenty-two poplar-trees, but they were cut down because of their old age and replaced with maples. Right in the middle of the street opposite the casino there was the monument to Lviv poet Corneliy Weisky (sculptor A. Popel, 1901), which, after the war, was moved to Szczecin. Here on this street you will get acquainted with the buildings, which to this day bear the traces of the glorious past.*

*Apartment building
formerly owned by A. Segal*

APARTMENT BUILDING OF A.SEGAL
4, Shevchenka Prospect

The apartment building (architect T. Obminsky), owned by the lawyer A. Segal, is one of the best examples of the Lviv Secession architectural style. The building's appearance, location and the popularity of its owner soon attracted respected tenants. The first floor was occupied by Marian Turski, the director of Eastern Auction. Although both the façade of the edifice and its interior decorations are equally impressive, the most remarkable are the fanciful stained-glass windows. Today, the ground floor is under the most popular Lviv grocery store.

ZALEVSKY'S MANSION
10, Shevchenka Prospect

This Neo-Baroque edifice crowned with two turrets and with a largest shop-window on the ground floor stands out among other mansions in the street. Completed in 1894 (architect Ya. Schultz, sculptor Herasymovych), up till 1940 it had been used as a residence and office premises for the famous Lviv confectioner V. Zalewski. Zalewski, who had been taught byJan Mikhalik from Krakow, transmitted the "sweet flair" and elegance of Krakow to Lviv. In 1928 the architect K. Pjotrovych designed the interior decoration of the ground floor and the shop-window in the "Art Deko" style. The window displayed the famous pictures made of chocolate and sugar. The factory's produce was exported to Paris

Zalevsky's mansion

and Vienna. After Lviv was joined to the Soviet Union, Zalevski was declared a capitalist and exploiter and exiled to Siberia, where he breathed his last breath. In one of his last letters to his wife he complained that all he longed for was at least one bite of something sweet.

*Next door to the Zalewski's mansion stands the **Sofia Grand Club** (12, Shevchenka Prospect). In 1810 on this spot was the St. Anna bathhouse. The water delivered from a particular spring to the bath was known for its curative qualities and the high content of minerals. Unfortunately, in 1850 the owner of the bath was forced to install a water-supply system. The history of a "quick passing moment" in Lviv could make a separate subject for research. It is known that visitors used several kinds of soap, the most popular being "the Greek, Turkish, Arabic and foreign soap". In 1422 King Wladislaw II conferred a bath opposite the monastery of the Franciscan order to the locals. Men, women and school students could take a bath on scheduled days. Students caused most of the problems; they splashed the water and broke the equipment. In response to the bath-owner's complaint, the Headmaster issued a decree, compelling the students to sing psalms while taking a bath.*

LVIV STOCK AND COMMODITY EXCHANGE

17/19, Shevchenka Prospect

The building's monumentality is the accomplishment of the architect A. Zakharievych. It was on the premises of Stock and Commodity Exchange that the most crucial decisions for the city and the region were taken. It was also the headquarters to the Eastern Auctions that attracted to Lviv the European beau monde. In the old days, hundreds of estate owners flocked to the Auction Market. Here they signed agreements, effected all sorts of bank payments and settled a good match for their daughters. The main aim of the Auction lay in promoting Polish goods on the Asian and Middle East markets. The rapid economic development

Queen Jadwiga

resulted in opening a regular flight between Warsaw and Lviv in 1922, and in improving railway communications. Today, the building houses the Office of Public Prosecutor. If an opportunity arises, have a look at its magnificent interior. A lasting impression is produced by the stained-glass windows and mosaic decorations of the stairs (architect C. Frych, 1909). On the first floor there is a conference room with the allegoric picture by F. Vygczyvalsky and the alto-relief by Z. Kurchynsky telling a story about the Man's life and fate.

BANK COLLEGE
9, Shevchenka Prospect

Many young hearts were broken in front of this building. The last-ditch attempts of Lviv young men to sneak onto the territory of the Queen Jadwiga city female school, founded in 1888, were foiled by vigilant guards, protecting the chastity of actions and thoughts of their students. The school was regarded as one of the best in the city, and the student-to-be and her noble parents spared no effort or money to secure a place in the establishment. The school's graduates were the most desirable brides in the city. A marriage with a school graduate promised to be lasting and happy. Unlike many other buildings, this one has inherited the airs and the elegance of its present owners. The future financiers from the Bank College contemplate the outside world thinking the same as Lviv young ladies once did. The only difference is that not fiacres but expensive cars are waiting for them at the windows. The guards are as vigilant and unapproachable as they were in the good old days. They safeguard bank secrets and their students.

"SHKOTSKA" ("SCOTTISH") COFFEE-SHOP

27, Shevchenka Prospect

At the end of the street there is a building constructed in 1909 in the late English Modern style by the architect Z. Bronhvich-Levynsky. The building was famous for the "Shkotska ("Scottish") coffee-shop located on the ground floor

"Skotska" house

(1909-1914). It was here that professors S. Banakh and M. Zarytsky created and developed their celebrated school of mathematical analysis. Lviv legend goes, that during their meetings in the coffee-shop these two University mathematicians used to write equations. The one who did not solve the equation had to buy a drink or provide some other reward for the winner. The only problem with these innocent pranks was that the professors did the calculations on paper napkins, which drove the waiter mad. Finally, Banakh's wife bought a note pad that went down in history as the "Shkotska book". Unfortunately, the latest reconstruc-

tions completely changed the interior of this building.

Across the street there is the monument to the famous historian and President of the People's Republic of Ukraine, Mikhail Hrushevsky.

THE POTOTSKYS' PALACE
15, Kopernika Street

The Pototskys' palace is the most luxurious palace in Lviv. Perhaps it was only the Pototskys, nicknamed the "little kings of Rus" for their numerous relatives, who could have afforded such lavishness. Having altered the

project by the French architect L. Doverne, the Lviv architect Julian Tsybulsky constructed a majestic edifice, which could easily rival castles in France. There are many fascinating stories about the palace, some of them occurring even now. During the recent restoration works it was found that in the old days there used to be a lake on this very spot. Workers discovered the remains of a ship. Some time ago attempts were made to build a subway in Lviv. Unable to withstand the construction, the palace cracked and sank to one side. Others affirm that this happened because the edifice was used as a registry office and in Soviet times there was a room where applications for marriage were submitted and birth certificates and death certificates were issued. Till this day the palace fosters numerous rumors. People say that here secret societies hold their meetings, that between the palace and the Art Gallery a passage will be built, and that soon an underground parking lot for administrative cars will be constructed.

Decorative motives of an entrance door

PEARLS IN THE LVIV'S CROWN

View on St. Yura's (George) Cathedral

■ *Having left Svobody Prospect behind and meandering in a westerly direction, we finally find ourselves in the "Imperial" Lviv. The majority of the buildings between Horodetskoho, Bandery and Franka streets were constructed during that period when Lviv was part of the Dual Monarchy. It was in the Austrian era that some of the edifices acquired a certain "air", which makes it worthwhile visiting them, if you are to discover the atmosphere of good, old Europe.*

FRANKO LVIV NATIONAL UNIVERSITY

1, Universytetska Street
📞 *296-4111*
🚃 *take trams № 2, 10, 9*
aor a marshrutka.

Allegorical composition of Halychyna

The building, initially designed to house the Halychyna Parliament, was constructed by the architect Hohberg in 1877-1881 in the time when, though being under Austrian rule, Halychyna enjoyed vast economic and juridical autonomy. The edifice is a typical example of the architectural fashion dominating in the latter half of the 19th century. To have a better look at the original exterior decoration take a few steps to the monument of Ivan Franko, that stands on the square in front of the University. Above the attic is an allegorical composition representing Halychyna

Main façade of the University

In 1799 in front of the Geht's mansion, which used to occupy the spot where the University is now, a wonderful park was laid out, with small bath-houses, a summer theatre, alleys and paths. In 1890 a fierce storm broke most of the trees, which were later replaced with new seedlings. A brass band gave weekly concerts in the park rotunda. The park was the favorite promenade place for Lviv aristocracy. Here were organized fireworks, festivities and other entertainments. The site, once occupied by the monument to Golukhovsky, today is decorated with a vase, an exact replica of the sculpture by the famous artist B. Thorvaldsen. And then there was the 20th century. In 1918 the park became the battlefield for the Ukrainians and Poles. The Germans built here a cinema. When in 1999 the Presidents of Central Eastern European states gathered in Lviv, the authorities finally managed to screw in light bulbs in the lamp posts and the Lviv inhabitants could at long last see the beauty of the park at night. In the mid-90s a deputy of the City Rada suggested building a fast-food store in the park. I wonder, what will happen next?

surrounded by the images of the rivers Vistula and Dniestr (sculptor T. Riger). Below are the female figures representing Love, Justice, Truth and Faith. The main entrance is decorated with the compositions "Education" (to the left) and "Work" (to the right) by the sculptor T. Riger. Unfortunately, the flowerbed in front of the University is only a feeble attempt to reproduce the long forgotten elaborate art of phyto-decoration. The adornments of the Neo-Renaissance staircase never cease to produce an astounding effect on the visitor (architect L. Marconi, 1880). The building became a University only in 1919. The then Jan Kazimierz University was famous for its schools of mathematics, philology and history. Today, the University maintains the traditions of one of the best educational establishments in Ukraine.

Professors of Lviv University. Early 20th century

THE RAILROAD ADMINISTRATION
20, Lystopadovoho Chynu Street

Few of the Lviv buildings were lucky enough not to change their functions. One of them is the Lviv Railroad Administration. The monumental edifice on the corner of Lystopadovoho Chynu and Gogolya streets, justly called one of the best examples of administrative architecture, was constructed in 1913 by the architect Z. Bronkhovich-Levynsky. An underground crossing, the only one in town in those days, leads to the building. Only the employees of the Administration had permission to get inside of the building. Yet, the fortunate commoners, who wandered down its halls and caught at least a glimpse of its spacious offices, felt assured that it was one of the best-designed administrative buildings in Old Europe. Over the main entrance ticks a huge clock. The wonderful illumination of the façade has turned the edifice into a lit island in the ocean of Lviv's dark alleys.

Entrance to the courtyard of the Scientific Society premises

SCIENTIFIC SOCIETY
6, Lystopadovoho Chynu Street

This building was constructed in 1897 as a casino for the gentry. Its location close to the Parliament proves that the place was chosen intentionally. The casino was a meeting

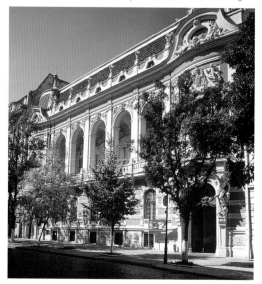

Scientific Society premises

place for the aristocratic elite, here they chattered leisurely about everything and nothing and won and lost vast fortunes. The lucky ones proudly walked back home, while the ill fated despondent wandered to the park nearby. The building was designed by the Vienna firm of Fellner and Helmer. The convenient driveway and the cozy courtyard invite the tourist to pop into the inner world of the edifice that proudly reveals its fanciful interior. The wooden stairs are rightfully regarded the most luxurious in Lviv. The light penetrates into the lobby through a glass cupola-like roof. The façade is decorated with four atlantes petrified in an expressive attempt to support the balconies.

Sculptural decorative motives on the façade

THE METROPOLITAN'S RESIDENCE OF SAINT YURA (GEORGE)

5, St. Yura Square

№ 2, 9, 10, 12

Future artists in front of the Metropolitan's Residence

The golden dome of the St. Yura's (George) Cathedral, conveniently located on the top of a mountain (321 above sea level), can be observed from any spot in the downtown area. The main sanctuary of the Greek Catholics was built in 1744-1761 by the prominent architect B. Meretyn. Decorated in the Rococo style, the cathedral bears traces of Ukrainian traditions in sacral design. The façade is adorned with the statues of St. Athanasius and Lev (by sculptor J. Pizel). The attic is crowned with the sculptural composition of "St. George the Victorious fighting the Serpent" by the same author. The Metro-politan's palace (architect S. Fesinger, 1762) together with the park and the cathedral create an integral architectural ensemble. The stairs decorated with the statue of an anchorite over the grotto lead to the cathedral's main entrance. In 1768 S. Fesinger assembled the Royal and Deacon Gates in the altar part. The altar icons were executed by

Cathedral's main façade

the artists Yu. Radyvylivsky and L. Dolynsky in the 1770s. In the 1850s the cathedral became the focal center in the political life of Ukrainians. Initially, anti-Russian tendencies dominated, which later were substituted with the ideas of Ukraine's independence. The crypts under the cathedral became the burial place for the most venerable church leaders. With the Soviets joining the Western Ukraine to the USSR, the Greek Catholic Church suffered hard times. The pseudo-synod, gathered by the Soviets shortly after Metropolitan Andrey Sheptytsky's death in 1946, proclaimed the Greek Catholic Church illegal and forcefully joined it to the Russian Orthodox Church. The majority of the priests and parishioners were subject to repression. The cathedral together with its property was passed over to new owners. The three gantries, placed in the garden, suppressed the "hostile" radio signals from the West and disfigured the city's panorama. It was only in 1989 that historical justice was finally restored and the Greek Catholic Church was made legitimate. It took much effort to renovate the neglected cathedral and the adjoining premises. During his visit to Ukraine in 2001, Pope John Paul II stayed in the Metropolitan's Palace by the St. Yura's Cathedral.

Sculpture of St. Lev

Metropolitan's Palace

Sculptural
decorations on the
façade of St. Yura's
Cathedral

Architectural section
of St. Yura's Cathedral

LVIV POLYTECHNIC UNIVERSITY

12, Bandery Street

The University's assembly hall is decorated with an allegorical picture, representing the Fire passionately kissing the Water and the birth to the boy called Steam, who grew up to become the driving force of technological progress. This as well as the other ten pictures in the hall were executed by the talented artist Ya. Mateiko. By the staircase are two allegorical figures resembling the mythical caryatids frozen in a loving embrace. The university

Sculptures decorating the stairs

is equipped with spacious lecture-halls and a rich library-museum. The stucco molding of the staircase and the allegorical bas-reliefs, representing Art and Science, add to the elaborate décor of the University. In the park there is a monument commemorating the professors and students, who died in World War II. On the outside walls of the ground floor there are plaques to the prominent alumni, among them V. Sikorsky, S. Vizental and S. Bandera. This imposing edifice of terracotta is the Lviv Polytechnic University, built in 1874-1877 by the architect Yu. Zakharevych. Anyone entering the building is closely watched by the symbolic sculptures of Architecture, Engineering and Mechanics by the famous sculptor Leopold Marconi. The portico slogan "Litteris et Artibus" ("To Sciences and Arts") inspires the youth to work and create. To the left of the main entrance is the first in Halychyna concrete bridge (engineer M. Tullier). Today, the University is one of the largest and most prestigious educational establishments in Ukraine.

Interior of St. Magdalena's church

ST. MAGDALENA'S CHURCH

8, Bandery Street

Completed in about 1630, the Catholic church was later reconstructed and redecorated by M. Urbanik, S. Fesinger and Yu. Zakharevych. The old altar in the apse, decorated with the scenes from St. Magdalena's life (by W. Kielar, 1634), and the modern alabaster altar (by Riechert-Toth, 1926) grip the visitor's attention. From 1917 through 1939 the adjacent premises housed a female correction school, where street girls were given their second chance. The church gave names to the "clients" of the establishments, who were known in the city as "Magdalenas". During the restoration works of 1995 a buried treasure was found in the church. Nowadays, the church is the Organ and Chamber Music Concert Hall. On Sundays and on religious holidays the Catholics offer mass here.

DWARF

At the intersection of Kopernika and Bandery Streets are the ruins of a rotunda erected over an old well. The ruins are guarded by two out of the eight lions that used to top the old City Hall (sculptor B. Dikembrosh). In their paws, the lions hold the emblems of the noble Lviv families of Campiani and Schloz-Wolfowiecz. Until the mid-60s the well was used as a sand pit for the sand to make the steep road less slippery in winter. Until an electric rail-switch was installed, the rotunda had given shelter to a dwarf, who had to switch the rails manually. The poor dwarf had a weird hobby. He used to go to the railway station, where he waited for a pretty and tenderhearted lady to help him with the toilet, since he was too short to do it himself.

THE CATHOLIC CHURCH OF ST. ELIZABETH

Kropyvnytskoho Square
🚊 № 1, 6, 9; 🚌 № 9, 12, 10, or a marshrutka

The Catholic Church of St. Elizabeth

The imposing 85-meter-tall edifice of St. Elizabeth's church was erected by the architect T. Taliovsky in 1903-1911 on the square by the railway station. The church in the Neo-Gothic style is the first thing that catches the eye of anyone arriving in Lviv by train. The church was consecrated in the name of Queen Elizabeth (1837-1898), the wife of King France Joseph I. The Queen, affectionately called by the commoners Sissi, retreated from politics after the tragic death of her only son. The more outrageous was her assassination by the Italian anarchist Luiggi Luccani. The only authentic decorations sur-

Franz Joseph I with his wife Elizabeth. An old postcard

viving are the composition of "John and Maria by the crucifix" (sculptor P. Vijtovych, 1910) and the central altar in the Art-Deco style (architects L. Diurkovych, Yu. Shostakevych and sculptor Ja. Riechert-Toth, 1928-1933). St. Elizabeth's church perhaps suffered more than any other church in Lviv during World War II. Its walls facing Horodotska Street still bear the scars of bullet wounds. The Soviet authorities used the church as storage for the May 1 transparencies. When in the 1980s officials ordered the crosses knocked down from the church, one of the "activists" fell from the dome with the cross he had just sawn off. The restoration works in the church commenced in 1990. Today, it is a Greek Catholic church of St.

The "Crucifix…" composition

Olga and Elizabeth. The sanctuary's interior was renovated by professors and students of Trush'College.

RAILWAY STATION

1,Dvirtseva
(Palace) Square
🚃 *№ 1, 9, 6*
or a marshrutka

The railway services between Lviv and other European cities were introduced in 1862, with the first line connecting Lviv and Przemysl (Poland). As the train remains the most popular

Railway station

means of traveling, the first acquaintance with Lviv, for the majority of tourists, takes place in the railway station. Built in 1899-1903 by the architect V. Sadlovsky, it was inaugurated on March 26, 1904. The metallic constructions of the platforms were manufactured in Czechia. In the old days one had to pay an admission fee to get on the platform. In 1918 the railway station became a battlefield for the Ukrainian and Polish troops. The station's façade is decorated with allegorical images of "Industry" and "Trade" (sculptor A. Popel). The portal is embellished with two figures symbolizing Lviv and Train Service (sculptor P. Vijtovych). The interior of the station has undergone several reconstructions. In 1946-1951 the architect V. Domashenko decorated the waiting lounges and the lobby in the Stalin Empire

style. Nowadays, the only memento of the Soviet architecture is the decoration of the fountain in front of the main entrance. To the left of the main entrance is a forge iron palm, presented to Lviv by Donetsk authorities. During the recent reconstruction of 2002-2003 an attempt was made to restore the station's original appearance.

The № 6 tram takes you back to downtown. Get off at the third stop, half way down Horodotska street. One may wonder why this run-down street has not been chosen for the terminal point of the famous Paris-Dakar rally. At the corner of Horodotska and Shevchenka streets is a small **Catholic church** by the name of **St. Anna**. Built in 1505 over the site of tailor apprentices' assassination, the church was reconstructed in 1673. The "innovative" Soviets shut down the church to open a furniture store on its premises. In 1991 the sanctuary was returned to the Greek Catholic Church.

The dreary, yet busy street of **Horodotska** will take you to the former **St. Anna School** (28, Horodotska), built in the Neo-Romanesque style by the architect Yu. Hochberger in 1884. Here by the former school a tragic accident occurred, when a tram ran into a crowd waiting at the tram stop. The stop was moved elsewhere, yet, the authorities kept back information on the accident. Next door to the school, at the corner of Leontovych Street, stands the **Jewish Hospital** covered with a parti-colored roof and crowned with an onion-like dome

Former Jewish hospital

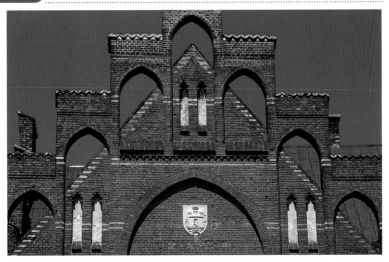

Façade of the former St. Anna School

(architect K. Moklovsky, 1898-1901). The hospital forms the center of the former Jewish district, the inhabitants of which were called the "krakidals" because of the district's close location to the Krakiwsky market. A hundred meters away from the school the notoriously famous Lviv prison of **"Bryhidky"** appears in all its "glory". In 1614-1784 the building belonged to a convent, which the king ordered closed down. Behind these walls it is believed many horrible things took place. A few hundred meters down the narrow and busy Horodotska, and we can finally disappear into the quiet alleys of the **Pidzamche** district. Apart from the above-mentioned churches of St. Nicholas and John the Baptist, be sure to visit the other sacred edifices of the Old Town.

THE CHURCH
OF ST. MARIA ON SNIZHNA
2, Snizhna Street
🚌 № 4, 6, 7

At the intersection of Bohdan Khmelnytsky, Horodotska and Krakiwska streets stands a monumental construction of the former German colonists' church. According to official documents the church was built in the 13th century. Martin Hruneveg mentions the church in his "Lviv sketches". Apparently, it was a wooden edifice. The reconstructions after the fires of 1623-1683 and the restorations of 1888-1892 reshaped the interior in the Neo-Romanesque style and left little of its original

look. Some Romanesque fresco fragments by Edward Liepshy still decorate the walls. In 1988 the edifice housed the Museum of Photography. Now it is the Greek Catholic church of the Holy Virgin's Incessant Help. Take a few steps down Snizhna Street and turn right into a cozy courtyard to feel the atmosphere of "little Paris".

THE CHURCH OF ST. ONUPHRY AND THE MONASTERY OF REVEREND BASILIAN

36, Bohdana Khmelnytskoho Street

Although we will never know the exact year of the construction of St. Onuphry's church, historians surmise that the wooden chapel was erected on this

The church of St. Onuphry

spot back in the 14th century. In the 1550s Prince Konstantin of Ostroh built here a stone church. Since then the church has undergone several reconstructions, with the most significant changes being introduced in 1680. F. Kulchitsky and F. Tresher adorned it with some exquisite decorations. In 1902, according to the designs by the architect Edgar Kovach, the constructor Ivan Levynsky attached the northern aisle to the main church. The interior

Abraham Koh

A courtyard in the monastery

THE LONG LOST WORLD

Close by the convent there is Stary Rynok (Old Market) Square, which, in times of Prince Danylo, the founder of Lviv, and his son Lev, was used as a huge market. After the city center had been moved to Rynok Square, and following numerous fires and reconstructions of the Zhovkivske outskirts, the Jewish community built the largest of Lviv's Progressists' synagogue, "Tempel", on the square in 1843-1846. The synagogue was the place for animated discussions between such intellectuals as Abraham Kohn and his son Gothilf over the Jews' future in Halychyna. Unfortunately, together with other Jewish sacred places, it was razed to the ground by the Nazis.

The majority of the Jews in Halychyna populated small towns, which were then called "shtetl". All the Jews divided into orthodox, conservatives and the uneducated poor. Among the most prominent Jews of Lviv community that stand out are F. Zukher, Sh. Samelson and Sholom-Aleichem. The Jews were predominantly involved in trading, different crafts and restaurant-businesses. It was the relations of the Jews with Halychyna serfs that were so vividly described by the Ukrainian writer Ivan Franko, who started his pamphlet with the words: «In the beginning was Vodka».

Lviv is the city of the eccentrics, whose living traditions are significant and go back in the centuries. Wars and economic depressions give boost to the number of "nonconformists". The "varyat", as they are called in Lviv, and those who only try to imitate their image, still meander around the city looking for a potential audience and financial sponsors. Today, you can bump into a young lady wearing sports shoes of different colors, who, mumbling something incomprehensible, would suddenly make an elaborate pas and shrink back tittering. On Rynok Square another young lady with a pretentious hat and sun- glasses is waiting for Polish tourists. She wants to tell them the heart-rending story about her being an adulterate daughter of General V. Jaruzielski and to beg the gullible tourists for money. In Krakiwsky market you might come across a man, whose long disheveled beard reveals which market rows he has just wandered by in search of his daily bread. Until recently, anyone could have asked an elderly woman, performing guitar concerts on Tarasa Shevchenka Prospect, to sing a hit-song. All these people are the potential clients of the famous Lviv mental hospital. There are many amusing stories about the cozy hospital premises and nearby shady alleys. For example, the "varyats", who, hiding from the Soviet Public Prosecutor, stayed in luxurious, well-furnitured rooms stocked with 'deficit' products (a Soviet term for the food products available only for the high-ranking few). Today, the Lviv mental hospital has saved the lives of a lot of businessmen. As a saying goes, businessmen never die of hunger, but only of fear.

A belfry in St. Onoufry's monastery. A. Kamenobrodzki

is noted for the iconostas of the early 20th century executed by the artist Ivan Sosenko. The fortified walls with loopholes surround the monastery and a belfry. In the 17th century the monastery also housed a hotel for Orthodox pilgrims, visiting the Orthodox Fraternity. The cemetery, located on the monastery's territory, became the burial place for many Fraternity members, including the famous printing pioneer Ivan Fedorov. In 1616 the monastery housed a print shop. The monastery was raised from ashes after it had been decimated by the Turkish army in 1672. The monastery also ran a hospital and a nursing home for the elderly and handicapped. Here even operated a beggars' "trade union", involved in raising money for the nursing home. After the monastery was returned to the Church, it underwent profound restoration, and the reverend Basilian print shop revived the printing traditions of the past.

THE CHURCH OF ST. PARASKEVA
77, Bohdana Khmelnytskoho Street
🚌 *No 6*

Located in the fringe quarters of the city, the church became the center of the Russins' community. The plaque and the Moldavian emblems on the façade indicate that the expenses for the edifice construction were covered by the Moldavian Governor Vasyly Loupou. The resplendent iconostas of the 17th century produces a profound impression on the visitor and is rightfully considered the most beautiful interior construc-

tion in Halychyna. The glittering gild of the iconostas matches the exquisite sacral paintings. Unfortunately, historians can only surmise as to the identity of the author of the masterpiece. The edifice was last reconstructed in 1908. Today, the church belongs to the Ukrainian Autocephalous Church.

THE BENEDICTINE CONVENT
2, Vicheva Square

Although unrightfully omitted in the "typical" tourist itineraries, the convent with the adjacent premises is probably one of the city's most interesting architectural monuments. The Benedictine convent was established in 1593, with the foundation of the main church being laid in 1597 by the architect Pavlo Rymlianyn.

After the conflagration of 1623 Jan Prokopovych reconstructed the sanctuary. The high walls around the convent, which sometimes mar the general aesthetic view, indicate that, if needed, the convent could have been used as a fortress. The monumentality of the buttresses supporting the convent's belfry is somewhat softened by a fanciful portal and pilasters, carrying a Dorian frieze. Stone sculptures decorate the monastery premises (1611-1687). In general, the convent is a vivid example of Lviv Renaissance architecture. Today, the original functions of the convent have been restored and it is a home to nuns. It also houses a theological and musical college and a kindergarten.

View on the Benedictine convent

THE LVIV TRAMPS' WORLD

■ *Lychakiv, Zamarstyniv, Levandivka, Bohdanivka and Klepariv. These outskirts reveal the mythical phenomenon of Lviv tramphood (Batiarka). The term "batiar" (tramp) might have been coined by Hungarian policemen, who came to Lviv after it fell under Austrian rule. In his memoirs Shniur-Peplovsky maintains that batiars inhabited Lychakiv and Pekarska districts and were part of the pickpockets' gang, which operated in the area in 1835. Yet the subculture, created by the batiars, still thrives and is a philosophy of life rather than mere hooliganism. Although batiars in the majority were politically indifferent, they sometimes demonstrated definite political preferences. Such was the case when in 1918 they took the side of the Poles in their fight for Lviv. The batiars' world originated in industrial districts, dark pubs and in the streets. The Polish researcher Yacubowska made an attempt to describe a typical batiar. He is a proletariat, perhaps a looser, and often a loner. Although sometimes he resorts to minor crimes to make a living, yet he is not deprived of noble features. He speaks his own slang. Unfortunately, the remains of the batiars' dialect have been substituted with the criminals' cant. The actors Tontz and Schepetz were the "visiting card" of the batiars' after the First World War.*

LYCHAKIV

Lychakiv is the oldest of the authentic Lviv names. The main artery of the quarter is Lychakivska street. The district used to be an estate of German colonists, the Lutzes. The names of the quarter's streets reflect the occupations of their inhabitants: Solodova (Malt), Pekarska (Bakery), Krupiarska (Cereals). The batiars' fame was marred only by the popularity of sauerkraut (sour cabbage) makers. Numerous fables reveal incredible stories about the merry atmosphere of Lychakivska Street. Mytna (Customs) Square separates the Catholic church of the Claris order (architect P. Rymlianyn) from the Hlyniana (Clay) Tower and the Benedictine monastery. It was under this square that the Turkish army dug a secret underground passage in 1672. Having learnt about the menace, the locals took measures to avert the danger and smashed the enemy. Soon the passage was forgotten, and it was only when the authorities were making the largest in Lviv underground crossing that the passage was discovered. Immediately the finding resurrected the legend that the passage had been used by the monks, who often visited the nuns in the convent across the square. Although the legend has no grounds whatsoever, it rooted firmly in people's

A view on the beginning of Lychakivska Street

imagination. Today, the church houses the museum of the famous artist Yu. Pinzel (tel. 756966; open: 11.00-16.00, daily, except Mondays). At № 3, Lychakivska street was published the first city newspaper, "Gazetta de Leopoli", in 1776. Nowadays, as well as centuries ago, Lychakivska remains a busy city artery. The tramline deprived the local fiacre carriers of their only way of earning a living. The memoirs about Lviv tell a story about the wife of one of the last fiacre carriers, Mrs. S., who, when she saw the first tram in Lychakiv "…by gestures made a sexual proposition, impossible to perform".

KURKOVE (TRIGGER) SOCIETY
23a, Lysenka Street

It was only in the 20th century that the Lviv Riflemen Society, founded in 1789, managed to find a permanent location in a house down Lysenka Street, initially called Kurkova, i.e. Trigger. And the trigger was the emblem of the Society. The historian I. Krypiakevych recalls that the Lviv Society used to own artillery till a cannon killed a person during a city festival in 1832. The key aim of the Society was to train people to defend the city in case of emergency. The first shooting-range was in the open air between the city ramparts, but later the Society acquired a separate shooting gallery. With time the initial aim of the Society lost its importance, and the organization turned into an elite club for the most venerable people in town, for the crème-de-la-crème. The annual election of the Trigger King reminded of splendid coronation ceremonies. The "King" was handed the power regalia, while the other society members swore their allegiance.

"VETERANS' CAVE " PUB

Here on Kurkova street was located the "Veterans' Cave" pub. The name of the pub is a modified surname of the Austrian general Veteranni. The pub enjoyed the ill fame not only for being the cheapest, and thus the worst, dance hall in Lviv, but rather for the inhospitality of its haunters, always eager to welcome a newcomer with a fist blow. The popular Lviv song about two civilians with tousled hair, who appeared in the pub right after midnight and beat the visitors without uttering a word, describes a definite place in the city.

THE CATHOLIC CHURCH OF ST. ANTONIO
49a, Lychakivska Street
🚋 № 2, 7

This church forms an imaginary border, dividing the street into Lower and Upper Lychakiv. For its closer location to the downtown, the Lower Lychakiv preserved a more "civilized" look, whereas the Upper Lychakiv stubbornly guarded its "authentic" inner world. Built in 1718-1765 at the request of K. Vyshnevetsky, the church of St. Antonio reconciled within its walls

I. Krypiakevych recalled that the statue of the Holy Virgin at Lychakivska Street was deeply revered by the locals. Once an Austrian official was passing down the street, when his carriage caught on the statue and an axle was broken. In a rage he ordered the statue thrown in a gutter by a fence. Next morning, he woke up blind. In the mid-19th century people constructed a chapel on the spot where the statue once stood. On the night of August 28, 1959, the chapel was pulled down.

all the district inhabitants. The façade was decorated by F. Kultchytsky. The luxuriant Baroque interior survives till these days, which could be explained by the fact that it, as well as the Latin Catholic Cathedral, has never been closed by the Soviets. The sculpture of the Immaculate Conception (sculptor S. Fesinger), placed by the foot of the staircase leading to the entrance, catches the eye of the visitor.

THE MILITARY HOSPITAL

26, Lychakivska Street

🚋 *№ 2, 7*

In 1659 Jan Sobieski allocated a large sum for the foundation of this monastery, where in 1687 was opened a hospital for wounded and elderly soldiers. The same year the French architect Benoit carried out the final reconstructions of the edifice. In the late 18th century the hospital was expanded. Not long ago a new military garrison hospital was added to the old construction, and the old building was left neglected.

OPEN-AIR MUSEUM OF FOLK ARCHITECTURE AND RURAL LIFE

1, Chernecha Hora Street

🚋 *71-2360*

🕐 *10.00-17.30, Tuesday through Sunday*

Monument to King Jan III Sobieski

The territory of the present Museum is known among Lvivites by at least two names. In the 18th century it was called Lionshanivka after the first owner of the estate Longchamps, the City Governor and a member of a Masonic lodge. In 1780 King Joseph II visited the estate and was profoundly impressed by its picturesque location. To commemorate the visit of the distinguished guest, Longchamps placed the statue of the Roman goddess Minevra and named the forest, "King's woods" (Kaiserwald). During the First World War, half of the forest was cut down and the statue disappeared. The former estate became a popular recreation place. Adjacent to the park were built luxurious villas and this area was known among common people as "Professors' colony". Since 1972 sixty hectares of the former estate have housed the Open-Air Museum of Folk Architecture and Rural Life. The museum features 124 architectural constructions and more than twenty thousand displays from different ethnic regions of Western Ukraine, among them **Boikivsky, Hutsulschyna, Lemkivsky, Podillya and Polissya**. One of the museum's most valuable exhibits is a hata (peasant house) from the village of Lybokhora, Skolivsky rayon, Lviv region. Built by Fedir Udytch in 1749 the house is the oldest residential construction in the Carpathians. In the center of the **Boikivsky** sector towers the famous St. Nicholas's church (1763), brought to the museum by the celebrated ethnographer, M. Drahan,

THE CHURCH OF ST. PAUL AND ST. PETER

82a, Lychakivska Street

🚋 *№ 2, 7*

The church of St. Paul and St. Peter towers over the intersection

Church of St. Peter and St. Paul

of Lychakivska and Mechnikova streets. Until 1668 it was just a small roadside chapel. In 1750 monks of the Paulin order built a bigger church on this site. Following the abolition of the order, in 1786 the church was handed down to the Jesuit community. In 1798 Fesinger reconstructed the building. In 1922 artists from the Northern Ukraine added some fresco decorations. Today, the church belongs to the Ukrainian Autocephalous Church.

A church from the Lemkivsky region

from Kryvky village, Turkivsky rayon, Lviv region. Today, monks of the Studit order maintain the church and conduct their masses. Next door to the church is a village school (1880) from Busovysko village, Sambirky rayon. The school consists of the two-room teacher's quarters, a kitchen and a classroom. While in the classroom, pay attention to the "donkey's" desk (the last desk in the row reserved for dumb students) and the birch rods on the teacher's desk, which apparently were to improve students' learning abilities.

The most interesting exhibit in the **Lemkivsky** sector is a farm from Zaricheve village, Perechynsky rayon, Transcarpathian region. The Lemky are one of the numerous region's ethnic groups, which

inhabited the territory amid the Uzh, San, Poprad and Dunaits rivers. During the ethnic cleansing conducted by the Soviet and Polish governments after the Second World War, the Lemky suffered more than any other ethnic group. A few years ago a church was constructed by the Lemky Diaspora to honor the memory of the perished.

Hutsulschyna is a Carpathian region full of myths and legends. The people of Hutsul inhabited the most remote nooks in the Carpathians

and thus managed to preserve their traditions and identity. Hutsulschyna still lures those who want to experience authentic rural life. Among other examples of Hutsul folk architecture the most significant is a fenced yard, the hradzha, from Kruvorivna village, Verkhovynsky rayon. The

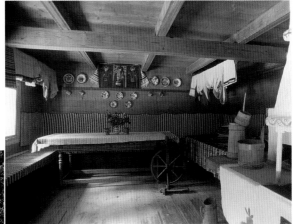

The interior of a peasant house in the Boikivsky sector

hradzha is a self-sufficient farm protected from the weather and wild animals by a fence.

Decorations, bright colors and the artistic lay out of houses distinguish **Bukovyna** from other Carpathian regions. The most vivid examples of Bukovyna folk architecture are the farm from Berezhonka village, Vyzhnytsky rayon, Chernivtsy region, and the 19th century farm from Toporivtsy village, Novoselytsky rayon, Chernivtsy region. The museum is popular for afternoon strolls and folk festivals, held in the open-air theatre. The ceramics store offers a wide range of exquisite ceramic products. Next to the store is a small, improvised zoo. At the start of the 1990s the museum held numerous festivals that promoted national renascence.

A church from Kryvchytsy village

THE CHURCH OF THE PROTECTING VEIL OF THE HOLY VIRGIN

the former Catholic church of the Holy Virgin Ostrobramska 175, Lychakivska Street

🚌 № 2

The former Turkul-Comelo's palace

The tall, imposing church tower dominates Lychakivska Street. The church (architect T. Obminsky) was commissioned by Archbishop Boleslav Tvardovsky, who vowed to build a church if Lviv was saved from the cavalry commanded by General Budiony. The construction was completed in 1938. Unfortunately, little survives of its original decor. In 1946-1991 the church was used as a warehouse with a monument to a Soviet tank safely guarding the entrance.

Among other attractions of the Lychakivsky district is the former **Semensky-Levytsky's palace** at 19, Pekarska Street. Its size and the grandeur of the French Baroque design make it a worthy rival of the famous Pototsky's palace. In 1879 and 1892-1894 I. Levynsky, Ya. Kudelsky and A. Wagner reconstructed the palace. A richly decorated driveway leads to the entrance. Today, the palace houses № 102 secondary school.

To the right of Pekarska Street is seen a dome of the three-aisle basilica, which used to be part of the Sacrament monastery. The basilica was constructed by the celebrated architects B. Meretyn, A. Minasevych and V. Sadlovsky. For a lengthy period of time the church was left abandoned, which led to the destruction of a large part of the interior decoration.

The former Semensky-Levytsky's palace

Next to the monumental building in the Soviet style, occupied by the **Gzydsky Academy of Veterinary Medicine** (50, Pekarska Street; tel. 2986889), stands the former **Turkul-Comelo's palace**, yet another exquisite attraction of the district (50 a, Pekarska Street). Commissioned by Countess Didushitska, the palace was built in the early 19th century in the Venetian Gothic style. It faces Pekarska Street backwards, thus, you have to walk around the palace to have a closer view of its elaborate façade.

Brother Albert

The Lviv famous deadpan joke goes that it is no surprise that **Lviv State Halytsky Medical University** (69, Pekarska Street; 722660) is located close to the Lychakivske cemetery. According to a saying,

Lviv Medical University and the monument to doctors killed during World War II

doctors' mistakes are hidden deep in the ground. Most of the University premises were built in the late 19th century. In 1894 the Medicine Department was finally opened in Lviv University. After World War II the department was singled out as a separate institution. The prewar surgical traditions of H. Ostrovsky, H. Shram and L. Ridiger are maintained by the followers of the professor Karavanov's school. The University boasts several medical museums, with the Anatomy museum being the most interesting.

*There are numerous stories from the past about Lviv's outskirts. The **Klepariv** district was founded in 1419 by the merchant Stano Klopper. In the 15th century the area was famous for the vineyards, as well as for cherry trees, which were under the city authority's protection. The adventure-seekers may risk a stroll down Kleparivska Street, which begins not far from St. Anna's church. A magnificent panorama of the city opens up the "Mount of Executions", which project over Kleparivska Street and Krakiwsky market. There on the mountain stands a small monument commemorating two Polish rebels – T. Wisniowsky and Ju. Kapustynsky. Almost at the foot of the mountain, right over Kleparivska Street, nestles a tiny building, which used to house an asylum for the poor, founded by brother Albert and constructed in 1891 by the architect J. Hochberger. Brother Albert, known, prior to joining the monkshood, as Adam Khmeliovsky (1846-1916), was an interesting personality. A gifted artist, one of the first exponents of Impressionism in Poland, he withdrew from politics and devoted himself to supporting the poor. After his death a convent of the Albert's order was organized.*

A view on Kleparivksa Street

Lviv brewers.
The latter half of the 19th century

LVIV BREWERY
18, Kleparivska Street

Lviv has always been famous for its beer. Although some individuals enjoyed the right to produce the beverage, yet, the beer brewed in monasteries was always considered of a higher quality. The Lviv brewery was established in 1715 and was very well known for its produce. The factory's premises

Lviv brewery
emblem

A joke. Friends of the Lviv brewer come to his wife to tell her that her husband had drowned in a beer barrel. "I hope he did not suffer much", said the wife. "No", answered the friends, " While getting drowned, he jumped out of the barrel three times to go to the rest-room".

were constructed in 1896-1912. The brewery became even more famous in the Soviet era, when it could rival one of the best beer brands in the USSR, the Russian "Zhigulivske". People used to come to Lviv just "to have a pint". Its popularity is reflected in the Lviv saying: "Lviv beer is top-notch, it makes a layman an ace". The brewery used to have a beerhouse, which now is under reconstruction.

THE HOUSE
FOR DISABLED VETERANS
35, Kleparivska Street

The house for disabled veterans

Finishing your stroll down Kleparivska Street, admire the former house for disabled veterans. Built in 1855-1869 by the architect T. Hansen, the house lodges the Institute for Fire and Technical Engineering, which will hopefully protect the construction from any calamity. Some Lviv scientists believe that the building was constructed in the Medieval Italian palazzo style. The premises are kept in an impeccable state, which allows us to admire the elaborate bas-reliefs of Mars, the god of war, Venus, the goddess of peace, and griffins (sculp-

tors Ts. Godebsky and A. Perier), which decorate the building's facade of yellowish-red bricks.

* * *

If we keep going in an easterly direction, we will inevitably wander into the Lviv district city guides prefer not to show to tourists. It is **Zamarstyniv**, the world of two-storied apartment buildings and intertwining streets. The district developed from a village, which was engulfed by the fast growing town. In 1389 Jan Zommerstein founded and inhabited a small hamlet. Interesting enough, but the author of this book was once told by district dwellers a legend about a mythical mister Tyniv, who in the winter walked out of a pub drunk, fell down on the snow and froze to death. To freeze to death in Ukrainian is "zamerzat", which is consonant with the modern name of the district, Zamarstyniv. Yet, the story remains a legend. Until 1940, about 35 per cent of Lviv's population lived in this quarter. Here dwelled those who came to Great Lviv in search of a job.

BACZEWSKY
114/116, Bohdana Khmelnytskoho Street

The patriarch of this celebrated family was L. Baczeles, who moved a vodka distillery from Vybranka village to Lviv. In 1856 his descendants expanded the factory and made its produce well known in the world. Leopold Baczewsky was granted a gentry title in 1908, the year

The former Baczewsky's factory

when King Franz Joseph II celebrated his 60th anniversary of enthronement. Adam Baczewsky (1829-1911) was the first to use liquor bottles of different colors, thus leaving behind his competitive rivals. The factory was destroyed in 1939 in a Nazi air raid. The trademark, revived after World War II in Vienna, never managed to regain the popularity it had once enjoyed. The factory's premises, which still survive, lodge a factory of diamond tools. The two lions by the main entrance gate are the reminder of the glorious past.

The "Vezha" restaurant in the Stryisky Park

The Baczewsky factory had an unconventional approach to advertising its produce. When Lviv held a General Halychyna Exhibition in Stryisky Park, they built a 20-meter tall tower and filled it with bottles. This wonder stirred a sensation among the city inhabitants, who came in crowds to admire the construction. Early in the morning the drunkards with lilac noses crowded around it, calculating how long all this liquor would suffice to quench their thirst. In the afternoon, the respected citizens with their families arrived and, having marveled at the wonder-tower, headed for the local pavilion to have a shot of "Baczewsky" vodka.

TRAMWAY DEPOT
3, Sakharova Street

Close by the district, known in the old Lviv as Kastelivka, are situated the hangars of the old tramway depot (architect Kamenobrodsky, 1894, 1906), which are still in use. The tramline, connecting the railway station and the exhibition in Stryisky Park, opened in 1894. In 1909 electric trams superseded the horse-driven. The same year season tickets were introduced with the owner's picture attached. The fare was the same for all parts of the city, except for the ascent up Horodotska Street. To pull a tram up the steep slope another pair of horses was harnessed, which raised the fare. All tram drivers wore uniforms and the profession was considered highly prestigious. Trams operated from 6 a.m. to 11 p.m. Right behind the old tramway depot is the first city power-station (1894-1900).

An old tram on a Lviv street

THE NEW WORLD OF OLD LVIV

"Ostroverkhova" Villa

■ *In the course of its history, Lviv has experienced several construction-booms, which changed the city's face beyond recognition. Due to the fires of the 16th century the elegant European Renaissance supplanted the Gothic style. In the mid-19th century, the Imperial architectural style came into fashion. The Functionalism and Secession of the early 20th century added new sensual grace. The railway depot is the right place to start the tour of Lviv's new world. The planned development of the district started in the late 19th century, when the picturesque hills were to be built up with villas and cozy family houses. The First World War and the following economic crisis partially foiled the bold plans of the architects Yu. Zakharevych, I. Levynsky and T. Obminsky. Nonetheless, the area deserves a closer study, which will reveal to the curious the traces of architectural freethinking.*

THE STREET OF THE MILITARY

The modern Hvardeiska (Guards) Street connects the tramway depot and the Military Institute of Lviv Polytechnic University. The street's old name of Kadetska (Cadets') indicates that the military have always been the masters. Climbing up this rather steep slope, pay attention to the facades in the Secession style. The building **№ 6** is famous for the fact that Pilsudsky, a marshal and the head of Polish State, lived in the house for several years. The **№ 28a** (1957) is a typical example of the Soviet Realism style. Luxurious summerhouses, which used to belong to Soviet officials and now are owned by Ukrainian authorities, down the shady Hlinky Street triggered numerous legends. The modern **"Lion's Castle"** hotel (7/9, Hlinky Street) and the villas, surrounded by Bohdan Khmelnytsky Park, form a cozy and comfortable nook.

Boy-Zhelenskoho Street leads to **Vooletska hill**, where stands a modest monument commemorating one of the most horrible events in Lviv's history. In 1941, right after the Germans had invaded Lviv, a large group of Lviv University professors was executed on the hill. Later,

"Zamok Leva" (Lion's Castle)

the witnesses to the shooting made it public. Among the executed were such prominent scientists as T. Boy-Zhelensky, A. Cieszynski, H. Hilarowicz, and W. Sieradzki.

Having left Vooletska hill behind and crossed Saharova Street, we reach the intersection of Chooprynky, Kyivska and Kotlyarevskoho Streets. It is the best place to observe the peculiarities of the beautiful **Kastelivka district**. The number one attraction is building **№ 27**. Starting in 1930, it was under the USSR consulate. Diplomats frequently gathered Lviv intelligentsia in their attempt to lure Lvivites by sumptuous banquets. It was here that M. Lemyk, a member of Ukrainian Nationalists Organization, attacked the consul Mailov, thus demonstrating his protest against the famine of 1932-1933 in Eastern Ukraine. Across the street, right at the intersection, is a splendid villa (**21, Chooprynky Street**) (architects Yu. Zakharevytch, I. Levynsky and M. Kovalchuk), which since the 1990s has hosted the Shevchenko Scientific Society. The house was once owned by the famous art collector M. Ostroverkhov, whose sudden death fueled the discussions of the peculiar approaches used by "aliens from the East" (as they call in Lviv anybody who comes from Eastern Ukraine or Russia) to accumulate art collections.

Entrance to the Khmelnytsky Park

It is hard to believe that the peaceful Bohdan Khmelnytsky Park conceals an atrocious secret. During the Nazis invasion, the premises of the modern Military Institute were under a hospital and the hill's slopes became a burial place for many German privates and officers. After the war, the Soviet authorities ordered the cemetery razed to the ground and set up a park. The recent reconstructions revealed the wretched secret. Negotiations are being carried out to restore the remains of German soldiers to a decent burial.

Monument to Lviv University professors

The "Fortress" building

A HOUSE AND A FORTRESS
50/52, Chooprynky street

Facing this elaborate edifice (architect Yu.Sosnovsky, 1901) one might imagine that he has moved back in time to the Middle Ages. In this medley of styles a connoisseur of art would track Gothic motives masterfully interlaced with the elegance of Renaissance fragments. A corner tower turns this apartment building into a real knight's castle. Yet, the locals gossip that the heating here is as poor as it was in a Medieval castle.

THE CHURCH AND CONVENT OF THE BAREFOOT CARMELITES
70, Chooprynky Street

The brick church and convent of the barefoot Carmelites were constructed in 1893-1895 in the Neo-Romanesque style. The project was executed by the construction factory of I. Levynsky and according to the designs by the architect F. Stap Junior. After World War II, the former monastery housed the city communication station. It was only in 2004 that the former house of worship was returned to the parish. Today, it is a Greek Catholic church of St. Clement.

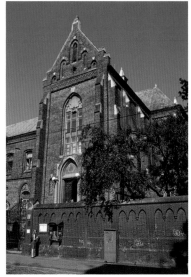

The convent of the Barefoot Carmelites

THE QUEEN OF PLASTER
13, Melnyka Street

It is perhaps one of the most elaborately decorated villas in the quarter. Until 1939 it belonged to the owner of plaster-producing factory Yu. Franz. The factory gave its name to a nearby street. This luxuriant Neo-Baroque edifice was designed by the architect Ya. Peros and sculptor Plishevsky. After World War II the estate was expropriated, and since then it has been used as a hospital.

Konovaltsa Street will take you back to the downtown area. The names, which the street bore in different periods, reflect the landmarks of Lviv history. Routed in 1892 by the owners of the aforementioned factory, it hosted the aristocracy and the wealthy. Until 1940 it was called November 29 Street, in commemoration of the Polish Patriots' Anti-Tsar Uprising. The Germans gave it a new name, Germanstrasse. The Soviets called it Engels Street, and the Ukrainian authorities named it after Konovalets, a leader of the Ukrainian Nationalists Organization. Unfortunately, the splendor of villas and mansions has been marred by recently built multi-storied apartment blocks. Pay attention to the Art-Deko decorations of the mansion at **№22-22a** (the former "VITA" health center), and stroll around the villas down Hipsova, Zalizniaka and Kokorudzy streets.

Lost among other quite alleys of this cozy district, Yaponska (Japanese) Street stands out for the fact that its old names allow to trace down all the vicissitudes of political struggles in the city. In 1945 the conflict between the Soviets and Japan made the authorities give Yaponska Street another name, Khasanska. Two months later it was called Yaponska, and in 1950 – Khasanska, it was only in the 1990s that the old name, Yaponska, was returned to this street.

Villa of Yu. Franz

NECROPOLISES IN LVIV

■ *The level of any civilization is estimated by several factors, one of which being the way cemeteries are kept by the descendants of the buried. In this respect, Lviv is a distinguished town and stands on a par with such cities as Paris, Prague or Warsaw. Yet, it has not always been this way. Having visited Lviv, King Franz Joseph II called it a town of cemeteries and monks. Until 1772, by any sanctuary there was a cemetery, which could have at any moment triggered an epidemic. The most celebrated Lvivites, for example, the Campiani or the Boims, were buried in family chapels or in crypts under churches. Others were buried in churches' or synagogues' yards. Although the decree prohibiting any burials within the city bounds was issued in 1783, it has only been since 1786 that the dead were buried in places designated by authorities. Numerous city reorganizations and re-planning razed the Paparivka, Stryiske and Horodetske cemeteries, yet left for posterity the two oldest graveyards of Lychakivske and Yanivske.*

CEMETERY-MUSEUM

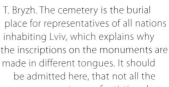

The Statue of Kneeing Christ by the entrance to the main alley

The Lychakivske cemetery reflects all the trends and changes in the European fashions for city graveyard arrangements. The cemetery was laid out in the form of a park. One of its architects, Karol Bauer, strictly divided the burial areas by alleys, paths and fields. Titus Thozhewski also took part in arranging the territory. In his days the graveyard covered 40 hectares. Since 1885, cemetery officials have been registering the burials. The city authorities have always advocated the importance of proper tomb-maintenance. It was forbidden to make use of any means of transportation in the cemetery and the coffins were moved in specially designed carriages. Tomb monuments were executed by such prominent artists as H. Vitver, A. Kuzhava, P. Filippi, Yu. Markovsky, T. Baronch, H. Kuznevych, S. Lytvynenko and T. Bryzh. The cemetery is the burial place for representatives of all nations inhabiting Lviv, which explains why the inscriptions on the monuments are made in different tongues. It should be admitted here, that not all the monuments are of artistic value. Commencing in 1944, even more hideous monument-slabs of gray uncut stone have been placed in the graveyard. The barbarian attitude of the Soviets led to the destruction of many old monuments, and some family crypts were forced "to house new hosts". In 1975 mass burials in the Lychakivske cemetery were abolished. Since then, to bury a deceased person, relatives must now obtain a City Rada permit. The exception is made for the most celebrated Lvivites as well as for those families, who have their own crypts. On July 10, 1990 the City Rada made a decision to turn the Lychakivkse cemetery into a historical and cultural reserve.

ⓘ Entrance fee for adults is 3UAH. Discounts are made for children and students. You can hire a guide in the excursion office by the main entrance. Booklets about the cemetery's history are available in different languages.

Maria Konopnytska (1842-1910), famous Polish children's writer.

Gabriel Zapolska, (1859-1921), famous Polish writer and public figure. Her tomb is decorated with the names of her 56 novels and dramas.

Wladislaw Belza, (1847-1913), poet, writer, publicist, the author of "Catechism for Polish children".

Mikhal Mikhalski, (1846-1907), public figure; President of Lviv.

Stefan Banakh, (1892-1945), founder of the functional analysis school, professor of Lviv University.

Zygmund Gorgolewski, (1845-1903), architect; designed Lviv Opera House.

I. Vilde, (1907-1982), prominent Ukrainian writer.

Ivan Krypiakevych, (1886-1967), Ukrainian historian, professor of Lviv University.

Z. Gorgolevsky's grave

Stanislaw Sczepanowski, pioneer in oil and gas production in Halychyna; banker.

Antony Dursky (sculptor V .Havlinsky), founder of the "Sokil" Polish youth sport organization.

Julian Ordon (sculptor T. Baronch), rebel, hero of the 1831 Lviv defense.

Severyn Goschynsky, (1801-1867), poet, participant of November uprising. Introduced Hutsul folklore in Polish literature.

The monument over Maria Konopnytska's grave

Ivan Franko, (1856-1916), (sculptor S. Lytvynenko), prominent poet, writer and political figure.

Markian Shashkevych, (1811-1843), (sculptor G. Perie) , participant of "The Russian Three", co-author of the "Rusalka Dnistrova" (The Dniestr Mermaid) collection.

Juzefa Markowska "Sleeping young woman" (sculptor Yu. Markowski, 1887)

The Baczewski's chapel, the family of prosperous entrepreneurs, owners of Lviv vodka distillery.

The Barczewski's chapel ,(sculptor V. Galytsky, 1887), the largest family chapel at the Lychakivske cemetery (220 square meters), built in Pseudo-Byzantine style with Romanesque fragments. The chapel was constructed for one of the wealthiest people in the Podillia region, Perobus Petro Wlodzimierz of the Samson Barczewski (1833-1884) emblem. A large part of his estate was bequeathed to charity.

The chapel of the Dunin-Borkowkys ,(sculptor G. Vitver). Commissioned in 1812 by Count Leopold Vincent Dunin-Borkowky as a burial place for his wife Ignatsia. The chapel is considered the most lavishly decorated crypt at the Lychakivske cemetery.

Volodymyr Barvinsky, (1850-1883), (sculptor Levandovsky) – prominent political and public figure; the founder of the "Prosvita" (Education) Organization.

Joseph Torosevych, (1784-1869), (sculptor E. Yaskulsky) – Doctor of Medicine, the founder of the orphanage for Armenian children.

Arthur Grodger, (1837-1867), famous Polish artist, known in Polish literature for his ardent love to Wanda Mane, a daughter of a local painter.

Solomia Krushelnytska, (1873-1952), talented opera singer, soprano. She was the first to introduce Ukrainian folk songs into opera repertoire. In 2000 Lviv Opera House was named after her.

Stanislaw Liudkewicz ,(1878-1979), famous composer.

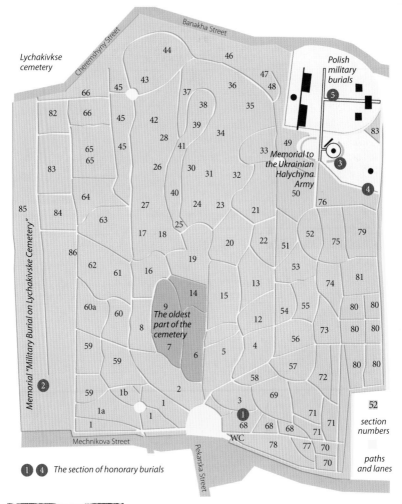

Banakha Street

Lychakivkse cemetery

Cheremshyny Street

44
46
47
48
43
45
36
37
38
39
35
49
33 Memorial to the Ukrainian Halychyna Army 50

Polish military burials

5

82
66
66
45
45
45
42
41
28
34
40
30
31
32
26
27
24
23
21
52
75
79

65
65
64
84
63

85

83

86

62
61
16
14
15
13
53
74
81

60a
60
8
9
The oldest part of the cemetery
7
12
54
55
80
80
73
80
80

59
59
6
5
4
56
57
80
80

59
1b
2
58
72

1a
1
1
3
68
69
71
71

1
68
68
68
71
70

WC
78
77
70
70

Mechnikova Street

Pekarska Street

52

section numbers

paths and lanes

Memorial "Military Burial on Lychakivske Cemetery"

2

3

4

76

51

20
22
17
18
19
25

83

1 4 The section of honorary burials

A. Dursky's grave

Isaak Isakovych, (1824-1901),

Samuel Stefanovych, (1755-1858), Archbishops of the Armenian Christian Church.

V. Chukarin, (1921-1994), (sculptor Ya.Chaika), twice the Olympic champion (XV, XVI), honorary Lviv citizen, coach of the USSR national gymnastics team.

Ihor Bilozir, (1955 -2000), famous Ukrainian composer.

Volodymyr Ivasiuk, (1949-1979), (sculptors V. Posikira and L. Yaremchuk, 1990),composer,

"Mythical Orpheus" on Solomia Krushelnytska's grave

Ju. Ordon's tomb,
by sculpture S. Havlinsky

Monument over Joseph
Torosevych's grave

A. Grodger's tomb

the author of the songs "Chervona Ruta" and "Ya pidu daleko v hory", which made national trademark.

Franz Smolka, (1810-1899), lawyer, Ambassador of the Vienna Parliament, initiated the construction of the memorial mound to the 300th-anniversary of the Liublin Union, an exceptionally bright personality.

The "Lviv orliats (eaglets)" memorial is the most controversial burial at the Lychakivske cemetery. The memorial holds the tombs of young Polish soldiers, who died in the 1918-1920 Polish uprising against the Ukrainians and Soviets. It was commissioned by the parents and families of the deceased. The idea of the memorial, initially called "White Roses," was suggested by R. Indrukh, an assistant at Lviv Polytechnic University. The memorial is the tomb for 2859 soldiers, including 3 American pilots and 17 French military men (16 bodies were exhumed and taken to France). In the 1970s the Soviet authorities partially destroyed the burial. The reconstruction commenced only in 1989. The Latin inscription on the main column says: "They sacrificed their lives for your freedom". The remains of an unknown soldier were exhumed and reburied in the Unknown Soldier grave at Pilsudski Square in Warsaw. The memorial's official inauguration is postponed due to the Ukrainian authorities' refusal to renovate all the inscriptions, which used to decorate the monument before it was damaged.

The Memorial to the Ukrainian Halychyna Army and to the Struggle for Independence of the Ukrainian People (sector # 76). The memorial's construction, im-

Monument on the communal grave of the 1863-1864 Uprising participants

plemented by the sculptors M. Posikira and D.Krvavych, architect M. Fedyk and artist I. Havryshkevych, commenced in the mid-1990s. The monument consists of two parts – a symbolic grave of the Ukrainian Halychyna Army soldiers and a communal grave of victims of the 1940s Stalin repressions.

"Masons"
on I. Franko's grave

The tall column, dominating over the lower field, is topped with the statue of Archangel Michael. The plates, surrounding the monument, bear the names of the deceased in their struggle for Ukrainian's independence. Recently, the remains of D. Vitovsky and doctor V. Tysowski, the founder of the "Plast" Ukrainian scout organization, were reburied in the memorial.

Monument over Samuel Stefanovych's grave

The Pantheons to the January and November Uprisings are on the opposite sides of the Lychakivke cemetery. Unfortunately, the Pantheon to the January Uprising of 1863-1864

The "Lviv Orliats (Eaglets)" monument

(sector # 40) is off the main alley and is difficult to find behind the thickets of wild growing bushes and trees. Following the decision of the City Rada (Administration), the construction of the monument commenced in the latter part of the 19th century. One of the initiators of the project was the catholic priest Ludwig Ruczka. The society of National Guardianship was set up to raise money for the construction. The central monument of the mound, which is the burial place for 230 rebels, was executed in the Zgursky's studio in 1906. It is a statue of Simon Vizumas Shidlowsky holding a Lithuanian flag he had seized in a catholic church in Surz and had had it with him in several battles. In his memoirs Yu. Vittlin recalls the veterans of the January Uprising, greeted by the public, marching down Lviv streets, thus honoring the deceased fellow-fighters. The other pantheon, commemorating the November Uprising (sector # 71), is the grave for 47 participants of the Polish rebellion. The

grave is topped with a symbolical sarcophagus decorated with an eagle, uhlan helmet, national emblems of Poland, Lithuania and Russ and an inscription, saying, "The avenger should rise from our ashes". Among other rebels, the grave holds the remains of Joseph Reitsenheim (1809-1883), a son of a venerable Austrian official, and the remains of Bohuslaw Longchamps de Berier (Franz Longchamps was a Lviv mayor). The tomb has recently been renovated and brought into order.

The monument to the victims of NKVD (People's Commissariat of Internal Affairs) terror (sector # 82). This communal grave holds the ashes of 205 Ukrainians, 21 Poles, 6 Germans, 14 Jews and 5 Russians, who fell victim to the NKVD terror raging before the Second World War. All the deceased were political prisoners.

Monument over V. Barvinsky's grave

Olha Basarab, 1890-1924.
*An active participant
of a Ukrainian patriotic
military organization, she
was tortured to death in
prison by the local police.*

Modest Sosenko,
1865-1920. A painter

YANIVSKE CEMETERY

128, Shevchenka Street
🚌 № 7

The Yanivske cemetery is definitely off the beaten tourist track. Unlike the Lychakivske, it lacks a developed scientific and research infrastructure, which makes it difficult, but not impossible, to find interesting grave monuments. Nonetheless, a visit to the cemetery is a must, if you want to see convincing evidences of Lviv's turbulent history.

The main entrance to the Yanivske cemetery is from Shevchenka Street. In 1883 this site was appointed for the burials of the Lvivites, who inhabited the western part of the city. Today, there are about 200,000 graves. Since 1980, the burials at the cemetery have required a permit from officials. Given the amount of military graves, this cemetery

rivals the Lychakivske. Here there are tombs of soldiers of General Denikin and General Vrangel armies, the tombs of Austrian and Russian military who died in the First World War. In 1920, 226 soldiers of the General Budiony cavalry

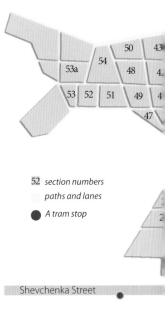

52 *section numbers*
    paths and lanes
🔴 *A tram stop*

Shevchenka Street

were buried here. Yet, the largest military pantheon (filed #38) is the memorial to one thousand soldiers who died in the 1918 Ukrainian-Polish war for Lviv. In the grave, together with privates, rest such prominent political figures as Myron Tarnavsky (1869-1938) and Kost Levytsky (1859-1941). Not far from the pantheon there is a small memorial to Polish warriors. In the 1970s officials ordered the memorials destroyed for political reasons. In the early 1990s the restoration of the graves commenced.

The Yanivske cemetery is the last resting place for the victims of political repressions. On field # 44 is a monument honoring the martyrs of the Soviet Holocaust. Until 1943 the cemetery was under a Nazis concentration camp, where together with Jews the Germans held prisoners representative of other nations. The grave for the NKVD victims is on field # 1. Here on this cemetery there are tombs of German (sector # 53) and Slovak warriors.

Commencing in 1855, a new Jewish cemetery was opened close by the Yanivske, when the old Jewish cemetery on Kleparivska Street was closed for new burials. With time, the new Jewish cemetery became part of the Yanivske. After the Second World War it was opened for non-Jews as well.

Wladislaw Kozak, *1913-1936, a Lviv unemployed, he was killed by the police during an anti-governmental demonstration. His funeral turned into mass manifestations and street fighting, which brought more casualties.*

Juzef Bilchevsky, *1860-1923, Catholic bishop in Lviv, beatified by Pope John Paul II in 2001.*

Bohdan Ihor Antonych, *1909-1923, A prominent Ukrainian poet. (Sculptor T. Bryzh)*

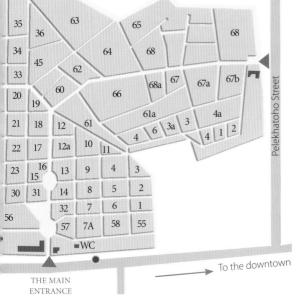

THE MAIN ENTRANCE

To the downtown

WC

Pelekhatoho Street

LVIV PARKS

■ *Although all the Lviv parks, with the exception of a few, have been left neglected, this very desolation adds to the romantic air of Lviv in spring and autumn and has preserved cozy and quiet nooks, where one can find shelter in summer heat. Yet, the past of "the city's lungs", as parks are often called, is much more interesting than the present. Today, the parks, because of the absence of a river in town, remain a popular recreation zone.*

STRYISKY PARK

15, Stryiska Street
📞 76-3202
🚌 № 4, 🚌 № 5

Stryisky Park

Stryisky Park was laid out in 1876-77, following the City Rada's decision to organize a recreation zone on the picturesque hills in the suburbs. Arnold Rering was appointed administrator of the project. First the landscape architect was to demolish the old Stryiske cemetery and plan out alleys and lanes. Trees and plants were brought from all over the world to plant on the hills. At the foot of the hill, by a charming pond, which is a home for a couple of swan families, is a monument

① *If you get lucky, for a small fee a greenhouse guardian might take a picture of you with a blooming palm-tree or a cactus, which blossom only once a year. What a coincidence that you visited the city on the day of blooming!*

to the Polish rebel Ya. Kilinski (sculptor Yu. Markowski, 1894). Exotic plants (the boards underneath each plant provide their names) could be observed in the greenhouse (1895) and around the pond. Once there used to be a good restaurant. One-hundred-thirty pavilions, built for the 1894 General Halychyna Exhibition, were located in the upper part of the park. The most popular were the pavilions of Polish radio, of the Baczewski factory and a fountain illuminated by multi-colored lights. The 120 meters wide and 15 meters high patriotic panorama of the battle at Ratslavytsy, by Ya. Styka, V. Kossak and Z. Rozvadovsky, drew the attention of the curious public. The quick-changing regimes did not touch the panorama. The Soviets regarded it as anti-monarchic propaganda, and the Germans saw it as an anti-Russian agitprop. After 1945 the panorama was moved to Wroclaw. The premises where it was exhibited today house a gym of the Lviv Polytechnic University. Another construction which has lasted till our time is a tower, where once was located a top-notch Soviet restaurant.

Monument to the Polish insurgent Ya. Kilinski.
Old photo

Lychakivske cemetery, offers recreation for all ages and tastes – a children and youth club for kids and a Lviv distillery for adults (26, Pohulianka; tel. 755646).

"POHULIANKA" (STROLL) PARK

Vakhnyanyna Street
🚌 № 7

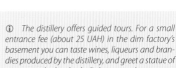

ⓘ The distillery offers guided tours. For a small entrance fee (about 25 UAH) in the dim factory's basement you can taste wines, liqueurs and brandies produced by the distillery, and greet a statue of a person, who has had a little too much.

The name of the area speaks for itself. In 1800 the Lviv lawyer Franz Venglensky acquired the spot and built a restaurant. Later, the area was sold to the restaurant chain owner Distle. Here in the summer time one could have a pint of beer in one of the numerous beer pavilions or go for a row on the lake. The Pohulianka Park abounds in spa springs. In the winter the Pohulianka hills became a Mecca for skiers. Today, the Pohulianka Park, which borders the

The Pohulianka borders the **Ivan Franko Botanical Garden** (44, Cheremshyny Street; tel. 766587). It is believed that the founder of the garden was the famous magnate Ignaty Zetner, who, for his ardent love of botany, laid out a park with exotic plants and cozy recreation places. The park outlived its creator and is a living memorial to the aristocrat and botanist.

ZALIZNI WODY (IRON WATERS) AND SOPHIIVKA PARKS

Its name, Zalizni Wody (Iron Waters), the park derives from springs rich in iron. Today, it is rather the woods than a park. All the attempts to spruce it up failed, yet it is the park's "wilderness", which constitutes its primary attraction. The neighboring Sophiivka Park was named after the former owner of the site, Sophia Henleva. In 1614 she commissioned the construction of **St. Sophia's church**, which in 1765 was renovated in the Baroque style. In 1839 Underka, a Czech by origin, laid out a park and opened a restaurant, which soon gained popularity among the locals. Since 1894 the site has been built up with deluxe villas. Close to the park is the **Ivan Franko memorial-museum** (150, Ivana Franka Street; tel. 767770) and the **Mikhail Hrushevky memorial-museum** (154, Ivana Franka Street; 767852).

BOHDAN KHMELNYTSKY PARK

4, Bolharska Street

📞 *72-7931*

🚎 *№ 3, 5, 9,* 🚌 *№ 5*

In the Soviet era the park, whose official name was the Park of Culture and Recreation, was truly the best recreation place in Lviv. You can get to the park through the main entrance from Vitovskoho Street, or through the Stryisky park, past the Monument of Glory (a memorial to the victorious Soviet Army). The park covers twenty-six hectares. Laid out in the 1950s-1970s, the park was designed to fit all tastes in recreation activities of Soviet proletariats. There was a children's area, the "Junist" (Youth) stadium and a youth club "Romantyk" (Romanticist). The authorities did not leave out ideological propaganda and placed a Lenin's monument in the park. The Lvivites do not mind the relics of the so-called Stalin Realism decor. Today,

the park hosts numerous festivals, children's feasts, beer contests and sport events.

VYSOKY ZAMOK (HIGH CASTLE) PARK

Uzhorodska Street

📞 74-3269

A grotto in the Vysoky Zamok Park

No other park in the city rivals the tranquility and the splendid panoramic view offered by the Vysoky Zamok Park. The park hills, built up with fortifications overgrown with vines, used to host political demonstrations. Today, the park stretches down in two terraces. In 1957, a television tower was constructed on the upper terrace. Lit at night by multicolored beams, the tower reminds one of the Eiffel Tower in Paris. The lower terrace is planted with chestnut trees. Among the park's architectural attractions, special attention is drawn to a house for a park warden, who looked after the exotic plants. After a long stroll, relax in the recently renovated restaurant "Vysoky Zamok" and enjoy the famous grilled chicken. In 1845, here from the balcony of the coffee shop (the restaurant then was a cozy little coffee-shop), King Franz Joseph II enjoyed the superb view of the city and the road to the Castle, lit by 18,000 gas lamps. The park boasts a crypt, decorated with emblems of celebrated Lviv families (sculptor B. Dickembosh, 1619).

*Panoramic view over Lviv
from the Vysoky Zamok Park*

LIONS OF THE CITY OF A LION

Trips
out of town

All journeys have one feature
in common, which at the
same time is an indispensable
constituent of happiness–
they broaden the traveler's
knowledge with fascinating
discoveries.

C. Paustovsky

TRIPS OUT OF TOWN

■ *If time permits, indulge in one of the exciting outings to Lviv's suburbs. The trip promises to be equally thrilling for those traveling by car, as it is for the adventurous lot, eager to brave public transport and experience the "supporting" shoulder (or back, or an elbow) of fellow travelers.*

LVIV-ZHOVKVA-KREKHIV

Embark on a bus trip to the "ideal town" of **Zhovkva** from Bus Station # 2. The bus fare is 2,50 UAH. The 32-kilometer drive to Zhovkva and the 16-kilometer drive to a Basylian monastery in Krekhiv guarantee an educating 5-6-hour journey back to the past and into the present.

On the way to Zhovkva you will pass by the village of **Kulykiv**, famous for its glorious past and the amount of sacred constructions. The catholic church of St. Nicolas (1538) is the only reminder of the fortified castle, which once occupied the site. The church was left abandoned for an extended period of time; yet, today there are reassuring signs of it being spruced up by the local religious community. Until the outbreak of the Second World War, Kulykiv was famed in Halychyna for its bakeries. The Kulykiv bread was praised in songs of Lviv batiars and vendors. In the 1960s the locals commenced producing the famous Kulykiv sausages. Kulykiv is the birthplace of the prominent Ukrainian actor Bohdan Stupka, known to the Ukrainians and Poles by his brilliant performance in the Hoffman's movie "By the Fire and a Sword".

Basylian Monastery

Stanislaw Zhulkewski

A dozen kilometers down the highway to the Ukrainian-Polish border-crossing at Krakovets and Rava-Ruska, you finally reach Zhovkva. The town nests under a cliff of the picturesque Rostochia mountain ridge, and at the foot of Haray Mountain, which rises one hundred fifty meters up over the valley. Archeologists affirm that the first settlements existed here as early as the late Stone Age. The first written evidence of the city, then known under the name of Vynnyky, dates back to 1368. The local population was predominantly involved in wine production. The topographic names of different settlements around Lviv prove that a thousand years ago vine was a common plant in Halychyna. Yet, the town's official history starts with its foundation by Hetman (General) Stanislaw Zhulkewski in 1594. The city's modern name is a derivative from its founder's surname. Clearly understanding the town's strategically favorable location and the possible advantages it entailed, Stanislaw Zhulkewski commissioned designing the city-plan to one of the best architects of those days, Pavlo Schaslyvy. In 1603 the city was granted the Magdeburg Right.

Zhovkva reached its peak of prosperity during the reign of Jan III Sobieski, who viewed this town as his favorite residence. It was in the Zhovkva castle that he celebrated, at the fireworks cannonade and panegyrists' praise chants, loss of the Royal town status, Zhovkva became a small provincial settlement, whose grandeur expressed in historical monuments has only recently begun to attract tourists.

When arriving in town, the cute little

Zhovkva castle

the victory over the Turks in the battle at Vienna in 1676.

In 1740 Zhovkva became the property of the Radziwils. In the late 18th and 19th centuries the majority of the town's population were Jews. Zhovkva was typical for a Halychyna Jewish settlement, a stetl, with one of the largest Jewish print houses. The second largest community was Ukrainian, next was Polish and a scanty German population. Today, the square, where the central city market was, bears little evidence of a once hustling place. Zhovkva inhabitants experienced all the turmoil of both World Wars. It was over the Zhovkva field that in 1914 the Russian pilot Nesterov made his world-famous loop. Later in 1951, to commemorate the pilot and his achievements, the Soviets named the town Nesterov. Its historical name the town received in 1991. With the

New City Hall

church of the Nativity of the Blessed Virgin (1705) cannot escape your attention. It is a working church with a resplendent iconostasis. It is better to start you acquaintance with the town at the old market square, which today is called Vicheva. The square most vividly demonstrates the convenient design of the city's historical center. In the past, the market was surrounded by apartment buildings, with the ground floors lodging shops of all kinds. Several preserved porticos used to encircle the square, thus allowing people to do their shopping whether rain or snow. The old houses that survive only accentuate the ugliness of modern postwar constructions on the square. In one corner of the square the signs of recent excavations, which revealed the foundations of older houses, are still visible. The town was spruced up for the 400th anniversary of the Magdeburg Right. Then the square was cleared of all the Soviet symbols, which had decorated the town for sixty years.

The castle's construction commenced on the cusp of the 16th and 17th centuries. Although there is no convincing evidence as for its architects or builders, yet, it has been proved that Stanislaw Zhulewski invited such celebrated architects as Pavlo Schaslyvy, Pavlo Rymlianyn, Ambrosi Prykhylny and Petro Beber to work out the designs. In the 1740s the castle was redecorated in the Rococo style. Since the Austrian authorities had turned it into an administrative building, the castle gradually fell into decay. After World War II the castle was

College of St. Vavzhynets the Martyr

used as barracks and later as a residential block for officers and their families. Today, most of the tenants have been given new apartments elsewhere, and the castle will house a museum. Although in 2003 the facade and the roof were renovated, one still can trace the remains of the castle's modern history.

The town used to have four entrance gates – Lvivsky, Zhydivsky, Hlynsky and Zvirynetsky. Towards the end of the 18th century, Austrian officials ordered the Lvivsky and Zhydivsky gates demolished. The Hlynksky gate was pulled down in the 1960s, because it was too narrow for Soviet tanks to get through. Lately, the gate has been re-built by the Society for the Cultural Monuments Preservation. Close to the gate is the **church of St. Laurenty the Martyr**. Constructed by the architects Pavlo Schaslyvy, Pavlo Rymlianyn and Ambrosi Prykhyly in 1606-1618, it tops an artificial mound, raised by captive Muslims. The size and the resplendent décor of the

Monuments to Stanislaw and Jacob Zhulkewskis

"Leaning Tower of Pisa"

Zhovkva is at the threshold of new discoveries. Several years ago, a secret underground passage connecting the castle and a riverbank, was revealed right behind the ditinets (fort town). Under the Soviet regime the town was a center of NKVD (People's Commissariat of Internal Affairs) "activities", which is proved by numerous mass graves of unlawfully executed people. During construction works an excavator fell into a basement filled with old wines and treasures. So bear it mind that wandering around the "ideal town" you might unwillingly become a discoverer.

church rivals some of the better-known edifices. Right after the Second World War the church's premises served as a warehouse for fertilizers. Most of the works of art, including the pictures by M. Altamonte, were preserved in the museum in Olesko. Today, it is a working church, well looked after by the Polish Army and the restoration unit of the Warsaw Polytechnic University. Adjacent to the church is a leaning belfry, nicknamed the Leaning Tower of Pisa.

Behind the church of St. Laurenty the Martyr stands a Greek Catholic monastery and **the church of the Holy Trinity** (1612), which underwent considerable reconstructions in 1906 (4/6 Vasylianska Street). Of special interest are the Neo-Byzantine murals, executed by the artist Yu. Butsmaniuk in the 1930s.

The Church of the Nativity of the Blessed Virgin

In the vicinity of the bus station there is a neglected and decaying synagogue, constructed in 1692-1700. Built in the Renaissance style, if the need required it, the synagogue could have been used as a fortress. Jan III Sobieski partially subsidized its construction. During World War II the synagogue was burned down by the Nazis. Recently, feeble attempts

View over the Dominican Cathedral

Entrance Gate. Krekhiv

have been made to reconstruct the house of worship. Next door to the synagogue rise the monumental walls of the Dominican Cathedral. The sanctuary was constructed in 1653-1655. Little has remained of the once luxuriant exterior décor. Today, the cathedral belongs to the Greek Catholic Church. Until the Second World War the cathedral had been famous for a miracle-working icon of the Holy Virgin, which was later moved to Warsaw.

St. Nicholas. Relief on a church façade in Krekhiv

Sixteen kilometers away from Zhovkva is the village of **Krekhiv**, known for the ancient **Basylian monastery of St. Nicholas**. To get to the village, take a minibus at the terminal by the church of St. Laurenty the Martyr. The bus ride will prove to be short and exciting. To your right opens a magnificent view of hills covered with the woods. In the village there is a wooden parish church, built in 1724 by I. Khomiuk. The monastery is situated at the foot of Pobijna Mountain. The

monastic complex surrounded by ancient fortification walls consists of St. Nicholas's church, a belfry, cells for monks and utility premises. Legend has it, that two monks from the Kiev Pechersky (Cave) Lavra, Ioil and Silvestr, dug a cave in the mountain, which later was called after one of the reverends, "The Ioil's Rock". The

Church of St. Peter and St. Paul

top of the mountain was crowned with the chapel of the Protecting Veil of the Holy Virgin and a small church of St. Peter and St. Paul. In September 1672 a Tartar squadron attempted an assault on the monastery, but stumbled at the valiant resistance on the part the defenders. Historians found evidence that among the casualties incurred by the aggressors was a Khan's nephew. To commemorate the glorious victory over the Tartars, a three-meter column with a pedestal was placed 1.5 kilometers north of the monastery by a field road. After the Soviet takeover, the monastery was closed and lodged a boarding school. Today, it is a Basylian divine seminary. Visible are signs of the monastery being under reconstruction.

Built in 1776, the monastery's Baroque entrance gate was connected with the other side of the fortification ditch by a stone bridge. The church, surrounded by other monastery premises of the 18th century, was erected in 1751. The north-

east fortification tower, constructed in the latter half of the 17th century, in 1759 was transferred into a belfry. Of special interest for a visitor is a beautiful park, laid out by the best Lviv landscape architectures and assiduously maintained by monks today. The Krekhiv monastery, famous for the Absolutions, was frequented by believers from all over the world. After the monastery resumed its functions in 1990, monks worked hard to revive the old Basylian traditions. Hundreds of believers pilgrimage to the monastery to participate in the festive services on the St. Nicholas's days of May 20-22. The restored ritual path, called the Path of Christ, leads from the monastery walls to the top of the mountain.

The monastery in Krekhiv

LVIV-OLESKO-
PIDHIRTSY- ZOLOCHIV
THE ITINERARY CONSTITUTES PART OF THE SO-CALLED
"GOLDEN HORSESHOE" ROUTE

View over the Olesko castle

Telephone code
for Olesko **Tel. 8-264**

"Olesko" hotel
73, Shevchenka
Street **Tel. 25-299**

"Ukrainsky Shinok"
(Ukrainian pub) café
In the hotel
9.00-23.00

"Hrydnytsa" restaurant
In the Olesko castle
11.00-20.00,
daily,
except Mondays **Tel. 25-264**
Lviv office **Tel. 70-5664**

OLESKO

To get to Olesko, take marshrutka (privately run bus services) # 279 or any other bus going to Brody at Bus Station # 2. The fare to Olesko is 6 UAH. The distance from Lviv to Olesko is 71 km. If you are traveling by car take the M06 E40, Kiev direction. The trip will take about one and a half hours.

Olesko is a tiny town that rather reminds one of a village. Yet, to see all the architectural and cultural sights it offers, you might want to stay for a day or two in a small hotel in the downtown area. So as not to drop dead of hunger while getting acquainted with the town's history, stop by the "Lubart" café on the way to the castle, or in the "Hrydnytsa" restaurant inside the castle. Needless to say, the privilege to enjoy food inside the ancient fort will be more expensive. To have a snack and a beer, visit the "Chaina" (tea-house), where you can observe the national folklore and meet the locals. Perhaps Olesko inhabitants, direct descendants of the grandees, will have something to add to the stories told by the museum guides.

In the town there are two pharmacies, a post-office and the "Lubart" café (open: 10.00-23.00).

On the way to the Olesko castle, down the Kiev highway, you pass by the village of **Didyliv**, a former residence of the notorious Stanislaw Stadnytsky, nicknamed the Devil from the Lantsutsky castle for his frequent forays on the neighbors' manors. In **Novy Myliatyn village**, by the highway, stands a chapel commemorating the victory of the village-dwellers over a Tartar squadron in the 17th century. To the right of the main highway is the town of **Boosk**, first mentioned in chronicles under the year of 1097, which in the times of the Halychyna-Volhyn Principality was a defense fort. The Boosk paper-mill, famous for its produce far beyond the Halychyna borders, was established in 1540. A stork, in West-Ukrainian dialect a "busiok", is the town emblem.

St. George the Dragon-Slayer.
Icon from the Lviv
National Museum

OLESKO CASTLE
34, Zamkova Street ☎ *(264) 25-280*
🕐 *10.00-16.30, Tuesday through Friday,*
11.00-16.30, Saturdays and Sundays.

The oldest of the survived Halychyna castles, the Olesko castle is situated on the top of the 50-meter-high hill in the southwest part of the Boosk lowland. The castle's history is

The Olesko Castle. *An old engraving*

*Monastery of the
Capuchin order*

Close to the castle is the monastery of the Capuchin order (1739), with the church of St. Joseph and Antonina, founded by the Zhevuskis.
The Capuchin order was established towards the end of the 16th century. Perhaps, the most prominent order representative was Marco d'Aviano, chosen to conduct negotiations between Protestants and Catholics several days prior to the battle with the Turks at Vienna. People say, that he was the first to brew coffee of the color matching a monk's cassock. Later, the beverage was called cappuccino.
The capuchins, famed for their pharmaceutical skills, walked barefoot and grew beards, which was not customary for Catholics. In Olesko monks practiced the so-called "Bones Cult". The body of a deceased monk, placed in one of the monastery's five pavilions, was buried only after the flesh decomposed and nothing remained but bones.
Once, when the Catholic Church was celebrating the memory of St. Anthony, one of the monks drowned himself in a well and ruined the festival. According to legend, his ghost still haunts the castle. Following the Austrian-Hungarian treaty, the monastery was shut down. Today, the monastic premises store a valuable collection of works of art, which in the future will be exhibited in the Olesko, Pidhirtsy and Zolochiv castles.

tightly connected with the political conflicts between Lithuania, Poland and Hungary. This explains the fact why the castle is frequently called the gateway to Halychyna and Volhyn. In the 13th century, after the Tartar Hordes had decimated the Russin settlement of Plisnesko, some of its dwellers moved to Olesko to construct another fortress. In 1340-1366 the castle belonged to the last Prince of the Halychyna-Volhyn Principality, Dmytro-Lubart Hedeminovych. From 1366 the town was the property of Oleksandr Koriatovych. Some historians evince that in 1390 Pope Bonifacius IX conferred the castle to a Halychyna catholic bishop. 1431 and 1432 were marked by the uprising of the Olesko region gentry (all being the adherents of Prince Svydryhailo), led by Ivashko-Bohdan Presluzhych from Rohatyn. For six weeks the castle garrison was stoically defending the town from the troops of the Lithuanian King Jagaila.

A water-spout on a wall of the former Capuchin monastery

In 1605 the castle together with the neighboring lands was taken over by the Russin magnate Ivan Danylovych. It was at that time that the father of Bohdan Khmelnytsky, Myhailo Khmelnytsky, served in the castle. It is assumed that Ivan Danylovych was one of the characters in the story, which today is considered more of a romantic legend than a historical incident. The Polish knight Adam Zhulkewski proposed to Ivan Danylovych's daughter. When the young man and the bride's father were playing cards, the latter point-blankly rejected the

Interior of the Olesko castle

Exposition in the Olesko castle

young man's proposal, who unable to stand the humiliation committed suicide.

In 1636, when all the Danylovyches died out, their huge estates became the property of Jacob Sobieski, the father of the future King Jan III. Yet another castle legend is connected with the latter. The future king of Poland was born on a stormy night in 1629, when the Tartars besieged the castle. When a midwife put the baby on a marble table, a mighty burst of thunder cracked the table and deafened the woman. The incident immediately triggered the divinations of the boy's glorious future. (Jan III was the most celebrated King and warrior in Polish history). In 1639 another Polish King was born in the castle – Mikhal Korybut Vyshnevetsky. The castle, which in the reign of Jan III Sobieski became a royal residence, was richly decorated by the King's wife, Queen Maria Kazimierza de Arquillon, in the history of Poland affectionately known as Marysenka. After Jan III death, the castle passed into the ownership of his son, Jacob.

Jan III Sobieski

In 1725 Konstantin Sobieski sold Olesko to the family of Zhevuski. The dynasty, famous for all sorts of eccentricities, was engrossed in the pursuit of mythical treasures and philosophers' stone rather than in the mundane task of maintaining the estates. In 1820 the castle was left abandoned until the Society for Castle Maintenance took Olesko under its protection in 1882. The fortress suffered not only from the owners' negligence, but also from different natural disasters. Thus, in a sever earthquake of 1838 the walls split asunder, some cracks being wide enough for a human to squeeze through. In 1951 lightning burned down the castle to ashes. It was only in 1975 that the fortress was rebuilt and open to the public. Today, it houses a branch of Lviv Art Gallery and is justly considered one of the most interesting museums in Ukraine.

Maria-Kazimierza (Marysenka)

PIDHIRTSY

A courtyard in the Pidhirtsy castle

There is no direct bus to Pidhirtsy. To get to the Pidhirtsy castle take bus # 279 (Lviv-Brody) at bus station # 2. It is the same marshrutka that goes to Olesko. Take off at Yaseniv village and catch any bus going to Zolochiv. Pidhirtsy is about 10 km from Olesko.

Those traveling by car should take the M06 E40, Kiev direction. Drive past Olesko and hang a left at Yaseniv village on the T1418 to Zolochiv. If you are keen on nature and animals, bargain with a farmer, who, for a nominal price or any other reward, will give you a shortcut (5-6 km) on a horse-pulled cart. The ride will leave you with deep, indelible impressions. A small village full of antiquities, Pidhirtsy, unfortunately, lacks a hotel or any other civilized comforts.

To get to the Pidhirtsy castle (tel. (266) 90-540) continue down the Kiev highway until the turn on Zolochiv. A several-minute drive and on your right, up on a hill is the monument to the First Cavalry, which fought its way through Poland to get further into Europe. The monument is one of the few mementos of the Soviet Realism in Halychyna.

At the entrance to the fortress is **the St. Joseph's catholic church** (1752-1763). The two columns, decorating the church, are topped with the statues of St. Joseph and the Holy Virgin. Having walked through the gate, you will see the monument to soviet warriors, who died in the area during the Second World War.

Although the first records of the Pidhirtsy castle date back to 1445, the fortification walls were raised in 1635-1640 by the architect G. Beauplan. The construction was financed by Stanislaw Koniecpolski, who had bought the castle together with the neighboring villages from Janush Podhorecki. The two-storied palace was erected

Knights Hall. An old photo

by the Italian architect Del Aqua. In 1682 Stanislaw Koniecpolski Junior bequeathed part of his estate including Pidhirtsy to the

king's son Jacob Sobieski. The castle was later inherited by Konstantin Sobieski, the younger son of Jan III.

In 1720 the magnates Zhevuskis purchased the estate. It then became the place for incessant amusements and wild parties. The palace was crammed with multifarious art works (the portrait collection itself counted 72 pieces), books, weapons and furniture. A fragment of the table, where Jan III had been born, was moved to the palace. The mansion boasted the luxuriantly decorated Golden, Green and Chinese Rooms. To accommodate a steady flow of gentry visiting the estate, a guest-inn (the remains of which survived till these days) was built close to the castle. To entertain their numerous guests, the hearty hosts organized an orchestra and a theatre.

Having paid two hundred one thousand zloty for the castle and neighboring villages, S. Zhevuski became the new owner of Pidhirtsy in 1787. Yet, with time the castle gradually fell into decay and many valuable

View over the Pidhirtsy castle

St. Joseph's Church

art-works disappeared. The last owners of Pidhirtsy were the family of Sanhushko. At the onset of World War II Roman Sanhushko moved the costly exhibits of the castle's collection to Brazil, where they are preserved in the family foundation in San-Paulo. After the Soviet takeover, the rest of the property was plundered. Even the beautiful park statues were confiscated and moved to St.-Petersburg. The meager leftovers were kept in the Lviv museum storages. The fire of 1956 destroyed the palace, leaving only the charred bare walls of the edifice. In the 1960s parts of the mansion were restored. Later, the fortress housed a regional health center for consumptive patients. Since 1997, when the castle was handed down to Lviv Art Gallery, it has been under reconstruction.

ZOLOCHIV

Zolochiv. An old engraving

Having left the charming Pidhirtsy castle behind, we set off for the Zolochiv. Under the Soviet regime the town was covered in mystery and remained out of reach for tourists. Close to Sasiv village you still can observe the impressive giant space radars, which used to be part of the USSR military system. A picturesque hilly road takes you to the rayon center of Zolochiv with 25 thousand inhabitants. The narrow river of Zolochivka flows through the town.

The distance between Lviv and Zolochiv is 66 km. You can get to the town by bus, train or car (the M12 to Ternopil). In Lviv

THE ZOLOCHIV CASTLE MUSEUM

3, Zamkova Street
☏ *43-385*
🕐 *10.00–17.00,*
Tuesday through Sunday

Having left the downtown, we finally arrive at the castle walls. The Zolochiv castle was built on the ruins of an ancient Russ fortress, decimated by Tartar hordes. The town was raised on the trade route connecting Western, Eastern and Southern Europe. The first evidence about Zolochiv dates back to 1442. On March 15, 1523 the town was

General view and the interior of the Zolochiv castle

you can catch a commuter train at the suburban train station, or a train at the railway station to Zolochiv. To get from the railway station in Zolochiv, located in the outskirts, to your final point of destination take a bus or a marshrutka (privately run mini-bus service).

The Zolochiv bus-station is in the downtown area. There you can catch buses to Kiev and Ternopil, or a suburban bus to Brodiv, Pomoriany or Boosk. In Lviv the buses to Zolochiv take off at the bus station on Stryiska Street, or at a smaller bus station in the outskirts of Lviv on Lychakivska Street. The bus fare does not exceed 4 UAH. At the same bus station you can catch a marshrutka for 5 UAH. The journey will take about one and a half hours. It can take even less then that, provided the bus makes fewer stops on the way.

granted the Magdeburg right. At that time, a large Armenian community inhabited Zolochiv.

In 1532 the owner of Zolochiv Stanislaw Senynski sold the town to Andrey Hurkov, a Posnan castellan. Later, the town and the fortress became the property of Jacob Sobieski, who improved the fortress's defense system by adding four bastions. Each fortification wall was more than one hundred meters long and eleven meters high. Although the ditch around

Jacob Sobieski's emblem on a stone tower

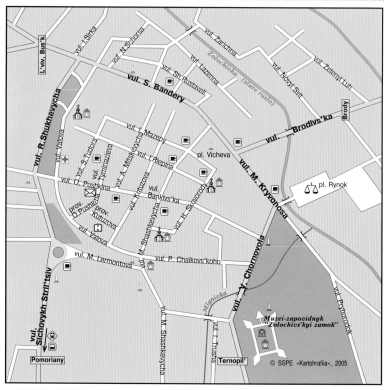

ZOLOCHIV

In the 17th century the Zolochiv castle was famous for the comfort it offered to its dwellers. There were several modern, for those days, water closets (for your reference, today in the Zolochiv castle museum there is only one rest-room). A secret passage led from the King's study to the Treasury. Researcher surmise, that the passage could also have been used as a so-called "long ear" – a system allowing eavesdropping of servants' conversations on the ground floor. Another secret passage led from the King's study to the fortification ramparts.

the castle had never been filled with water, its depth and the pickets in the bottom could easily halt the enemy. The ramparts were designed so that in case of an enemy's attack a cannon ball would hit the mound instead of the castle walls. In the 19th century the bastions performed a purely decorative function. Each tower was adorned with Janin, Hodzav, Ravycz and Herburt emblems on stone plaques together with the inscriptions J.S.K.K.S.K. A bridge connected the entrance gate with the other side of the ditch. The only tower-clock in town was placed over the gate. A secret underground passage led from the central tower elsewhere, thus allowing defenders to leave the sieged fortress. The Renaissance Royal castle and the so-called China palace is all that has remained from the old days.

In 1672 the fortress was defeated and demolished by Turkish troops. Yet, after the castle had been returned to Poland, the Turkish prisoners of war rebuilt it. After Jan's III death, the Zolochiv castle belonged to Prince Jacob, who died in 1737. Later, together with other manors it was the property of the Radzivils, who neglected proper castle maintenance. In 1802 Zolochiv was acquired by the landlord Komarnytsky, who transformed the castle premises into living quarters. In 1840 Komarnytsky sold the fortress to the Austrian government, which used it as barracks. In 1872 the former fort became a penitentiary. Yet, hard times hit the castle in 1939 when the Soviets turned it into an NKVD (People's Commissariat of Internal Affairs) prison. A museum exposition tells about the execution of seven hundred people, who were tortured here to death by the Soviets from 1939 to June 1941.

The latest accomplishment of the museum is the recent restoration of the China palace, built by the castle owners in their pursuit of the fashion. Following the vogue for exotics, the local gentry disguised their servants, little Petrus' and Ivankos, as Negroes or Chinese. Today, the Zolochiv palace displays part of the Oriental collection of Lviv Art Gallery. In the future, the administration is planning to perform tea ceremonies.

Another of the castle's attractions are the two huge stones, found close by the town in the village of Novosilky. One of the stones is covered with inscriptions in Gothic, while the other one depicts two intertwined wreaths, standing for "the life" and "the death", with a hole in the intersection of the lines. Unfortunately, all the attempts to give a plausible explanation of the nature and function of the stones produce no answers.

Telephone code for Zolochiv
tel. 8-03265

Directory inquiries
tel. 42-222

Railway Station
10, Voroniatska Street
tel. 42-101

Bus Station
46, Sichovykh Striltsiv Street
tel. 42-255

Car Service
Zolochivske car-service (car maintenance and repair)
3, M. Zalizniaka Street
tel. 42-423

"Ukraina" Hotel
4, Valova Street
tel. 42-142

TOURIST INFORMATION CENTERS:

"Zakhid-Show"
International Tourist Services;

"TAS"
Insurance Group;
"Kyiavia",
Airline Ticket Agency;
"Ilona",
Travel Agency
3, M. Kryvonosa Street, 2nd floor
tel. 50-235

Post-office
7, Pushkina Street
tel. 42-581, 42-441

BANKS:

Savings Bank Branch
1, Mazepy Street
tel. 42-163

Privatbank
10, Shashkevycha Street
tel. 42-248

"Nadra" Bank
22, Shashkevycha Street
tel. 5-00-67

CAFES AND RESTAURANTS:

"Yuniks"bar
2a, I. Trusha Street
tel. 50-133

Grill,bar
5, Pushkina Street
tel. 45-693

"Zorand"
café
1 b, Brodivska Street

"Kazanova"
café
3, M. Kryvonosa Street
tel. 44-162

"Yanina", café
17, Lermontova Street
tel. 45-268

"Lavanda", café
1a, Voroniatska Street
tel. 43-270

Zolochiv castle
3, Ternopilska Street
Open: 10.00-17-00
Tuesday through Sunday
tel. 43-385, 42-101

ENTERTAINMENT:

Billiard Hall
"Ukraine" hotel,
4, Valova Street
tel. 42-142

Disco club
"Yuniks" bar,
2a, I. Trusha Street
tel. 50-133

SHOPS:

«Vella»
shopping center
(Food products, textile, household chemical goods),
12a, Sichovykh Striltsiv Street
tel. 42-253

"Khyhy" book-store
1, Shashkevycha Street
tel. 42-276

"Smak"
supermarket
8a, S. Bandery Street
tel. 5-04
I. Trusha Street
tel. 50-133

LVIV-SVIRZH

■ *The trip to Svirzh village could be part of the "Golden Horseshoe" tour. To follow the tour route, take the Zolochiv-Lviv highway M12, turn to Peremyshliany at Pidhaichyky village (T1407), then, at Ushkovychy village turn to Bibrka. The total route distance to Svirzh is about 70 km. Yet, we suggest you reserve a whole day for the trip to Svirzh. The village is about 40 km from Lviv. You can get to the village by bus, marshrutka (privately run minibus service) or by car. Both buses and marshrutka to Svirzh take off at Lviv bus station # 5. The fare is about 3 UAH.*

If you finally manage to get out of the Lviv streets, avenues and lanes cobweb, a car trip to Svirzh will take half an hour. Take the Bibrka highway (P03) and turn to Peremyshliany at Bibrka.

A courtyard in the Svizh castle

The first written evidence about **Svirzh** dates back to 1427, when King Wladislaw II visited the village. In 1449 the castle was separated from the village of Svirzh. In 1530 it belonged to the Svirzkys. The present-day look the castle has had since the 17th century, when its owner Count Zetner reconstructed and redesigned the construction. The lover of botany (Count Zetner founded the Lviv Botanic Garden), he introduced

some major changes in the estate. The reconstruction and fortification of the defense walls he commissioned to General Pavlo Rodzinski, who then was constructing the Royal Arsenal in Lviv. One glance is enough to understand that the castle could not offer safe protection against a mighty enemy, yet, with a chain bridge raised, it was a family sanctuary from the hardships of everyday life. During the Cossack uprising led by Bohdan Khmelnytsky in 1648-1657, the castle was sacked by the rioters. Nevertheless, the fortress withstood the Turks assaults of 1672 and 1675. On the castle's territory is the Renaissance church, fragments of which date back to 1541.

The castle was the family home of the Zetners until the late 19th century. In the 20th century, Count Robert Lamason Silence decorated the castle with portraits and valuable furniture. It should be mentioned here, that in 1914 the Russian troops set the estate on fire. During the Second World War the castle was raided and in parts destroyed. The castle's modern history is tightly connected with the Society of Architects, when its members initiated here a cultural center. Unfortunately, in the chaos of the 1990s the castle was neglected. Despite their amicability, the guards do not always allow the curious tourists to peep into the castle's courtyard. Thus, if you are not one of the museum staff, all is left for you is to enjoy the tranquility of the surrounding landscapes.

Fortification tower

A shot from the film "D'Artagnan and three musketeers"

Unbelievable as it is, the fortress was presented in the film "D'Artagnan and three musketeers" as the fortress of La Rochel, a bone of contention between the Protestants and the Catholics. The "star role" in the film belonged to the defense tower by the castle.

The Svirzh castle

LVIV-DROHOBYCH-TRUSKAVETS

■ *The trip to Drohobych and Truskavets is comfortable and enjoyable. You can choose between trains (some of the carriages are similar to European standards) and marshrut-ka. Trains depart from the suburban train station, and marshrutka – from the bus-station between the suburban and long-distance train stations. The fare is 10 UAH.*

Church of St. Peter and St. Paul

Having left Lviv, on the way to Drohobych you pass by the town of **Mykolaiv**, once a defense fortress that belonged to the family of Mniszech. Unfortunately, nothing is left of the fort. Further down the road you pass the Mykolaiv cement factory, one of the largest in Ukraine, and cross the bridge over the Dniestr River. In the 17th century by the village of **Rozvadiv** on the river-island stood a fortress, which protected the locals from the enemy's assaults.

DROHOBYCH

Emblem of Drohobych

Drohobych is situated 100 km to the southwest from Lviv. You can cover the distance either by commuter-train, by marshrutka or by bus. Trains depart from the Lviv train station and the fare is no more than 4 UAH. Marshrutka fare is no more than 10 UAH. Buses leave from bus-station #8 and the fare is no more than 6 UAH. If you are traveling by car, take the M06 E471 to Stryi, and in Pisochna village turn right onto the T1410 to Drohobych. The trip will take about two hours.

The Drohobych railway station is located in the suburbs of the city. From here you can catch a train to the neighboring cities of Truskavets, Boryslav, Morshyn or Stebnyk.

Marshrutka is the most common public transport in Drohobych, conveniently connecting the old and new districts. The bus fare depends on the distance and is about 0.50-0.70 UAH.

Drohobych is a town with a rich and ancient history and the fascinating architectural monuments make it well worthwhile visiting. Since a one-day trip is too short for seeing all the sights, you can book a comfortable room in the "Tustan" hotel (1, Shevchenka Square) and have a rest before you continue with the journey.

Monument to Adam Mickiewicz

Today, the population of Drohobych consists of about one hundred thousand people. It is a town with a glorious 900-year-long history, friendly inhabitants and high aspirations for the future. In the old days the key to the town's well-being was salt, traded in Halychyna and Volhyn as well as shipped to many towns in Europe. Some archeological excavations found in the city are the oldest in the region. The ancient Russ settlement existed on the site in the times of Kievan Russ. Drohobych gained city status in 1422. The main attractions of the Rynok (Market) Square are the City Hall built

in the 1920s and **the monument to Adam Mickiewicz** (1892).

In the 15th century Drohobych was a region center. In 1722, following the first division of Poland, the town was overtaken by Austria. The first Halychyna Ukrainian Gymnasium was opened in Drohobych in 1775. In the mid-19th century the town saw an industrial boom. Commercial productions of ozocerite and later of oil and gas were developed in the town outskirts. In 1866 the first in Central Europe petroleum refinery was constructed in Drohobych. In 1910 another petroleum refinery was opened in the region. The Austrian-Hungarian Empire was ranked third in the world by the amount of oil produced in Drohobych and Boryslav. A railway service was started at the end of 1772 to facilitate industrial development.

In 1918 Drohobych was proclaimed part of the Western Ukrainian People's Republic. From 1919 until 1939 the town was under the state of Poland. Drohobych has always been an important political and social center. The town's inhabitants are proud of the fact that the life of the famous Ukrainian writer Ivan Franko was tightly connected with their native region and town.

In September 1939 German troops marched into Drohobych. A few days later the Soviet Red Army liberated the town from the Nazis. From July 1, 1941 until August 6, 1944 Drohobych was under Germany. In 1940-1959 the town was an administrative center of the Drohobych

An old street

St. Yura's (George) Church

Carved and gilded iconostas inside the church

region. The city is at the crossroads of highways, connecting it with Lviv, Stryi, Sambor, Truskavets, Boryslav and Stebnyk.

Unique are Ukrainian wooden churches in Drohobych. **The church of St. Yura** (George) (1654) at 23a, Soliany Stavok Street, was moved to Drohobych from the village of Nadievo in 1657, after a similar church had been burned

The town's character is defined by its dwellers. The beggars in Drohobych have always been distinguished for their ingenuity. Before World War II one of the homeless, Fevronia Sikorova, having saved enough money, ordered a monument to herself from the local craftsman T. Valigur. Every day the illiterate woman would come to the monument to pray, not suspecting that the local kids had played a trick on her and erased the first two letters on the epitaph. Korova, "a cow" in Ukrainian, was all that was left of the surname.

The Church of the Exaltation of the Holy Cross

down by Tartars. The three-framed church is topped with three octahedral domes. The inside walls are all covered with murals. The altar part is decorated with gilded carved iconostasis. Today, the church houses the Drohobychyna (Drohobych region) ethnographic exposition (tel. 28-242). Despite that, public worships are held on religious holidays.

Another sacral edifice, located close by, is **the church of the Exaltation of the Holy Cross** at 7a, Zvarytska Street. Originally built as a defense tower, its present-day appearance is the result of the 1661 restoration works carried out after a Tartar's assault. Being considered a masterpiece of the Halychyna Medieval architecture, the church is protected by the state.

One of the oldest Drohobych architectural monuments is **the Catholic church of St. Bartholomew** (1392) at 12, Danyly Halytskoho Street. Previously, there had been a Russka fortress, which is proved by the remains of foundations. Famous for the luxuriant Baroque altar and stained-glasse windows by Ya. Mateiko and Yu. Mehoffer, the church still bears distinct characteristics of a fortification construction. Under the Soviet regime the edifice was used as a print-house, and still later as a museum, until it was returned to the Catholic community in the late 1980s. Unfortunately, only few fragments of epitaphs and several massive foundation tables have survived through the years.

Next door to the church is a monumental **defense tower**, the foundations of which date back to the 12th century. In 1551 Ivan Hrendosh, a constructor from Przemysl, built on another tier. In 1979 a plaque was installed on the corner of the tower, commemorating the Cossacks victory in the 1648 battle for the town.

A fair on Rynok Square.
An old photo

Not far from the tower stands the monument to one of the most prominent town inhabitants, Yuri Drohobych (Cotermak). A famous scientist, he headed the Boulogne University in 1481-1482. The town's

history is tightly connected with such celebrated figures as Cornylo Ustyanovych, I. Lukasevych, Vasyl Stefanyk, Les Martovych, Modest Mentsynsky, Bruno Schultz, Kazimierz Wiezinski, and Hryhory Kossak.

Like many other provincial towns in Halychyna, Drohobych was the epitome of paradise for the Jewish community until the outbreak of World War II. The first

View on the monument to Yu. Drohobych and the fortification tower

synagogue in town was built as early as the 17th century. By 1939 the Jewish community was about fifteen thousand people, which constituted almost half of the total town population. There were about twenty synagogues and Jewish houses of worship. The majority of Jewish financiers acted as intermediary agents in oil production and trade. The Nazis resorted to brutal reprisals against the local Jews – most of them were killed or imprisoned in concentration camps. At 6, Orlyka Street is a synagogue (1842-1865) modeled after the synagogue in Kassel, Germany. The Soviets used its premises as a furniture store. In 1993 the synagogue was returned to the Jewish community.

The life and art activities of the celebrated artist **Bruno Schultz** (1892-1942) were closely tied with Drohobych. His works "The Crocodile Street", "A Cinnamon-store" and "A Sanatorium under the Clepsydra" were influenced by the atmosphere of those days in Drohobych. Famous far and wide are the murals Schultz painted as a decoration for the

An anecdote tells about a Hartenberg, an entrepreneur who made his fortune by trading oil and who had a whim to decorate the floor in his study with gold coins. Yet, there was a problem. On one side of the coin there was the portrait of an Austrian King and on the other – the state emblem. Unable to solve the dilemma himself, he wrote to the King, asking how he should place the coins. The King replied: "Place them on the rib".

Bruno Schultz. Self-portrait

Holy Trinity Church

with the Empress Maria-Teresia's approval, a monastery of Basylian order was constructed on the site. Destroyed by the conflagration of 1825, the church was rebuilt and sanctified in 1828. In 1944 the HKVD opened a transit detention center for political prisoners in the monastery's premises. It was only in 1990 that the church was returned to the catholics.

At the corner of Truskavetska and Boryslavska Streets, close to Rynok Square, stands **the church of the Holy Trinity**. Constructed in 1690 as a church of the Carmelite order, in different periods it housed city administration offices and an educational establishment for children. It was only in 1813 that the sanctuary was finally returned to the Greek Catholic parish. The monks of the Basylian order opened here a four-year school, where the famous Ukrainian writer Ivan Franko received his primary education.

bedroom of a child of the German official F. Landau. Under mysterious circumstances the remains of the murals turned up in the Jad Vashem Museum in Jerusalem. On the corner of 12, Drohobycha Street is placed a memorial plaque to the artist. Bruno Schultz was killed in a Nazis' round-up in 1942.

At 3, Stryiska Street is the Greek Catholic church of St. Peter and St. Paul. In the 1770s,

DROHOBYCH

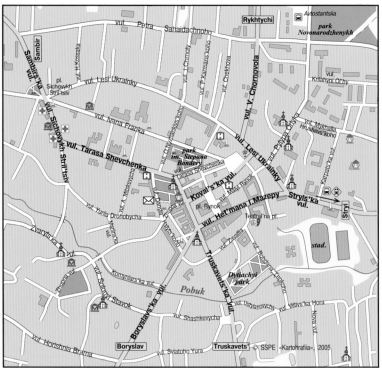

Telephone
code
for Drohobych
tel. 03244

Information Service
tel. 09

Railway station
1, Majdan Zluky
tel. 21-638, 22-589
Information Service
tel. 22-589

Bus stations
Bus station № 1,
Stryiska Street
tel. 23-333
Bus Station № 2,
Orlyka Street
tel. 23-310

Drohobych
Telephone Office
21, Danyly Halytskoho
Street
tel. 35-552, 38-549,
20-329

COMMUNICATIONS
"Ukrtelecom" Electronic
Communication Service
Center № 2
21, Danyly Halytskoho
Street
tel. 20-037, 35-220

"Mobitel "
Mobile Communication
Service Center
21, Danyly Halytskoho
Street
tel. 27-359

BANKS:
"Aval"
21, Danyly Halytskoho
Street
tel. 50-166, 21-562

"Nadra"
82, Boryslavska Street
tel. 35-775

"Ukrsotsbank"
26, Shevchenka Street
tel. 35-439, 39-134

"Tustan" Hotel
1, Shevchenka Square
tel. 35-884, 20-049

TOURIST AGENCIES:
"Globus"
10/1, Mazepy Street
tel. 50-090

"Magellan"
2, Drohobycha Street
tel. 33-838

PHARMACIES:
№ 116
15, Shevchenka Street
tel. 21-523

№ 115
15, Rynok Square
tel. 37-028

№ 117
26, Truskavetska Street
tel. 22-005, 29-000

№ 260
31, Rynok Square
tel. 20-632

City Hospital
for Children
11, Sheptytskoho Street
tel. 38-861

City Central Hospital
9, Sheptytskoho Street
tel. 23-416

"Usmishka" (Smile)
dental clinic
2, Drohobycha Street
tel. 39-031

City Central Policlinics
22, Sichovykh Striltsiv
Street **tel. 20-522**

"Perlyna Prykarpattya",
Health Resort
83, Truskavetska Street
tel. 35-938, 22-557

HAIRDRESSERS':
"Svit Krassy "
25, Rynok Square

"Elegant"
9, Rynok Square
tel. 38-348

CAFÉS AND
RESTAURANTS:
"Ukraina",
restaurant
1, Kovalska Street
tel. 22-885

"Berizka", restaurant
5, Zavallya Street
tel. 22-317

"Tustan", restaurant
11, Shevchenka Square
tel. 20-060

"Zatyshok", café
8, Rynok Square
tel. 33-871

"Choomatsky Shliakh",
café
6, Rynok Square
tel. 39-069

"Julia", café,
internet-club
27, Rynok Square
tel. 21-603

"Bistro", café
21, Rynok Square
tel. 39-175

"Drohobytska Cahva",
coffee-shop
8, Mazepy Street
tel. 22-066

CULTURAL
ESTABLISHMENTS:
"Drohobychyna"
Museum
32, Franka Street
tel. 22-035

St. Yura's (George)
Church, Museum of
Wooden Architecture
tel. 22-639

Picture Gallery
18, Sichovykh
Striltsiv Street
tel. 33-798

Lviv Regional
Yuri Drohobych
Musical and Drama
Theatre
1, Teatralna Square
tel. 23-264, 23-228

ENTERTAINMENT:
"Prometei" Cinema
1, Shevchenka Square
tel. 23-711

"Frankova Zemlia"
Drohobych Radio
Station **tel. 21-143**

"Traffic",
computer-club
20, Rynok Square
tel. 37-588

Billiard club, bar,
slot-machines
8, Kovalska Street
tel. 38-855

"Drohobytsky
videocentre"
video rental services
8, Rynok Square
tel. 33-473

"Grand"
fitness club
1, Mickiewicz Street
tel.38-433

C-club
youth club-chain
2, Mickiewicz Street

SHOPS:
"Svitoch"
27, Rynok Square
m. 33-734

"Prodoocty"
rocery store
27, Rynok Square
tel. 21-603

"Romashka"
supermarket
22, Rynok Square

Photo express services
21, Rynok Square
tel. 50-076

"Vyshenka"
(household equipments,
grocery, tobacco goods)
15, Rynok Square
tel. 35-563

"Haberdashery and
souvenirs"
31, Rynok Square
tel. 21-279

"Legenda"
(souvenirs and perfume
store) 10, Rynok Square

"Orchid"
(jewelry and souvenir
store)
16, Rynok Square
tel. 39-177

TRUSKAVETS

The resort town of Truskavets is situated in the picturesque foothills, nine kilometers from Drohobych. The town, whose unique atmosphere one can readily feel when approaching the downtown area, is buried in verdure.

Truskavets is situated 100 km to the South of Lviv and 90 km away from Ukraine's western border. The railway service connects it with the largest cities in Ukraine, the CIS and Europe. You can get to Truskavets by all means of transportation. Catch one of the three commuter trains at the suburban train station (consult the train schedule), a bus at bus station #8 by the railway station, or marshrutka (the fare is 8UAH, additional fee of 1 UAH is charged for heavy luggage). Those traveling by car should take the M06 to Styi, turn right at Pisochna village onto the T1410 to Drohobych, and then, short of Drohobych, onto the T1413 to Truskavets. The trip from

Truskavets emblem

Lviv to Truskavets will take about two hours.

The Truskavets train station is located in the town center. It is a large building with a recreation lounge, restaurant, bar, hotel complex, information bureau, pharmacy, luggage-room, currency exchange office, public telephones, toilet facilities and a tourist agency, where you can purchase a package tour to a health resort of your choice. Crowds of enterprising women will attack you on the platform offering rooms and apartments. Prices range from 10 to 35 UAH per night, depending on the location and facilities offered. But be aware that there might be a huge gap between reality and what you have been promised.

The bus station is situated on Drohobytska Street, at the outskirts of the city in the Drohobych direction. It is a modern building equipped with all the necessary services. Coaches from the train and bus stations take vacationers to health and resort centers.

Marshrutka # 1, 2, 3 (the fare is 0.50 UAH) operate within the city from 8.00 to 21.00.

The first written evidence about Truskavets dates back to 1469. Scarce remains verify the fact there once was an ancient Russ fort town. On the Baba hill, which is now within the city boundaries, was a pagan temple in the old days. The origin of the city's name still stirs up heated discussions in scientific circles. Despite all the debates, the "official" year of the city's foundation as a resort is considered 1827, when the premises for the first eight balneal baths were constructed.

The curative characteristics of the Truskavets sources have been known since long ago, when in 1578 the King's doctor Voitcec Ochko first wrote a treatise about their medicinal powers. Extensive research in the field was carried out by the German scientists N. Fithel and B. Hake. In 1836 Theodore Torosevych, an Armenian by origin, was the first to conduct a chemical analysis of the "Naftusia" mineral water. In 1892 an inhalation center was constructed in town. When Halychyna was under Austrian rule, the resort easily rivaled Riehengal and Wiesbaden by the level of services offered in health centers and the chemical ingredients of the Truskavets mineral waters.

In view of the possible advantages this might have entailed, private hotels, villas and health resorts sprang up rapidly. To attract more investments, a joint-stock society headed by the famous entrepreneur Raimond Jarosh was organized in 1911. Under his leadership the town was the first in Halychyna equipped with electric power. In 1912 a new train station was constructed for the convenience of vacationers. Train lines connected Truskavets with Lviv, Vienna, Krakow, Poznan, Prague, Warsaw and Berlin. In 1913 Truskavents was awarded the Large Golden Medal for the considerable achievements in the development of resort infrastructure. New services and amenities were introduced in the city to fit all tastes and demands. The lake for bathing was equipped with modern facilities; new tennis courts and sport grounds were constructed. The following facts vividly describe the growing popularity of the resort: in 1923 it was visited by 6,080 vacationers, in 1927 – 12, 633, in 1931 – 14, 659 and in 1933 – 17, 000.

Among historical edifices in Truskaverts, special attention is drawn to the "Hopliana" wooden villa (1928). It was constructed in the so-called "Zakopane style", which was then en vogue in Poland. The style developed from the traditional Carpathian wooden architecture. Today, other edifices close to the villa are being reconstructed.

In the 1930s Truskavets was visited by the USA Ambassador in Poland, Presidents of Turkey and Estonia, and many other honorary guests. Today, Truscavets is a favorite

The "Hopliana" wooden villa

holiday place for Ukrainian Presidents. Presently, the "Hopliana" villa hosts the museum of the famous Ukrainian artist Mikhail Bilas (open: 10.00-17.00, Monday through Saturday).

In September 1939 villas, health centers, spa hospitals and restaurants were expropriated by the state. During the Nazis invasion the resort was turned into a military hospi-

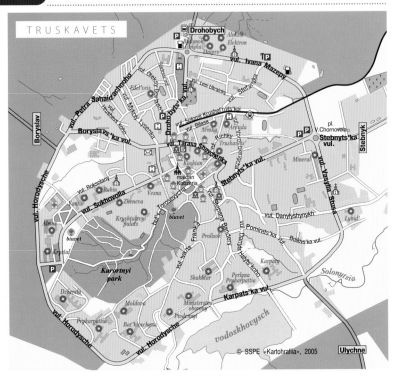

TRUSKAVETS

tal. After the Second World War the Soviets put one of the well-known resorts in Europe into new use as a collective farm. It was only in 1950 that Truskavets was given town status, and commencing with 1952 it was pronounced "an all-Soviet Union health resort". About 350 thousand vacationers come to Truskavets annually, which makes it one of the biggest health centers in Europe.

Today, Truskavets is a large resort, which can accommodate fifteen thousand holidaymakers. If you are in town on a two, three-day business trip you can stay in a hotel or a health center.

Truskavets is well known all over the world, as is the "Naftusia" mineral water for its medicinal powers. The mineral water bal-

Miner water pump room

TOURIST AGENCIES
**Traveling
and excursion bureau**
2, Shevchenka Street
Tel. 51-119

"Halintur"
12, Bilasa Street
Tel. 51-628

"Haluchanka"
1, Sichovykh Striltsiv
Square **Tel. 51-183**

"Jurgen"
1, Sichovykh Striltsiv
Square **Tel. 54-695**

"Truskavettourist",
excursion center
2, Shevchenka Street
Tel. 51-384, 51-119

HOTELS
"Arcada"
21, Richky Street
Tel. 66-683

"Truskavets"
7, Drohobytska Street
Tel. 69-291

"Chervona Ruta"
6, Stusa Street
Tel. 55-436

APARTMENT BUREAU
5, Shevchenka Street
Tel. 54-413, open daily

"Truskavetscurort"
13, Bilasa Street
Tel. 52-415, 51-414

**Mineral water
pump-room #1**
5, Torosevycha Street
Tel. 51-098

**Mineral water
pump-room #2**
67, Sukhovolia Street
Tel. 54-572

Central City Pharmacy
Heroiv UPA Street
m. 51-505

Pharmacy #325
13, Stusa Street
Tel. 51-109

Pharmacy #329
2, Mazepy Street
Tel. 51-395

"Horytsvit" Pharmacy
3, Bandery Street
Tel. 51-234

CATERING ESTABLISHMENT
"Berizka"
Dietary canteen
10, Roksolany Street
Tel. 53-366

"Babylon" , café
9, Heroiv UPA Street
Tel. 51-538, 55-411
11.00-24.00

"Zoria" ,canteen
2, Drohobycha Boulevard
Tel. 51-601

"Polonyna"
dietary canteen
8, Torosevycha Street
Tel. 51-675

"Zhadka" , café
1, Shevchenka Street
Tel. 67-060

"Hrazhda" , café
2, Karpatska Street
Tel. 62-244

"Sas", restaurant
1, Heroiv UPA Street
Tel. 51-319

"Stara Brovarnia"
restaurant
25a, Stebnytska Street
Tel. 53-512, 68-936
11.00-23.00, open daily

ENTERTAINMENT
"Chervona Kalyna"
cinema
29, Stebnytska Street
Tel. 51-420, 55-064

"Mir"
entertainment center
47, Boryslavska Street
Tel. 50-740

**City and Resort
Museum**
14, Sichovykh
Striltsiv Street
Tel. 52-237

**Mikhail
Bilas Art
Museum**
3, Kobzaria Square
Tel. 50-002, 54-235
10.00-17.00

**Shevchenko
Entertainment
Center**
8, Kobzaria Square
Tel. 51-727, 50-723

**Truskavet City
People's Hall**
36, Shevchenka Street
Tel. 51-317

"Oho!" sport and entertainment complex
10, Roksolany Street

Casino
"Karpaty" sanatorium
17.00-6.00

Entertainment center
1, Bilasa Street

"Beskyd" restaurant
disco, sauna
3, Drohobytska Street
Tel. 55-450

SHOPS AND MARKETS
"Zodiak" market
25, Stebnytska Street

"Knyhy" book-store
2, Bandery Street
Tel. 51-590

"Knyhy" book-store
1, Boryslavska Street
Tel. 51-590
9.00-18.00, Monday
through Saturday

Souvenirs
4, Shevchenka Street
Tel. 53-770
9.00-18.00, Monday
through Saturday

**"Vyshenka"
grocery store**
16, Sahaidachnoho Street
Tel. 50-387

Shopping Center
12, Sukhovolia Street
Tel. 51-598

COMMUNAL SERVICES:
**"Kashtan"
fashion house**
2, Symonenka Street
Tel. 51-020

"Lilia" dry-cleaner's
31a, Bandery Street
Tel. . 51-547

Photo studio
5, Stebnytska Street
Tel. 66-930

**"Charodika"
hairdresser's**
2, Heroiv Upa Street
Tel. 55-095, 55-092

"Sophia" beauty shop
2b, Sichovykh
Striltsiv Street
Tel. 69-505

"Yulia" hairdresser's
5, Shevchenka Street
10.30-19.00, Monday
through Saturday

**Telephone code
for Truskavets**
Tel. 03247

Information service
Tel. 09

Railway station
1, Vorobkevycha Street
Information services
Tel. 55-092 booking-
services

Bus Station
35, Drohobytska Street
Information services
Tel. 50-263

Air-tickets
1, Heroev UPA Street
Information service
Tel. 54-216 reservation
1, Borobkevycha Street
(at the railway station)
Tel. 68-530

Communications
11, Heroev UPA Street
Tel. 68-687

"UTEL", Lviv branch
11, Heroev UPA Street
Tel. 67-070

Intercity phone calls
Tel. 07

**Telephone telegrams
reception Tel. 06**

BANKS
"Aval"
20, Suhovolya Street
Tel. 68-085

"Privatbank"
Heroev UPA Street
Tel. 66-074, 66-080

"Ukrsotsbank"
2, Mazepy Street
Tel. 54-681, 51-470

Taxi Tel. 0-65, 0-53

Car Service Station
73, Stebnytska Street
Tel. 51-151

Car Park Tel. 69-297

ances metabolism, contributes to the renal calculi excretion, reduces bile lithogenicity, fights inflammations in kidneys and liver, excretes radionuclides, and regenerates liver cells as well as performs other healing functions. The picturesque landscapes that attracted the first settlers have changed little since then. Truskavets is beautiful regardless of the season. Natural medicinal features influence the body's defense reaction and strengthen the immunity system.

There are 20 spa resots (known as "sanatoriums") and about 20 health centers in the city. The largest are "Carpathians", "Dnipro-Beskyd", "Moldova", "Perlyna Prykarpattia", "Almaz", "Rubin", and "Kryshtalevy Palace". The health centers conduct spa, ozocerite and climate therapies. Some sanatoriums are equipped with mineral water pump-rooms with non-contact heating cells.

The sanatoriums of the "Truskavetskurort" (Truskavets resort) meet the demands of all types of vacationers, who can choose between small wooden bungalows in the early 20th century style, new cozy 10, 15-room villas, or modern 8, 11-storied complexes, which can accommodate 450-900 people. Package tours include three meals a day, cooked according to your doctor's specifications. The most demanding tourists can order meals in the best restaurants.

The recently opened international hospital offering treatment according to the Professor V. Koziavkin's methods will lodge up to 1, 800 children.

Different underground mineral waters, varying in chemical ingredients and therapeutic characteristics, have been developed in Truskavets.

In the center of the resort, on Torosevycha Street, is the main mineral water pump-room of the closest sanatoriums (open: 7.00-10.00, 12.00-15.00, 17.00-20.00, daily, tel. 66-060). The information on the water's chemical composition is provided on boards by each tap. Nevertheless, it is advisable to drink only the water recommended by your doctor. Inappropriate treatment can have serious consequences and might spoil the impression of one of the best resorts in Ukraine.

Railway station in Truskavets

"PERLYNA PRYKARPATTYA"

*The Ministry
of Internal Affairs
Medical Rehabilitation Center*
71, Bandery Street
📞 50-649, 50-098, 61-670
fax 66-676
e-mail: perlyna@tr.lv.ukrtel.net
www.perlyna.lviv.ua.

One of the best and the most modern health facilities in Truslavets, "Perlyna Prykarpattya' is located in the city-center.

Highly proficient staff provide resort guests with qualified treatment and diagnostics in the clinical-biochemical, duodenal intubation, fibergastroscopy and X-ray laboratories. Patients can also undergo ultrasound and ther-movision diagnostics. The spa resort features a mineral water pump-room equipped with fast heating, mineral baths, ozotokeritotherapy, intestinal treatment, psychological and reflex therapy laboratories as well as massage parlors.

Upon the patient's request the canteen may offer dietary meals three times a day. The health center also features a restaurant. Guests stay in a modern 10-storied building, connected with the medical center by covered passages.

"KARPATY" (CARPATHIANS) SANATORIUM

2, Karpatska Street
📞 62-000, 62-129
fax 62-747, 62-939
www.san-karpaty.com.ua

The well-developed infrastructure of the 'Karpaty' sanatorium makes it one of the most comfortable health facilities in the resort. The spa center is located in the picturesque southeast outskirts of town, nearby a water reservoir and the woods. The nine-storied 'living building', connected with the club, canteen, medical center and sport complex with covered

passages, matches well the surrounding environment. The sanatorium offers single and double rooms with toilet facilities, a refrigerator, telephone (for internal, city and international calls) and satellite and regional TV. "Karpaty" also provides deluxe rooms for most exigent guests. All the rooms face South and South-West. A splendid view of the Beskydiv mountain range opens up from room balconies. The 'living building' accommodates 420 guests. A huge winter garden close to the concert and dance halls and canteen adds to the general relaxing atmosphere of the health facility.

Dietary meals are an essential part of the resort treatment. The sanatorium features a canteen and cozy bars, "Karpatsky" and "Sakura". In a picturesque park nook, decorated with sculptural compositions on the Carpathian mythology by the famous artist Roman Petruk, is the "Hrazhda" café, modeled in the Hutsul wooden architect style.

The mineral waters with diuretic and anti-inflammation properties, ozokerite (earth wax produced in the neighboring town of Boryslav), spa regimen, dietary food, physiotherapy, walking and climate therapy, all these factors contribute to healing kidney and liver diseases as well as metabolic disturbances.

"DNIPRO-BESKYD"

*Sanatorium
and Hotel Complex*
33, Drohobytska Street
📞 67-325, 52-261, 51-705
fax 66-191, 52-036
e-mail: post@beskyd.com.ua
www.beskyd.com.ua

The sanatorium and hotel complex is a unique resort center in Truskavet. Located in the ecologically clean part of town, it provides all the necessary diagnostics, treatment and leisure facilities. The sanatorium building has comfortable rooms, a dietary canteen, and mineral water pump-room as well as treatment and diagnostics center.

The "Beskyd" hotel accommodates 500 people in single, double and deluxe rooms. Guests enjoy express elevators and comfortable lounges. The hotel is decorated with Italian marble.

The package includes the following diagnostic analysis: medical and chemical bioanalysis based on conventional methods; intra-abdominal pH-scopy; duodenal intubation and lavage with "Naftusia" mineral water; X-ray, ultrasound and radionuclide diagnostics; fibre-gastroscopy; proctoscopy; chromium cystoscopy. Guests may receive consultations with gastroenterologists, gynecologists, nutritionists, cardiologists, neurologists, proctologists, psychiatrists, urologists and endocrinologists and undergo prescribed subsequent treatment.

"MOLDOVA" SANATORIUM

12, Horodische Street
📞 *69-352, 55-393; 51-337*
e-mail: moldova@reha.lviv.ua
www.bistyle.com.ua/moldova

The 'Moldova' sanatorium offers modern complex treatment for chronological liver, gall bladder, bile capillary, stomach, duodenum, intestinal and urogenital system diseases.

The treatment includes spa therapy, dietary cure, massage, ozotokerite therapy, balneo- and physiotherapy (Charcot douche, underwater massage, etc.), ultrasound and laser therapy.

The sanatorium is located in a park area and is surrounded by greenery.

Guests enjoy comfortable rooms with all facilities, a treatment and diagnostic center, club and canteen.

"LYBID" SANATORIUM

50, Danylyshynykh Street
📞 *54-118*
tel./fax 54-605
e-mail: lybid@isa.org.ua

The sanatorium features single and double rooms, two-bedroom suits, a fitness center, billiard hall and tennis court. The administration organizes excursions for the guests. All the rooms are equipped with a shower cabin, toilet facilities, a washbowl, refrigerator and TV. Cars are parked at a parking lot.

The sanatorium offers a mineral water pump-room.

The "Lybid" sanatorium has modern diagnostic facilities, including a medical and diagnostic laboratory, laboratories of ultrasound and computer cardiovascular system diagnostics.

The health facility provides a wide range of medical treatment: mineral water therapy, dietary meals upon request, ozokerite therapy, mineral, bal-

samic and effervescent baths, underwater douche-massage and air-massage, physical and laser therapy, therapeutic exercises, massage, inhalation and dental treatment.

The package includes accommodation, full board, meals and medical treatment.

"KASHTAN" SANATORIUM

11, Bilasa Street
📞 *51-304, 66-060*

The sanatorium is located in the downtown area of Truskavets. Guests may opt between staying in a comfortable villa of 10-12 deluxe rooms, or a modern eight-storied building, accommodating 450 people.

The diagnostics are conducted in the sanatorium, which has urology and gastroentero-

*"Yantar"
Sanatorium*

logical units. Close to the health facility is a mineral water pump-room and a health center BOL-1.

"Kashtan" features a lithotripsy center and rehabilitation units for people suffering from diabetics, urolithiasis and gastrointestinal disturbances.

Guests enjoy a tennis court, volleyball grounds and a summer dance floor.

"MARIOT"

Spa Hotel Complex
6, Roksolany Street
📞 *51-118; 66-127*

Guests are accommodated in 30 deluxe rooms and enjoy a billiard hall, swimming pool, sauna, fitness center, Jacuzzi and massage parlor. Meals are served in a bar and the "Central" restaurant. Treatment is available upon request.

INTERNATIONAL CLINIC OF REHABILITATION TREATMENT BY THE PROFESSOR KOZIAVKIN METHOD

37, Pomiretska Street
📞 *65-200*
fax65-220

"YANTAR" SANATORIUM

54, Sukhovolia Street
📞 *66-109, 66-060*

"Yantar" consists of two eleven-storied buildings connected by covered passages. The sanatorium is famous for the "Mother and child" unit for 200 people, where children of 4 to 16 years of age stay with their parents. The facility also offers urological and gastroenterological units, play grounds for children, a ticket-office, physiotherapy hall and sports ground.

Close to the sanatorium is a large treatment and diagnostic center - a resort policlinics and a balneo- and ozokeritehospital # 2, as well as a mineral water pump-room. The health facility is located not far from a resort park and the city-center.

Truskavets tourists are offered a wide range of entertainment activities, which are highly popular with the locals as well. In the downtown are located the Shevchenko and "Mir" entertainment centers, featuring films, concerts by famous singers, music groups and folk companies, as well as disco parties. On Ukrainian national holidays special entertainment programs are offered. The most popular holidays are the New Year, Christmas, Easter and the City-day, celebrated on the Day of Medicine. The most frequented cinemas are "Zlata" and the new digital cinema hall, "Millennium".

The sanatoriums' volleyball and basketball grounds, tennis courts and fitness-centers with modern equipment help you stay fit. Children are offered play-rooms and play-grounds with swings and slides.

The adventurous lot may try their luck in a casino, strip-bar, bowling and billiard halls and a disco-bar, or play slot machines in the modern sport and entertainment center under an intriguing name "Oho" or in the casino located in the "Karpaty" sanatorium. Guests can play electronic roulette or poker and win a prize in the entertainment center at 1, Bilasa Street. In the "Beskyd" restaurant are a night disco-club, sauna and swimming pool.

LVIV-SLAVSKE

■ *Slavske is a village in Skolivky rayon, Lviv region. Located in the valley of the Opir and Slavka rivers of the Eatern Beskydiv mountain range, it is one of the best ski resorts in Ukraine. Slavske is surrounded by mountains: Vysoky Verkh (1243m), T rostian (1232m), Klyva (1072m), Menchil (1072m), Ilza (1064m), Plitky (1037m), Pysana (1036m) and Makivka (1033m).*
Tourists get to Slavske by train, and in the winter season private buses take admirers of skiing from Lviv to the center of the village.

The region's past is covered with mystery. The first evidence about Slavske dates back to 1015. According to legend, after Sviatopolk Volodymyrovych had assassinated his brothers Boris and Hlib and another of their brothers had escaped to Hungary, Sviatopolk's servants overtook the latter and killed him in the upper reaches of the Opir (Resistance) River. However, the river could have acquired its name in the times of the Mongol and Tartar invasion of 1240-1241. These lands first were part of the Halychyna and Volhyn State, later – of the Great Princedom of Lithuania, until they were conquered by Poland. The village belonged to the family

Cozy guest houses for vacationers

of Pototsky. Later, the estate was acquired by a Evhen Kinsky, who soon sold it to Baron Hredel.

The "outside" world learned about Slavske in 1878, after the Stryi-Mukachevo train line was completed. The train has always been and still is the most popular and at the same time the most reliable means of transportation. Until recently, a so-called "cowboy" train plied between Lviv and Slavske. The train's conveniences, or rather their absence, remind one of the Wild West.

Among other historical sights the church of the Dormition of the Holy Virgin is worthwhile visiting (1901). Scientists affirm that the sanctuary was erected on the spot, where fitful gusts of wind had several

times brought down the cross from the old church.

Hard times struck the region when this part of the Ukrainian Carpathians became the front line between the Austrian-Hungarian and Russian Armies. The Legion of Ukrainian Riflemen (Legion Ukrainskikh Sichovykh Striltsiv, USS) distinguished itself in the war. A memorial complex was placed on the field of one of the fiercest battles by the town of Makivka. After the war and until 1939, Slavske was under Poland. In World War II and during the postwar period the Ukrainian Insurgent Army (Ukrainska Povstancheska Armia, UPA), which mainly consisted of locals familiar with the terrain, was given wholehearted support. The exposition of the private museum of Yuri Mykolsky reveals the history of the Ukrainian Insurgent Army (2, Sichovykh Striltsiv Street).

In the late 19th and early 20th centuries Slavske and the neighboring regions were gaining popularity as a skiing center. The first cableways and ski jumps were built in the 1920s-1930s. Yet the prime of its glory as a skiing resort Slavske reached in the 1970s, which then was the head trainingcenter of the USSR Olympic team. A chaircableway (2,750m) and 16 chair lifts are still in operation. Two chair lifts (800 and 1,300m) take skiers up Kremin Mountain. This slope is ideal for those who are new to mountain skiing. The western slope of Pohar Mountain, 700-800 meters long, is another skiing slope. Tourists may use two chairlifts, "Dynamivska" and "Nova", 800m

Slavske in winter

and 900m respectfully. The "Nova" is illuminated at night. Yet, it is Trostian Mountain that boasts the best skiing slopes and routes.

Recently, the diversity of private guesthouses and hotels turned Slavske into an alluring resort place. The local tourist industry possesses a distinct regional folklore atmosphere. For example, here pick-ups and mini-lorries (UAS and HAS-66) are the most popular means of winter

Snowmobiles – an elite means of transportation

transportation, second only to skis. Ingenious drivers have adjusted the cars to tourists' needs. For 5-10 UAH a pick-up with an open body will take you to the mountain

of your destination. Such Carpathian safaris, with the experience of high-speed travel through the impassible wilderness, guarantee you a mixture of everlasting impressions. The most demanding tourist can travel by carts or horse-driven sledges. Young carters welcome guests right at the railway station and volunteer to take them, for a reasonable fee, to the place of their destination. Once on top of the mountain, take a shot of hot wine and a bite of tasty snacks to regain your vigor. Slavske is no less beautiful in the summertime. The tranquil atmosphere and clean air promise a pleasant stay and a good rest. There is no doubt that you will be traveling back home with baskets full of mushrooms, bilberries, raspberries or blackberries.

Ready for a headlong slide

SPA TREATMENT

Mineral water pump room. Morshyn

■ *Several resort towns and villages, which constitute 5% of all the resort places in Ukraine, are located in the Lviv region. 7 of 8 Ukrainian mineral waters are produced here. Each resort is distinguished by its original character and uniqueness. The town of Truskavets is an absolute leader in the industry. A little smaller in size, yet no lesser in popularity is Morshyn. Small resort towns are Nemyriv, Shklo, Skhidnytsia and Velyky Liubin.*

Annually about 300,000 people come to the Lviv region to restore their health and vigor. Spa centers and guesthouses feature the most modern medical diagnostic equipment. In addition to that, the resort administration will take care of your leisure time – concerts, dance parties and new acquaintances will facilitate the medical treatment. Here you will get rid of your ailments and return home full of energy and vitality.

Those planning to undergo treatment in health facilities should first consult their doctors, who will advise you on the resort to choose. Book a package tour in advance and, with the hope of an unforgettable vacation, start packing your luggage. Guests can either stay and undergo treatment in the same establishment, or they can pay only for treatment, which is the same as for those on the full-board package, and book a room and dine elsewhere. Packages vary and may include treatment; treatment and meals; and treatment, meals and accommodation.

Most of the sanatoriums are located in ecologically clean and picturesque areas.

MORSHYN

The first evidence about Morshyn, and its salt-producing plants, dates back to the 14th century. Two people, Petro Morschtin and Yuri Morschtin, Germans by origin, leased the land from Polish King Kazimierz to run salt-producing factories. It is surmised that the city's name originated from their surname.

"Marmurovy Palace" sanatorium

In 1876 the merchant Bonifaccio Stiller arrived in Morshyn and, following the advice of his two friends, doctors Dzinkowski and Piasecki, opened a spa establishment, which then were en vogue in Europe. After a detailed assessment of the area and treatment conditions, a project was drawn to build spa resorts, modeled after similar mountain centers in Switzerland and Tyrol. The establishment was opened to the general public in May 1878 with the support of the Krakow Balneology Society.

In 1935 the construction of the "Kurortny Dom" (Resort House) sanatorium commenced, according to the designs by the engineer Nykodymovych. Today, the establishment is called "Marble Palace". Then the new spa hospital, inhalatoruim, solarium and mud-bath chambers were constructed and the roads were paved with asphalt. The primary attraction of Morshyn is the mineral water pump-room, where the water, supplied through underground pipes, is mixed with fresh water in various proportions and warmed up.

Today, the unique mineral water springs, ideal geographical location, convenient transportation system and clean environment make Morshyn one of the most well-known gastroenterological resorts in Ukraine as well as abroad. The resort

A sculpture in the park by the sanatorium

is surrounded by pine-tree forests. Once in town, you will immediately feel the cleanliness of the air. Due to its diuretic, bile-expelling and relaxing properties, "Morshynska" cleans the inside of the human body and increases the immunity, and has proved effective in balancing metabolism as well as curing digestive system and urinary tract diseases, and allergies.

Presently, the resort of Morshyn consists of six comfortable hotels, a balneological hospital and mineral water pump-room (all belong to the closed corporation of "Ukrprofozdorovnytsia") and four resort centers that belong to other establishments. According to official data of June 1, 2003, the resort accommodates 3,255 people, with 3,140 people staying in spa resort centers and 115 – in two guesthouses. In the village of Lysovychi-Bania are located two sanatoriums, "Niva" and "Prykarpatska Vatra".

Getting to Morshyn is fairly easy. The distance between Morshyn and Lviv is 85 km. Direct commuter trains to Morshyn depart from the train station. The fare is 3.70 UAH. The trip takes two hours. Busses, which depart from bus station # 8 by the train station (Ivano-Frankovsk direction), are another option. Bus fare is 6 UAH. A more comfortable journey is by marshrutka, which depart from the same bus station. The fare is 10 UAH. If you are traveling by car, take the M06 E471 and turn onto the T1422 in Styi.

An old mineral water pump room. Morshyn

"PERLYNA PRYKARPATTYA"

5, 100-richia
Kurortu Morshyn Street
📞 *60-412, 60-416,*
fax 60-412
e-mail: perlyna@ridnel.net
http://perlyna:ridne.net

Located in the center of the resort, the sanatorium is one of the most modern health establishments in Morshyn. "Perlyna Prykarpattya" is designed for people suffering from digestive system diseases.

A treatment and diagnostic center was opened in the sanatorium in May 1999. The center features a medical diagnostic laboratory, esophagogastroduodenoscopy, intestinal pH-scopy, ultrasound, electrocardiogram, intestinal oxygenation and psychotherapy laboratories as well as a massage parlor. Guests may use a physiotherapy laboratory equipped with the latest facilities.

Two living buildings, with single and double rooms with all facilities, semi-deluxe rooms and one and two-room deluxe suits, accommodate 201 people each. Dietary meals are served in the sanatorium canteen.

"MORSHYNSKI" SANATORIUM

5, Dzherelna Street
📞 *64-400, 64-365*
fax 60-707
Marketing
and distribution department
📞 *60-708 (-707) (24 hours)*
e-mail: dpsm@UKR.NET

Guests are offered double rooms with all facilities, rooms with a TV and refrigerator, deluxe rooms and two or three-room suits. They also enjoy cable TV, badminton and volleyball grounds, tennis courts, a discoclub, bar, parking lot, sauna, billiard hall, hall for table tennis and fitness center. Excursions are organized to picturesque places in the Carpathians. Within 500 meters from the sanatorium is a huge forest lake with spring water, where you can rent a rowing boat or a catamaran.

"Perlyna Prykarpattya" sanatorium

"Morshynsky" offers a wide range of treatment methods, including balneotherapy (spa and other kinds of baths, different therapeutic douches), ozotokerite and mud therapy, spa treatment, climate curing, physiotherapy, dietary meals, massage and alternative medicine (acupuncture, etc.).

"DNIESTR"

4, 100-richia
Kurortu Morshyn Street
📞 *60-539, 60-530*
fax 60-539

The sanatorium is a rehabilitation center for the victims of the Chernobyl disaster and people from polluted areas. Treatment is offered for fatty hepatosis, chronic hepatitis, gallbladder inflammation, cholangitis, pancreatitis, chronic gastritis, stomach and duodenal ulcer, metabolism disorder (sugar diabetics), osteochondrosis, gynecological disorders, neurosis and nervous exhaustion. Rehabilitation programs are designed for patients suffering from biliary and intestinal dyskinesia as well as for patients who had virus hepatitis and have undergone laparoscopic and intracorporal cholecystectomy.

Treatment includes spa therapy (mineral waters # 1, 4 and 6), massages (general, gynecologic and relaxing as well as massage of prostate gland), phytotherapy, mechanotherapy and physiotherapy. The sanatorium features endoscopy, X-ray and echography laboratories, dentist department and a laboratory for intestinal lavage.

Guests have a variety of menus offered at the local canteen: full-board, dietary, vegetarian and meals cooked at the request of the customer. Guests staying in deluxe rooms enjoy a separate menu, stipulated by the package.

"MARMUROVY PALACE" SANATORIUM

2, Parkova Square
📞 *60-508, 60-510,*
60-518
Tel./fax 60-517

Being one of the oldest sanatoriums

"Dniestr" sanatorium

in the resort, it was opened in 1938. Today, "Marmurovy Palace", equipped with the latest technologies, offers a wide variety of spa treatment services and diagnostics. All the services and laboratories are located in one building.

"ZORETSVIT" SANATORIUM
8v, Proliskova Street
📞 60-389, 60-388

Guests enjoy manual massage, hydromassage, relaxing massage and underwater douche, as well as the "Relax" spa saloon.

"CHEREMOSH" SANATORIUM
8, 100-richia Kurortu Morshyn Street

📞 60-489,
Tel./fax 64-502

"LAVANDA" SANATORIUM
33, Franka Street
📞 60-459

BALNOELOGICAL AND MUD TREATMENT HOSPITAL
3, Parkova Polscha Street
📞 64-336, 64-344

The Balneological and Mud Treatment Hospital in Morshyn offers the following packages – treatment; treatment and meals; treatment, meal and accommodation.

"SVITANOK" SANATORIUM
2, Dzherelna Street
📞 60-400

MINERAL WATER PUMP-ROOM
2, Parkova Ploscha Street
📞 64-023
🕐 7.00-10.00, 12.00-15.00, 17.00-18.30

"MORSHYN" GUESTHOUSE
48, Franka Street
📞 60-454

"LUBOMYR" RESORT COMPLEX
Motel, Russian baths, sauna, bar
village Bania-Lysovetska
15, Shkilna Street
📞 (03245) 68-357
2 km from Morshyn down Morshyn-Bolekhiv highway

Telephone code for Morshyn
Tel. 03260

Information service
Tel. 09

Railway Station
Advance booking ticket office is open 24 hours a day. Tourists enjoy a hotel, café (open: 10.00-22.00), automatic lockers and toilet facilities (0.40UAH).
1, Vokzalna Street
Tel. 64-539, 64-492

"Ukrainian Airlines" Agency
39a, Franka Street
Tel. 64-325

Bus Station
1, Vokzalna Street
Tel. 64-522

Parking
Guarded covered parking lot, car maintenance, emergency service
3a, Ozerna Street
Tel. 63-371

"Stryiposhta"
post office,
Morshyn branch
"Stryitelecom"
telecommunication
agency, Morshyn
branch

48, Franka Street
Tel. 4864-463, 64-380

Intercity telephone communications
Tel. 07

BANKS:
"Aval"
60, Franka Street
Tel. 64-045

Prominvestbank
60, Franka Street
Tel. 64-153, 64-052

Pharmacy
47, Franka Street
Tel. 64-324, 64-468

City Hospital
18, 50-richia UPA Street
Tel. 64-391

"Zviazkivets" Hotel
48, Franka Street
Tel. 63-620

CAFES AND RESTAURANTS
"Vatra" *café*
64, Franka Street
Tel. 63-622

"Nostalgia" *bar*
3a, Parkova Street
(inside the balneological and mud treatment hospital)
Tel. 63-329

"Dzyha" *, bar*
52, Franka Street
Tel. 64-280

"Zeleny" *café*
Franka Street, opposite the "Lavanda" sanatorium **Tel. 64-280**

"Grill" *bar*
44, Franka Street
Tel. 64-361

"Kashtan" *restaurant*
48, Franka Street
Tel. 63-663

"Kolyba" *café*
village Bania-Lisovytska
108, Kurortna Street,
opposite the «Vesna» sanatorium

Travel agency
65a, Privokzalna Street
Tel. 64-095, 64-096

ENTERTAINMENT CENTER
Dance Hall, Small and Large Concert Halls and Library)
52, Franka Street
Tel. 62-177, 62-181

SHOPS:
"Fuji foto"
43, Franka Street
Tel. 8 (050) 581-8465
"Kristal"

Ceramics, souvenirs and goods for photography
39, Franka Street

"Svitoch" *confectionery*
43, Franka Street
Tel. 60-757

"Sryiski Delikatesy" *Store*
Franka Street

"Kovbasy" *Sausage Store*
Franka Street

COMMUNAL SERVICES
"Roksolana"
Fashion atelier
39, Franka Street
Tel. 60-751

"Viktoria" *Hairdresser's*
39, Franka Street
Tel. 60-753

"Spokuska"
Beauty Parlor
39, Franka Street
Tel. 60-768

Shoe repair
Franka Street

Dentist's office
39, Franka Street

Jewelry store
Production, repair and exchange
39, Franka Street
Tel. 60-764

NEMYRIV

Nemyriv is a so-called urban village (a settlement too big to be called a village and too small to be called a town). Nemyriv bus station is located right in the downtown area, as are a café, hotel and store. You can get to Nemyriv by bus or by car. Buses to Nemyriv depart from Lviv bus station # 8 (busses to Rava-Russka or Yavoriv). The fare is about 5 UAH. Those traveling by car should take the M 10 to Yavoriv, and turn onto the T 1417 after Yavoriv to Nemyriv through Verbliany. Another option, which is 10 km longer, is – the Zhovkva M 09 to the E 372 to Rava-Russka and turn onto the T 1417 to Nemyriv.

The sanatorium is one and a half kilometers from Nemyriv.

"NEMYRIV" RESORT
1, Kurortna Street
Nemyriv, Yavoriv rayon,
Lviv region
📞 *27-515, 27-547*
fax 27-500

One of the most popular balneological resorts, "Nemyriv" is located in a large forest 320m above sea level. The resort's isolation from large urban settlements guarantees fresh air, saturated with ozone, micro-elements and ethereal oil. The water, rich in hydrogen sulfide and widely applied in therapies, produces a positive effect on the main body functions and heals inflammation processes. This spa treatment has been known for 200 years. The Nemyriv resort boasts the "Anna" mineral spring, the water possesses similar properties to that of "Myrhorodska" mineral water in the Poltava region. The water stimulates secretion, facilitates in regaining vigor, increases intestinal motility, bilification and bile extrusion, as well as possesses anti-inflammation properties. Spa treatment includes massage, water massage, reflex therapy, ozotokerite applications and inhalations. The sanatorium features laser therapy, phytotherapy, functional and ultra sound diagnostics and X-ray laboratories, as well as dental surgery and orthopedic laboratories.

The resort provides not only qualified treatment, but also spare time entertainment. Entertainment and dance parties, concerts and excursions are held to make your stay pleasant and memorable. Average package tour is 12 to 24 days.

Tips
for the tourist

A journey is considered successful if the traveler goes on his own, without friends, and obstacles do not hinder his path

Sholom-Aleichem

TRANSPORT AND COMMUNICATIONS

■ *If you travel a lot and enjoy doing it, then you already know whom your travel-companion will be and how you are going to get to Lviv. Indeed, you can get to Lviv by any imaginable means of transportation, except for boat, as there is neither river nor sea in the vicinity.*

RAILWAY STATION

If you want to feel the atmosphere of Lviv prior to setting your foot on Lviv ground, then choose the train. Having stepped out of the carriage, you find yourself inside the majestic rail station, an architectural monument of the early 20th century. The building has been recently restored and is ardently loved by both tourists and Lviv natives.

The central train station is conveniently located in the southwest part of the city close to the down-town area. A monumental arch-like roof covers the platforms, which match the general ensemble of the train station and are the disembarking area for international and domestic trains. Exits to the city are located in the middle of the station premises (just descend down the stairs) and to the left and right of the building.

In the terminal building there are waiting lounges and the passengers' service center, constructed in compliance with the latest European standards and equipped with the most modern technologies and furniture. The first-class waiting lounge, where passengers can watch a film while waiting for their train, features a children's play-ground, billiard and chess table, as well as a lunchroom, where travelers can order meals. A small fee, 3 UAH for 3 hours and less, is charged for a stay in the lounge, which operates 24 hours. We advise you to make use of the lounge services, relax and have a cup of coffee, while your children will finally leave you alone and play with toys in the play ground.

The rail station offers waiting lounges for commuter passengers and the military.

The central ticket office is located on the ground floor, where travelers can purchase tickets for international and domestic trains. Separate ticket counters are designated to sell tickets for commuter trains. The left wing is under a restaurants, which is open from 10.00 to 22.00 hours and offers meals at reasonable prices. On the ground floor you can also find a police post, pharmaceutical kiosk, currency exchange point (the exchange rate is lower here, so it is advisable to wait a little and exchange money somewhere in the downtown area), lunchrooms, newsstands with the latest issues of newspapers and magazines, a mini-market, bars, a shooting gallery, TV-room, Express-bank, public phone booths, slot machines, information desk (the charge depends on the information provided),

A forge iron palm, presented to Lviv by Donetsk authorities

toilet facilities (0.60 UAH), two left-luggage rooms (open: 24 hours; 2 UAH per 24 hours per item) and automatic lockers (open 24 hours, closed 11.00-12.00 and 2.00-3.00 a.m.; the charge depends on the size of the luggage and ranges from 2 to 4 UAH). If you still have some time to kill before your train departs, leave the luggage in the lockers (which are 100 per cent safe) and go sightseeing. If

you are in Lviv on an important business trip, then you should look impeccable. In this case the hairdresser's is what you need. Timetables in the central ticket office provide information on the departure and arrival of international and domestic trains. The timetable of commuter trains is in the commuter train ticket office. Electronic boards are installed in both waiting lounges, in the passage tunnels and by the platforms.

In the left wing of the first floor is the Service Center offering the following services: tickets booking and delivery, information services, reservations for luggage courier services, porter services, reservations in guarded parking lots, organizing sightseeing excursions, booking rooms in hotels, telecommunication, fax and Xerox services, booking the VIP conference hall for conducting business meetings, and car rental services. At the Center passengers can also purchase

On a train station platform

Central Train Station
1, Dvirtseva Street
Information Service (24 hours)
tel. 0-05, 226-2068
*Service Center of the Central
Train Station*   **tel. 226-1903**
*Hotel-type
Rooms*   **tel. 226-2065**

**Suburban
Train Station**
116, Horodotska
Street   **tel. 226-5120**
Booking Services **tel. 226-5276**

**Advance
Booking Office**
20, Hnatuka Street **tel. 226-5276**

Waiting lounge

a train-timetable brochure and place an order for food products delivery.

The left wing of the first floor also features 11 hotel-type rooms including deluxe suites, and separate recreation rooms for mothers with children and for disabled passengers. Meals served in the room, porter, laundry and ironing, these are some of the services provided to tourists staying in hotel-type rooms. If you are exhausted after a long trip, and you are traveling with a kid, it is advisable to stay in one of the comfort-able hotel-type rooms or in the room for mothers with children. Dirty clothes will be cleaned and ironed for you. A short rest, and you are fit to proceed with the journey.

In the right wing on the first floor are located a post office and a public telephone office.

To the left of the station is the heavy luggage department. The ground floor of the building is under a first-aid post.

350 meters from the central station is the suburban-train station, which constitutes an integral part of the railway station ensemble. The suburban-train station is a terminal for trains of the westerly direction – Mostysk, Khodoriv, Stryi, Morshyn, Truskavets and Sambir. For passengers' convenience the station features 10 ticket counters, an information center, hairdresser's, two waiting lounges, a first-aid post, police post, bar, café, telephone booths, slot machines and toilet facilities (0.60 UAH).

All the services in the central and suburban-train stations operate 24 hours a day.

By the train station is a parking lot, a petrol station and a car wash.

To get from the central train station to the downtown area, take trams #1, 6 and 9 (the fare, regardless of the distance and amount of stops, is 0.50 UAH and is paid to the conductor) or marshrutka # 66 (the fare, regardless of the distance, is 1 UAH and is paid to the driver). Taxi is another option. Taxis can be called by phone ("Radar service" taxi agency – tel. 000 or "Navigator" taxi agency - tel. 002). Beware, that private taxi drivers more often than not overcharge.

BUS STATION

Traveling by bus can also be thrilling. Although you are kept rooted to your seat, the driver will always make a stop at your request. And the scenery beyond the window does not change that fast, so you have time to enjoy the view. The Lviv's bus station, seen from the distance, serves almost all large cities in Ukraine, as well as in Russia and Europe. There are several bus lines offering services: "Neoplan", "MAN", "Mercedes" and others.

The central bus station is located on the edge of town on one of the longest streets, Stryiska. Built in the

---

"Lviv" Central Bus Station
109, Stryiska Street   **tel. 63-2531**

BUS STATION :
2
22, Khmelnytskoho Street   **tel. 552-0489**

3
11, Petliury Street **tel. 292-2332**
5
2, Luhanska Street   **tel. 70-2785**

6
154, Lychakivska Street   **tel. 71-8151**

8
1, Dvirtseva Square **tel. 238-8308**

late 1980s, the bus station, unlike the glittering and shiny train station, reflects the spell of hard times and negligence.

The inside of the spacious three-storied building consists of three tiers. The first and second floors circle around a large foyer. On the ground floor there are three ticket counters, two of which operate round the clock, and the third one is open only when queues are too long. The offices sell tickets to both domestic and international buses. Departure and arrival times are indicated on the television information board. By a click on the remote control you can get the information on the bus of your choice: the departure time, route, seats available, the bus line, estimated arrival time to the terminal, the fare to the place of destination, insurance information and the departure platform. If you want, you may even place an advertisement or a greeting. Nearby is a huge board indicating departure and arrival times. Opposite the ticket office are freight service offices: "Autolux" company ships heavy luggage to Kiev and Borispol and "Miss-Tour" – to Donetsk. Having purchased a ticket, the passenger is insured from the moment he arrives at the bus station until he reaches the place of destination. The station is guarded by the police, so here you feel safe. Beggars and homeless, common

visitors of stations, do not frequent this place. Yet they siege the entrance gate, so, beware of pick-pockets and hold tight your belong-

Bus station by the railway station

ings. Having purchased a ticket, you will be given a free is-sue of the "V dorohu" newspaper featuring information on the bus and flight schedules, advertisements and entertainment reading. Bus tickets can also be booked via Internet: www.bus.com.va.ua. Each bus line offers a discount for "group" tickets. Children and disabled get discounts. The left-luggage office, open 24 hours, is to the right of the ticket counters. The charge per item per 24 hours is from 1 to 3 UAH. Next to the left-luggage office is the WC (0.75 UAH, open 24 hours). On the first and second floors are two waiting lounges (accessible free of charge) with a limited capacity. A small outlet, where you can buy food and travel necessities, is on

the first floor. However, it is advisable to do shopping in a supermarket. Nearby is an information office (open from 9.00 to 19.00, closed for lunch at 14.00-15.00). All the enquiries are free of charge (tel. 63-24-97). For 10 UAH you can have a lunch at the grill-bar located on the same floor (open: 8.00-23.00). On the second floor

EMERGENCY SERVICES:

Fire	**tel. 01**
Police	**tel. 02**
Ambulance	**tel. 03**
"Bohdan" ambulance	**tel. 0-56, 97-8759**
Gas Service	**tel. 04**
Directory Enquiries	**tel. 09**
City Information Services	**tel. 0-89**
Speaking Clock	**tel. 0-60**
Emergency road-side assistance	**tel. 0-61**
Pharmacy Information Services	**tel. 0-67**

Airport
168, Lubinska Street
tel. 69-2500, 69-2985, 69-2216
Fax **297-1155**

Lot, Polish Airlines
Airport
tel. 69-2985, 69-2500, 297-1155

Ukraine International Airlines
Airport
tel. 69-2744, 298-6977
11.00–17.00
www.ukraine-international.com

Lviv airlines
Airport
tel.69-2112

Booking office
5, Hryhorenka Square
tel.72-7818

"Avia" Agency and
"Grand Tour"
Train Services Agency
Booking office
13, Svobody Prospect
tel.76-9170, 72-7665
9.00–18.00

"Gal-Expotour" Tourist Agency
30, Vynnychenka Street
tel.76-5988, 76-3373
e-mail: getour@galexpo.lviv.ua
htpp:\\www.getour.lviv.ua

"Halintour"
Lviv Regional
Tourist Agency
1, Krushelnytskoi Street
tel.72-1941, 297-0821
Airline Ticket Agency
27, Zubrivska Street
tel.221-3619
29, Naukova Street
tel.69-2982

Kiy-Avia
Airline Agency,
Lviv Branch
tel.74-3027
Fax **297-6563**
e-mail: lvov@Kiyavia.com

"Mist-Tour" Joint Ukrainian-Ca-
nadian Tourist Agency
34, Shevchenka Prospect
tel.297-0852

Universal
Flights Sales Agency,
Lviv branch
5, Henerala Hryhorenka Square
tel.74-4344, 297-0630

is a small café, where you can have a cup of coffee and a cake, although it will be a little more expensive. While sipping coffee, you can study the schedule of intercity buses, indicated on a large information board. In the bus station there are representative offices of international bus lines. On the first floor are located the "Vinev" company (open: 10.00-19.00, lunch break: 13.00-14.00; daily, except Sundays. Tel. 63-25-31) and the "Euroclub" company (open: 10.00-19.00, lunch break: 13.00-14.00; on Saturdays and Sundays open from 16.00 to 18.00. Closed: Monday. Tel. 97-66-60). The "ACTON" company (open: 10.00-16.00, on Saturdays: 11.00-14.00, daily except Sundays. Tel. 98-25-47, 64-97-39) is on the second floor. On the same floor is a first-aid post. In the beauty salon the qualified staff not only neatly execute male and female haircuts, but also make beautiful hairdos, manicures and pedicures. The administration office is on the same floor. UTEL public phones are on the first floor. City telephone booths are located by the main entrance to the station. The currency exchange office is on the platforms' area. The exchange rate is lower here than in town. Near is a newsstand, selling not only the latest newspaper and magazine issues, but also books and some travel necessities. If you have time to spare, play

a game or two on slot-machines.

State and private bus companies conduct domestic and international transportations. The main international destinations are Poland, Spain, Holland, France, Germany, Italy, etc. There are no facilities for the disabled in the bus station, although a wheel-chair is offered to carry the handicapped from the platform to the ticket office.

To get from the bus station to the downtown take trolleybus # 5 (the fare is 0.50 UAH), bus # 37 (the fare is 0.80 UAH) or marshrutka # 71, 80 or 57 (the fare is 1 UAH). The "Navigator" (tel. 000) and "Radar" (tel. 002) taxi agencies have contracts with the bus station administration and offer their services 24 hours a day. A taxi ride to the downtown

area with these companies is 10 UAH, if you hire a private taxi or a taxi of a different firm it might be even more expensive.

In front of the bus station are several food outlets and road-stands, a café, a tobacco kiosk and shoe repairing office.

THE AIRPORT

If you value your time so much that you are eager to pay extra just to save a few hours, then traveling by air is for you. Besides, the bird's eye view of the city from the plane will give you an idea of what to expect.

Lviv's airport is located on the edge of town, right at the end of Lubinska Street. If you want to have lunch in Frankfurt-am-Mein, Warsaw or Vienna, dine in Moscow, Kyiv or Sevastopol, or have a cup of coffee in Paris, all you have to do is hop a plane.

The central airport building is comfortable and cozy, although there is only one waiting lounge, decorated with frieze murals in the best traditions of the Soviet realism style. All the services are in the waiting lounge. Two exits lead to the departure and arrival terminals with check-in, customs and passport control counters (the latter two are for international flights). Opposite the main entrance are the information desk, post office and tourist agency. The information desk operates 24 hours a day (enquiries are free of charge; tel. 69-21-12). A small post office is open from 9.00 to 18.00. Next to the post office is a tourist information office (open: 12.00-17.00; tel. 69-20-59). In the same premises, but in a small separate room

are located two domestic and international ticket

A road sign pointing the way to the Airport

offices (open: 06.30-19.00). Discounts are given on the tickets issued for children, disabled, etc. Tickets bought in advance are cheaper than those purchased on the flight day. Tickets can be acquired three months prior to the departure date. If you have already settled on the date, than do not hesitate to take advantage of the discounts. The airport also features a duty-free shop, open at the time of flights' departure and arrival. The first aid is rendered at the first-aid post. The VIP-hall for official delegations is open round the clock. If you have to make an urgent domestic or international call, telephone booths are in the waiting lounge as well as by the main entrance. If your luggage is lost, there is nothing to worry about – the lost-luggage trace service is in the waiting lounge right by the ticket offices. In order not

to miss your flight, consult departure and arrival times indicated at the information board. Arrive 1 hour in advance for a domestic flight and 2 hours – for an international flight to complete the check-in formalities. It is worthwhile studying the customs information table as well. There are no cafes or restaurants inside the airport, but three cafes and a restaurants are located close to the premises. Thus, if you have time to spare and feel like having a bite of something or a cup of coffee, leave your luggage in the left-luggage office (1 UAH per item per 24 hours) and visit one of the catering establishments. The only toilet facility is in the passengers' sector. Another public toilet facility is close to the airport (accessible at 0.50 UAH fee). The currency exchange office, located in the airport premises, is open from 9.00 to 18.00. As it is the case in all airports, the exchange rate is low,

*Road sign
"Attention! Evacuator!"*

CAR EMERGENCY SERVICE:

T&B
135, Pasichna street   **tel. 70-1400**

112 Ukraina
6, Pidstryhacha Street
(Registry)   **tel. 64-8628**

Emergency Road-Side
Assistance   **tel. 0-61**

CAR MAINTENANCE CENTERS:

Audi, Seat, Volkswagen
13, Buzkova Street   **tel. 70-0676**
9.00–18.00

Avtozaz Daewoo, VAZ, GAZ, Fiat
5, Sichynskoho Street
9.00–18.00   **tel. 228-2777**

BMW
1, Piasetskoho Street   **tel. 62-9322**
9.00–19.00

Ford
43, Horodnytska Street
9.00–18.00.   **tel. 297-1441**

Hundai, KIA, KAMAZ, Subaru,
UAZ, ZIL
15, Bohdanivska Street
9.00–19.00   **tel. 294-0282**

Isuzu, Mazda, Suzuki
230, Kulparkivska
9.00–19.00   **tel. 65-9104**

Mercedes, Toyota, Ford
359, Horodotska Street
9.00–18.00   **tel. 62-0164**

Mitsubishi
44, Bohdanivska Street
tel. 298-0888, 298-0855
9.00–18.00, Sa 9.00–15.00

Opel, UAZ
282, Horodotska Street
9.00–18.00   **tel. 62-6056**

Peugeot
4, Hlibna Street   **tel. 221-6705**
9.00–19.00

so wait until you get into town. Several airlines fly to Lviv, these include Lviv airlines, Ukraine International Airlines and Aerosvit airlines. Economy class tickets are cheaper, but if you are used to comfort, then book a seat in the business class.

The newly constructed administration building is next door to the departure and arrival terminals.

The "Tustan" hotel, offering rooms at a reasonable price, is just one stop from the airport (trolleybus #9) . Tel. 69-28-82.

To get to the city center take trolleybus # 9 (the fare is 0.50 UAH), the # 95 marshrutka (the fare is 1 UAH), or a taxi (the fare depends on your negotiation abilities, the bottom price being 10 UAH). To get to the train station, take trolleybus # 9 (2 stops) and change to marshrutka # 67 or 2. To get to the central bus station, take trolleybus # 9 (two stops) and change to trolleybus # 3, marshrutka # 57 or bus # 37 (the fare is 0.80 UAH). The bus station is at the terminal stop.

TRAVELING BY CAR

Many prefer to reach Lviv by car, which may be more convenient when traveling with the whole family. If you want to have a closer look at a flower, drink water from a spring, or see an architectural sight, all of which abound in the Lviv region, you can

always make a stop. In this case, apart from your own luggage, you must have all the required documents: driver's license, a customs declaration for the car and the registration certificate. Also do not forget a first-aid kit, a fire extinguisher and an emergency warning triangle – you will feel more secure with these things. If you are planning trips out of town, it may be wise to fill your petrol tank in Lviv – an empty petrol tank is a bad companion. Otherwise, you are bound to wait, whether rain or heat, for a "kind old man" to take mercy on you and share with you a splash of the valuable liquid, or pull your car to the nearest petrol station. On the second thought, there are plenty of stations down the road, so you can push the car yourself, just ask your fellow-companions to give you a hand. Most petrol stations operate round the clock. Payment is in cash. All the stations have pump attendants, so there is no need to get out of the car and dirty your hands. Yet, to pay for the petrol you do have to leave your car and take a couple of steps to the cashier-desk. Most petrol stations have toilet facilities and small shops selling basic necessities. Yet, at certain times your wish to make use of the toilet facilities may not be granted due to the water-shortage problem in Lviv. Then follow our advice and find a petrol station by high and thick shrubs, where you can "merge with mother-nature" for free.

PARKING LOTS

Parking lots are plentiful in Lviv and all are run by private owners. Any thrifty entrepreneur, who considers himself a successful businessman, organizes a small parking place for several cars in his yard. Such services are in high demand especially in the downtown area and other busy districts. Parking cost ranges from 5 to 10 UAH,

A Lviv's tram

depending on the location. However, you can always negotiate with a security guard of an enterprise or establishment, who for a small charge of 2 UAH will let you park your car in their parking lot. The only disadvantage is that you have to retrieve your car by 8 a.m., so that the administration of the establishment does not notice the intruder. And if the guard has a cup of hot tea and falls asleep, then your car is not safe from thieves. Thus, take our advice and park the car at official parking places.

Renault
105/a, Zelena Street
tel. 41-8295, 41-8291
9.00–19.00, Sa 9.00–13.00

Skoda
407, Zelena Street   **tel. 70-2420**
9.00–19.00
13, Buzkova Street   **tel. 70-0676**
9.00–18.00

CAR WASH FACILITIES:

PIT-STOP
153, Pasichna Street   **tel. 78-4587**
open: 24 hours, tire repair,automobile service shop, WC

Car-wash
11, Hrabovskoho Street   **tel. 72-3801**
open: 9.00-19.00, vacuuming the inside of the car, WC

Bristol
6, Hnatiuka   **tel. 297-4114**
open: 24 hours, window toning, alarm system installation.

«Diamant» car service center
44, Bohdanivska Street   **tel. 298-0888**
9.00–18.00, Sa — 9.00–15.00, car servicing, car dealer, WC

Lviv-auto
36, Nekrasova Street   **tel. 75-9072**
9.00–18.00, Sa — 9.00–15.00, vacuuming the inside of the car, engine wash, engine repair, anti-corrosion treatment, ultra-sound cleaning of injectors, chassis servicing, wheel configuration, tire recapping, welding, unbending and painting, installation of security equipment, scanner diagnostics; DAEWOO spare parts store, WC

Lvivenergoavtotrans
15, Kozelnytska Street   **tel. 70-9257**
8.00–23.00, vacuuming the inside of the car, car servicing, WC

Marlin
Varshavska-Pidholosko
tel. 52-0364
open: 24 hours, general car-service, car wash, shop, WC

AUDI-CENTER-ZAKHID
13, Buzkova Street   **tel. 70-0676**
9.00–18.00, car-wash, vacuuming the inside of the car, general car-service, car dealer, WC

PETROL STATIONS:

WOG
288, Horodotska Street
tel.62-6340
open: 24 hours; petrol pump attendant; a grocery and a household chemical and basic goods shop; WC
291, Khmelnytskoho Street
tel. 297-5698
24 hours; petrol pump attendant; grocery and basic goods shop; WC
67, Chernovola Prospect
tel. 52-0364
24 hours; petrol pump attendant; grocery and basic goods shop; WC
11, Bohdanivska Street
tel. 294-1129
24 hours; petrol pump attendant; grocery and basic goods shop; WC

AVIAS
5 – Stryiska Street
tel. 227-0980
24 hours; basic goods shop; WC

ALFA-LVIV
153, Pasichna Street
tel. 296-6260
24 hours; petrol pump attendant
2a, Naukova Street tel. 65-4022
open: 24 hours; petrol pump attendant; grocery and basic goods shop; WC

BUSINESS FINANCE
14, Professor Buika Street
tel. 70-5668
open: 24 hours; petrol pump attendant; basic goods shop; WC
50, Volodymera Velykoho Street
tel. 64-9555
open: 24 hours; petrol pump attendant; grocery and basic goods shop; WC
6, Khotkevycha Street
tel. 222-3309 *open: 24 hours; petrol pump attendant; public telephone cards; WC*
101, Kulparkivska Street
tel. 64-6905 *24 hours; petrol pump attendant; WC*
5, Washingtona Street
tel. 70-1788 *open: 24 hours; petrol pump attendant; WC*

Naftoproduct
Horodotska Siaivo Street
tel. 67-7120
open: 24 hours; petrol pump attendant; grocery and basic goods shop; WC

LOCAL TRANSPORT

Although Lviv is officially divided into six districts (Halytsky, Zaliznychny, Lychakivsky, Frankivsky, Shevchenkivsky and Sykhivsky), the city's inhabitants may use more names to designate historical parts of town: Bilohorscha, Holosko, Zamarstyniv, Znesinnia, Kamianka, Klepariv, Kozelnyky, Kryvchytsy, Kulparkiv, Lysynychy, Maiorivka, Novy Lviv, Riasne, Sygnivka,

"Navigator" Taxi Agency

Sykhiv and Sknyliv. Like in another city or town such unofficial district division is more popular and logical.

All forms of overland transport exist in Lviv: trams, trolleybuses, buses and marshrutka (privately run minibuses). The electric transport is owned by the state and thus is in deplorable condition. Nine tramlines connect the central and historical outskirts of the city. A few years ago new tramlines were introduced in the newly built districts, which are very convenient for passengers

– trams as well as buses and trolleybuses are the cheapest means of transportation. Apart from that, it is only by these means of transport that children and the disabled enjoy certain privileges. It is a generally excepted rule. Otherwise you might find yourself in an unpleasant situation when some muscled conductor, dressed in civvies, walks into the compartment and asks for your ticket. A fine is charged for fare dodging. You are

At a matshrutka stop

cepted rule to give seats to children and senior citizens. If an elderly woman happens to get on the bus and stand right by you, while you, comfortably seated, pretend to be utterly absorbed in watching something through the window, beware – all the fellow-passengers will openly manifest their disapproval. The fare for trams and trolleybuses is 0.50 UAH, regardless of the distance. Conductors, with huge pockets or bags dangling in front nicknamed "kangaroos", walk slowly up and down the bus aislesreminding the passengers to pay for the trip. When you pay the fare, a conductor will give you a torn ticket, which is to be saved until the end of the journey. It is advisable to stick to this

also supposed to pay for heavy luggage but nobody does or demands so. The bus fare is 0.60-0.80 UAH and depends on the distance and bus model. The fare is paid to conductors, when you get on the bus.

Privately run minibuses, otherwise known as "marshrutka" or "pyzhyk" (a colloquial derivative from Peugeot), have solved all the problems with public transportation. People welcomed the innovation, because the charge was reasonable and the advantages were numerous. This rapidly developing means of public transport is gaining in popularity. Today, the old part of the city with its narrow and intertwining streets has turned into "a course of survival competi-

TAXI:

VIKAR **tel. 298-3333**
8.00–2.00; each next kilometer:
1 км — 1,20 UAH,
starting price — 7 UAH.

VIRAGE
9/7, Kleparivska Street
tel. 233-8114, (067) 718-1238
24 hours; starting price: 5 км — 7 UAH,
each next kilometer — 1,20 UAH.

Desad-Service
3, Petrushevycha Street **tel. 75-4754**
24 hours; starting price 4 км — 7 UAH,
each next kilometer— 1,20 UAH, The
details about trips outside the city are
negotiated with the driver.

KROK
Zamkova Street, 4 **tel. 75-6180, 0-83**
24 hours; starting price 5 км — 7 UAH.
The details about trips outside the city
are negotiated with the driver..

MIF **tel. 41-9111, 41-9101**
24 hours; starting price — 6 UAH.

NAVIGATOR
109, Zelena Street
tel. 298-6002, 0-02, (067)949-3333
24 hours; starting price — 10 UAH.

RADAR SERVICE
tel. 0-00, 298-1995
24 hours; starting price — 10 UAH.

"Fortuna" radio-taxi
28, Krymska Street
tel. 40-5040, (067)990-0003
24 hours; starting price — 7 UAH.

VAT Fiacre
34b, Fedkovycha Street
tel. 238-2408
5.30–21.00, each next kilometer:
1 км — 1 UAH.

PRIVAT-TAXI
tel. 239-3434, 239-1222, 239-3333
24 hours; starting price — 7 UAH.

SHETERLIAK
tel. 40-4455, 40-4454
24 hours; starting price— 6 UAH.

Misto-Trans **tel. 299-1777**
24 hours; starting price — 7 UAH.

HERTZ car rental company
62, Horodotska Street
tel. 297-0052, 8 (050) 358-2861
e-mail: hertz@hertz.lviv.ua

LVIV WEB-SITES:

www.lviv.net
Information on everyday business, cultural and entertainment life in Lviv;

www.leopolis.lviv.net
Picture gallery about Lviv;

www.portal.lviv.ua
General information about modern Lviv;

Parking area

www.lwow.com.pl
The site about Lviv in the Polish language.
www.pro.lviv.ua
www.about.lviv.ua
Information about the business life in Lviv – services, companies and business cooperation.

tion", where only the dexterous will survive in the jams of cars, marshrutka's, trams and pedestrians. The "struggle for survival" reaches its peak at rush hours and weekends, when the central part of the city is closed for traffic and becomes a pedestrian area. A journey by marshrutka costs 1 UAH and the fare does not depend on the distance or comforts of the passenger section. Some marshrutka's are the old mini-lorries and lack basic comforts, yet the fare is the same as for a more comfortable vehicle.

You pay the driver when you get on, but do not expect him to give you a ticket. The routes outside the city limits are more expensive and the fare depends on the distance. The route number and street names along the route are indicated on the windscreen and side windows of the vehicle.

No doubt the taxi is the most comfortable means of transportation, which will take you to any destination fast. Lviv has a well-developed taxi service. You can book a taxi by phone, giving the operator your present address and the address of your destination, as well as your phone number. The operator will promptly call you back and inform you that the taxi is waiting for you downstairs. It takes about 10-15 minutes, in rush hours – 20-25 minutes, for a taxi to come and pick you up. The journey within

the city limits costs between 8 and 20 UAH. A taxi can be called to a motel or restaurants outside the city. In this case you have to pay for the booking, which is 7-8 UAH. About twenty officially registered taxi agencies operate in Lviv. Each agency sets its own service rules. The best taxi operators are "Radar Service" and "Navigator". If you are on a business trip and need a receipt for the journey, bear in mind that not all city taxis can offer this service. Only "Radar-Service" taxis are equipped with electronic counters, indicating the cost, distance, day and time of the journey. There is an extra charge if you need your taxi driver to assist you with the luggage. When the taxi is booked by phone the cost of the trip is set, but with private car drivers you bargain for a better price. Rates in the evening and nighttime are a little more expensive than in the daytime.

PARKING

If you want to have a look at an architectural sight or have a cup of coffee, but want to park your car first, watch for a parking sign. At the weekend and on holidays, finding a parking place turns into a strenuous exercise, especially in the downtown area and busy streets. Yet, it is not impossible. Before you have reminded your fellow travelers not to forget their purses and cameras, a man wearing a cap and dark-brown or black clothes with an inscription on his back "parkuvannia" (parking) will approach your car. He is a parking attendant in a uniform. He sees that cars are parked at the places designated by him, charging for the service 2 UAH an hour. Here you may expect a certain degree of security. Parking attendants' working hours are from 8.00 to 18.00.

CAR RENTAL

If you arrived in Lviv by bus, train or plane, you may eschew certain inconveniences, for example, searching for a parking place, a petrol station, etc. Despite all this, the advantages of traveling by car outnumber disadvantages, and you might want to rent a car. You can rent a car through the hotel you are staying at, provided the hotel

Post office

renders such services. The HERTZ car rental company, at 62, Horodotska Street, has a wide range of cars on offer (Skoda, Volkswagen, Ford, etc.). All you have to do is dial 297-00-52 or 8-050-358-28-61, or apply through the Internet (hertz@hertz. lviv.ua, www.hertz.ua). The prices start from 60 USD per 24 hours.

The central hub for public transport is Svobody Prospect. Here from the Opera House and up till the end of the street you can get a marshrutka to practically any spot in town. You can also

Public telephone booths at train station platform

catch a marshrutka at Ivana Franka Street from Halytska Square up to the end of Ivana Franka Street. Another busy transport cross-section is at the railway station, where you can get any means of public transport to any spot in town.

Central Post Office
1, Slovatskoho Street
tel. 97-0327, 297-0328
Manager   **tel. 72-1080**
Informational operator   **tel. 0-88**
e-mail: peredplata@post.lviv.ua
www.post.lviv.ua

"Ukrtelecom" central office
37, Dorosheka Street **tel. 74-2124**
Information   **tel. 298-6210**
"Ukrtelecom" customers'
service center   **tel. 297-1615**

UPS: mail and freight
express delivery
tel. 297-0748, 41-9070

UTEL:
Information Services   **tel. 8-198**
8+ Services   **tel. 8-196, 97-2000**
Telephone and telegraph exchange:
Inter-city Operator   **tel. 0-73**
International Operator   **tel. 0-79**
Telephone Massages
Operator   **tel. 0-66**

MOBILE COMMUNICATIONS

Mobile phone services are provided in Lviv by two Ukrainian operators: UMC and Kyivstar. Mobile communication services offer many brands of mobile telephones, phone cards and phone accessories for sale, and provide information about services they offer.

UMC Information Center
9, Yaponska Street
8-800-500-0-500, for mobile phone calls **111** (Phone calls received 24 hours a days. All the calls are free within Ukraine)
e-mail: umc@umc.com.ua
http:\\www.umc.ua

Kyivstar Information Center
6, Mateika Street   **tel. 297-4187**
297-4313, **40-8888**

MOBILE COMMUNICATION OUTLETS:

UMC
9, Yaponska Street
tel. 8-800-500-0-500
Mo-Fr 9.00–19.00,
Sa 10.00–18.00, Su 10.00–15.00

Eurotel
20, Kniazia Romana Street
Mo-Fr 9.00–19.00,
Sa 10.00–16.00   **tel. 297-4187**

Evant
18, Vitivskoho Street
tel. 40-3333

MOBILE COMMUNICATION CENTER
139, Lychakivska Street
tel. 298-0398
Mo-Fr 9.00–19.00,
Sa 10.00–17.00

MENCE
63, Kulparkivska Street
tel. 295-3434
Mo-Fr 9.00–19.00,
Sa 10.00–17.00
1, Stara Street   **tel. 296-6400**
Mo-Fr 9.00–19.00,
Sa 10.00–17.00, Su 10.00–17.00

Mobi-1
14, Lychakivska Street
Mo-Fr 10.00–19.00,
Sa 10.00–16.00   **tel. 76-6592**

Mobivim
7, Dudaev Street   **tel. 74-4166**
Mo-Fr 10.00–19.00,
Sa 10.00–16.00

Mobipark
8, Shevchenka Prospect
298-6800
1/3, Kopernika Street   **298-7142**
Mo-Fr 10.00–20.00,
Sa 10.00–16.00

"NOT" Centers
89, Bandery Street   **40-8110**
Mo-Sa 9.00–20.00, Su 9.00–18.00
3/b, Horodotska Street   **72-6581**
2, Zelena Street   **76-4868**
33, Franka Street   **296-5733**
26, Shevchenka Prospect **74-4177**
Mo-Fr 9.00–20.00, Sa 9.00–18.00,
Su 10.00–15.00

"NTON" Centers
25, Horodotska Street
tel. 72-8929
2, Doroshenka Street **tel. 297-4012**
17, Zelena Street   **tel. 298-1751**
3, Petrushevycha Street
tel. 78-1818
1, Shpytalna Street   **tel. 294-9176**
15, Krakivska Street   **tel. 72-7932**
2, Nevskoho Street **tel. 297-1133**
79, Franka Street   **tel. 76-9637**
40, Kulisha Street   **tel. 74-5530**

INTERNET RESOURCES

You can get an introduction to some Lviv establishments and services prior to arriving in "Ukrainian Paris". On the Internet, there are various sites with picture galleries of architectural and historical sights as well as sites with detailed information about hotels, restaurants, clubs and theaters, including details of services, addresses and specific details.
In the city there are a large number of internet-cafes and clubs, where you can check your in-box, send e-mails, work on the computer, serf the net or play computer games.

COMMUNICATION

If it happens that you are traveling alone without your family, do not despair – it has its own benefits. If you want to share your impressions of Lviv or send

a post-card, or maybe ask your relatives or friends to transfer money for the souvenirs you have not yet bought, go to the Central Post Office at 1, Slovatskoho Street, nearby the Franko University and Lviv Art Gallery. It is a majestic edifice of the early 20th century with spacious lounges, adorned with stained-glass windows and decorative greenery. From the Post Office you can send a telegram or a letter, make a money transfer, order for a mail courier service within Lviv (4 hours at the determined time; tel. 72-39-43), receive a money transfer through the Western Union system, send international or intercity parcels or packages, purchase a telephone card, buy publications and postal goods (stamps, postal cards and envelopes), and send or receive e-mails and faxes, as well as make a Xerox copy of a document. In the Post Office there is a currency exchange point of the "Aval" Bank, open on weekdays from 8.00 to 20.00, on Saturdays – from 9.00 to 16.00 and on Sundays from 9.00 to 14.00.

In the same building is the Ukrtelecom office (entrance from 37, Doroshenka Street). Here you can make use of Internet, fax, telegraph or place an international call. The office is open from 7.00 to 23.00.

Local post offices provide similar postal services. From any post office you can send a letter or parcel, buy postal goods or publications, and purchase an Internet card or an "Ukrtelecom" (national phone company) telephone card for both intercity and international phone calls. 20 post offices distribute electronic vouchers for mobile phone accounts. Some post offices cash money on Visa and Maestro cards through POS (point-of-sale) terminals. However, not all post offices are equipped with telephone booths for intercity and international calls. Be prepared for the fact that not all public phones in the city will allow you make calls with the prefix "8" (required for all long-distance calls and

many mobile phone calls). To call internationally or long-distance it may be best to make use of long-distance telephone offices that use digital phones and are equipped with contemporary communication systems; or to head for the Central Post Office, where a wide range of communications are offered. In Lviv six-digit numbers were the norm for a long time; however, today many phones operate with seven digit numbers. When dialing the seven digit number through the mobile or intercity communication systems the prefix digit "2" is omitted, while for in-city calls it must precede the number. In the telephone directo-

Lviv views on postcards

ries published some two years ago you still might come across phone numbers with the initial digits "33" or "9". Today, these numbers are preceded with "2". The numbers starting with "35" have been changed; for details consult the information service (tel. 09, 089-Lviv information service). Emergence phone numbers have less then six digits.

PRESS, RADIO AND TV

You can get more detailed information about local events and festivals from the local media, which boasts a wide variety of publications. The "Vysoky Zamok" (High Castle) newspaper, published daily except for Sundays, is a colorful family newspaper featuring different supplements: politics, culture, sports, humor, health, nature,

Newsstand

Lviv periodicals

INTERNET CAFES:

"Integrator"
35, Bandery Street **tel. 297-0251**
Services offered: computer (1hour
– 1 UAH), printing, scanning,
lamination and Xerox-copying.

"Bunker"
61, Volodymera Velykoho Street
tel. 40-2026
9.00–23.00
Services offered: computer games,
lazer printing, scanning, Internet.

"S-Club"
1/2, Krushelnytskoy Street
24 hours   **tel. 40-3135**
Services offered: printing, computer, scanning, computer games,
Internet. Internet – 4 UAH per hour.
Games – 3 UAH, Internet – 15 UAH
per night, games – 6 UAH.

"S-Club"
101, Chornovola Street
tel. 40-7222
24 hours, Services offered: printing, computer, scanning, computer games, Internet. Internet – 4
UAH per hour. Games – 3 UAH,
Internet 15 UAH per night, games
– 6 UAH.

"S-Club"
1, Antonenka-Davydovycha
Street   **tel. 227-3365**
24 hours, Services offered: printing, computer, scanning, computer games, Internet. Internet – 4

UAH per hour. Games – 3 UAH,
Internet 15 UAH per night, games
– 6 UAH.

"Pavuk"
7, Svobody Prospect **tel. 72-5084**
24 hours
Services offered: Internet, computer games. Internet – 4 UAH
per hour; 15 UAH per night. Copy
and Print Center, open: 24 hours.
Services offered: printing, scanning and typing.

PUBLIC PHONE CENTER

"Svit Rozvah"
(Entertainment World)
1, Shevchenka Prospect
tel. 297-4128
9.00–23.00
Services offered: typing, scanning,
printing and computer games.

Service-Center
36a, Lychakivska Street
8.00–21.00   **tel. 76-1849**
Services offered: Internet, printing, typing, scanning, computer
games. Internet – 3 UAH per hour.
Games – 2 UAH.

Internet-Club
12, Dudaeva Street **tel. 72-2738**
24 hours
Services offered: Internet and all
computer services. Internet – 4
UAH per hour in the daytime and
2 UAH at night.

children column, complete
TV program (including programs of satellite channels),
etc. The daily "Postup" newspaper covers political and
cultural life, gives reviews
and previews of cultural
events and features daily
subject supplements, including a color supplement with
a complete TV program.
The "Lvivska Hazeta" (Lviv
newspaper) with five issues
a week and daily subject
supplements features the
latest political, cultural, and
economic news, as well as
comments, exclusive inter-
views, TV programs, information on the real estate
market, etc.

On radio, there are several
Lviv FM music, entertain-
ment and news stations:
"Radio Man", "Lvivska Kh-
vylia" (Lviv wave), "Lux" (First
Class) and "Nezalezhnist"
(Independence). There are
also some national stations
broadcasting on Lviv radio:
"Gala-Radio", "Auto FM",
"Nashe Radio" (Our Radio),
"Melodia" (Melody), etc. You
can easily tune to AM Polish
stations, because of Lviv's
close location to Poland.

Lviv has a well-developed
television network; along-
side the local television
companies (LTB, TRK Lux,
TNT and Mist), network
television transmits 42
national and international
news and entertainment
channels ("Inter", "Novy
Canal", STB, "1+1", ORT, RTR
and "Discovery") as well as
special music (MTV, OTV
and others), children and
sports channels.

MEDICAL FACILITIES,
DRY-CLEANERS AND SHOE-REPAIRS

■ *"Don't take good health for granted". We must not scorn this saying. However, it is only when we are in emergency, we can appreciate the saying's wisdom. When we are in a strange city and do not know where to turn, the situation might become critical.*

DIAGNOSTIC CENTERS

Despite the best specialists they provide, the state medical institutions in Lviv, as in any other town in Ukraine, leave much to be desired. All is because of the lack of finances. If you happen to be taken to a state-run hospital, be prepared to receive a list of the medicines you have to purchase, starting with analgin (a common pain-killer) to more complicated drugs. Private medical facilities are more expensive at a much higher level. If you are well-off and need a doctor, call the "Bohdan" ambulance, which arrives promptly and the doctors render immediate and qualified help (a visit costs 100 UAH, paid in Hryvnia prior to the doctors' assistance). In the "Bohdan" medical center, tests and treatment are carried out on the premises in a comfortable environment with pleasant wards and

"Bohdan"
Medical Canter
33 b, Khmenytskoho Street, Birky
tel. 59-3674

International Consultation and Diagnostic Center at the Lviv hospital for the railway personnel
3, Ogienka Street
tel. 748-2284

"Prostir" Scientific and Consultation Center"
33, Svobody Prospect
tel. 296-5480

"Svit Zdorovia" (Health World)
32, Doroshenka Street
tel. 74-0677

Simeks-Sono
Ultra-Sound Diagnostic Center
7/1 Karmeliuka Street
tel. 75-9207

"Metropol" Medical Spa Center
2, Stusa Street
tel. 299-2333
Services offered: Russian and Rome steam baths, solarium, sauna, Jacuzzi, massage, restaurants, recreation lounges.

Interior of the pharmacy-museum

PHARMACIES

If you are confident in your medical knowledge and know which medications you need, Lviv pharmacies are at your service. Today, pharmacies spring up like mushrooms in Lviv. Some pharmacies operate round the clock. In the information center you can check the availability of different medicines in pharmacies. The oldest pharmacy in Lviv is the pharmacy-museum at Rynok Square. Here you can not only acquire the needed drug, but also view the exposition of tools for preparing medications and learn the history of pharmacy in Lviv. And, of course, here you can buy the famous "Iron Wine", the universal remedy for all ailments.

SAUNAS

Saunas are a healthy way of recreation. People say that saunas relieve the pressure and help get rid of a couple of kilos of flesh. For an additional charge masseurs will massage your body and dispel black thoughts. Later you can rent a room and wallow in luxurious linens and feather pillows, and have a pint of beer, or some other beverage. The cost of a visit to a sauna is about 50 UAH.

Information on availability of different medicine in pharmacies   **tel. 0-67**

"Your drug availability information"   **tel. 298-9898**

PHARMACIES:
"Market-Universal" Pharmacy
19, Halytska Street
tel. 74-2006
24 hours

St. Nicholas's Phyto-Pharmacy
23, Hrushevskoho Street
tel. 72-3874

"Tiso"
3, Dudaeva Street
tel. 72-5087
24 hours

"By the Black Eagle"
Pharmacy-Museum
2, Drukarska Street
tel. 72-0041

St. Trinity Pharmacy
28, Shevchenka Prospect
tel. 72-3713

courteous staff providing the best possible care. The "Simeks-Sono" center conducts complete ultrasound diagnostics and the leading specialists are available for further consultations. The Women Health Center at the Lviv hospital for the railway personnel provides qualified diagnostics, consultations and treatment. However, it should be borne in mind that the high level of service is reflected in the price.

"Iron Wine"

"Eurochystka" dry-cleaning

DRY-CLEANERS

If you want to clean your worn suit, then pack and take it to a dry cleaning establishment. When you hand in an article of clothing to a dry cleaners' today, you can rest assured that the buttons will not fall off, or some other mishap does not occur. If, ab-sorbed in sightseeing, you have not noticed when ice cream dropped on your clothes, or a clumsy somebody poured a glass of wine on you, there is nothing to worry about. Just take the article to a dry-cleaner's. The qualified staff will rescue your mood and will quickly deal with stains, even with the old spots, you have always tried to disguise.

SHOE-REPAIRS

Lviv cobblestone streets will destroy any shoes, let alone young ladies' stunning high heels. More often than not heeltaps stick in the stones and thus get buried forever in Lviv's history. However, Lviv footwear repairers are always there for you, holding hammer and nails. While repairing your shoes, they will entertain you with an amusing story or a joke. Time will fly fast and soon your shoes will be ready

SAUNAS

Grand Hotel
13, Svobody Prospect
tel. 72-4042

Grand Resort
Village Basivka, Pustomytivsky rayon,
15 km from Lviv

Dniestr
Tourist Hotel Complex
6, Mateika Street
tel. 297-4317

Eneas
Hotel
Sauna, massage
2, Shimzeriv Street
tel. 76-8799

"Metropol" Medical Spa Center
2, Stusa Street
tel. 299-2333
solarium, sauna, Jacuzzi

DRY-CLEANERS

"Eurochistka"
61, Franka Street
tel. 76-2779, 28-2825

"Snizhynka"
2, Shevska Street
tel. 74-2321
Mo-Fr 8.00-19.00, Sa 8.00-14.00

SHOE-REPAIRS

"Kabluchok"
14, Franka Street
tel. 72-5786

"Pidkivka"
2, Kniazia Romana Street
Mo-Fr 8.00-19.00, lunch break 14.00-15.00, Sa 8.00-14.00

"Kabluchok-Obnova"
4, Kniazia Romana Street
Mo-Fr 8.00-19.00, lunch break 14.00-15.00, Sa 8.00-14.00

Sign pointing the direction to a tailor's shop

WHERE TO STAY

Grand Hotel

■ *Hotels in Lviv reflect the Ukrainian society. There is no middle-class layer. You have to choose between up-market, expensive hotels for VIP clients and old hotels built in the Post-Soviet style and decorated in the so-called European fashion, unknown to the rest of the world.*
You can also opt for private accommodation, the owners of which will heartily welcome the guests. You will be recommended apartments, private houses in the green town area or luxurious houses with all services. The price of the accommodation depends on the standard of the facilities offered.
Real estate agencies can provide any information on the available accommodations, services and prices.

The following signs, indicating the facilities offered by Lviv hotels, prove helpful when choosing an accommodation

	room service		room air-conditioned
	24-hour service		room with a telephone
	business center		refrigerator
	conference hall		bath
	internet		accommodation with pets
	restaurants		gym
	bar		swimming-pool
	casino		sauna
	discounts for children		massage parlor
	facilities for the handicapped		beauty parlor
	currency exchange		hairdresser's
	parking area		laundry
	car service		cable TV
	car rental		credit cards accepted

TOP END HOTELS:

GRAND HOTEL ****

13, Svobody Prospect
📞 72-4042, 72-7665,
Fax 76-9060
e-mail:
grand@ghgroup.com.ua
www.ghgroup.com.ua

Staff speaks — English, Polish.
Breakfast included.

Visa, Maestro, MasterCard, Visa Elektron, Diners Club, EuroCard, American Express.

The hotel is located right in the heart of the city, near the Lviv Opera and Ballet House and some other historical and cultural sights. Built in the late 19th century, the hotel combines the classical elegance of that epoch and the comforts of a modern 4-star hotel. After the reconstruction, the hotel still preserves original architectural decorations of the interior. The inside of the building is adorned with splendid stained-glass windows by famous artists. Refined cuisine, service and comfort of the highest standards are the main benefits of the restaurants and bars in the Grand Hotel. The hotel offers the highest level of recreation and entertainment activities in the "Sofia" Grand Club.

GRAND RESORT ***

Lviv region,
Pustomytivsky rayon, Basivka village.
📞 297-1606, Fax 297-1605

Staff speaks — English, Russian.
Breakfast included.

MasterCard, Visa, American Express, EuroCard.

DNISTER ****

Tourist and Hotel Complex
6, Mateika Street
📞 297-4317, 297-4306
Fax 297-1017
e-mail: tour@dnister.lviv.ua
www.dnister.lviv.ua

Breakfast included.

MasterCard, Visa, American Express.

The luxurious hotel complex similar to European standards is located close to the city center in the park area by the Franko National University. In 1998 the presidents that participated in the Summit of Central Eastern Europe stayed in this hotel.

ENEY***

2, Shimzeriv Street 📞 76-8799, 76-8370
e-mail: eney@mail.lviv.ua
www.eney.lviv.ua

Staff speaks — English, Polish, Czech.
Breakfast included.

MasterCard, Maestro, Visa, VisaElektron, EuroCard, Diners Club.

The coziest hotel in Lviv, the Eney is located close to the city center in the green park area by the Botanic Garden of the Medical University and within a couple of meters from the Lychakivsky Museum. The hotel offers a high level of services and a warm and

The "Aeneas" hotel interior

friendly atmosphere. The Eney provides all the facilities for business and leisure activities and features
14 comfortable single and double rooms. Because
of a small number of rooms, the staff devotes closer
attention to the guests' needs and habits.

ZAMOK LEVA
(LION'S CASTLE)
7, Hlinky Street
297-1563
e-mail: Lions_castle@org.Lviv.net
www.Lionscastle.com

Staff speaks — English, Russian, Polish.
Breakfast included.

MasterCard, Maestro, Visa.

8 persons · 12 persons

BURGER-CLUB ★★★★
Lviv – Obroshino
21, Franka Street
298-2430, 239-6843

Staff speaks — Russian.
Breakfast included.

MasterCard, Visa.

25 persons · 25 persons

NAVARIA
THE "NAVARIA NOVA"
Hotel Complex
Lviv region, Pustomytivsky rayon,
Navaria village
227-2727
Fax 227-2597

Staff speaks — English.
Breakfast included.

20 persons

The "Navaria Nova" hotel complex is located in a picturesque nook by a lake 7 km from Lviv. Its exquisite
style is emphasized by the interior decorated with
modern works of art, beautiful stained-glass windows and exotic plants. Each of the 20 hotel rooms is
equipped with all the facilities needed for a comfortable stay.

OLENA
5, Balabanivka Street, Lviv – Briukhovychy
59-3470, 59-5181
Fax 293-9879
e-mail: olena@is.lviv.ua
www.lato.com.ua

Staff speaks — English, Polish.
Breakfast included.

MasterCard, Maestro, Visa, VisaElectron, EuroCard.

AT THE BURGER
73, Franka Street
296-6569, 76-9580, 76-1251, 75-4954

Staff speaks — Russian.
Breakfast included.

Visa, MasterCard.

12 persons

BUDGET HOTELS:

SUPUTNYK***
116, Kniahyny Olhy Street
📞 64-5822, 65-2421, Fax 64-1523

HETMAN***
50, Volodymyra Velykoho Street
📞 64-9981, 230-1320
e-mail: hetman@mail.lviv.ua

Staff speaks — English, Russian.

MasterCard, Maestro, Visa.

50 persons 300 persons

GEORGE**
1, Mickiewicz Square
📞 72-5952, 74-2182, 297-4255
Fax 72-2925
e-mail: geoh@mail.lviv.ua
www.georghotel.org

Staff speaks — English, Derman, Polish.
Breakfast included.

Visa, MasterCard.

20 persons

Located in the city center by the monument to Adam Mickiewicz, the hotel is one of the oldest in Ukraine. The edifice is an architectural monument of the early 20th century with a facade in the Neo-Renaissance style with some Baroque decorations.

NTON***
154 b, Shevchenka Street
📞 233-3123, 233-7172, 291-2711
Fax 233-7168
e-mail: hotelnton@ukr.net
www.hotelnton.Lviv.ua

TUSTAN
168 a, Liubinska Street
📞 69-2881, 69-2882
Fax 69-22-16

The "George" hotel. An old photo

VLASTA**

30, Kleparivska Street
233-3427, 233-3430
Fax 233-3430

BOHDAN

33 a, Khmelnytskoho Street,
Birky village
59-3227
e-mail: c_bogdan@LITech.net

Staff speaks —*Italian, Polish, English.*

Maestro, MasterCard, Visa, Visa Elektron.

24h 90 persons

KOLYBA

14, Burdenka Street,
Lviv-Briukhovychy
59-3141, 293-7082
Fax 293-9879

Breakfast included.
Hotel features a zoo and a children play-ground.

TOURIST

193, Konovaltsa Street
35-2391

50 persons

LVIV

7, Chornovola Prospect
79-2272, 79-2270
Fax 79-2547

20 persons

Staff speaks — *English, German, Polish.*

"HALITSIA" MOTEL

Sokilnyky village,
295-1268

VIKING

Pidbirtsi village,
Lviv region
76-1280

Breakfast included.

Visa, MasterCard.

ECONOMIC:

NEZALEZHNIST (INDEPENDENCE)

6 a, Tershakivtsiv Street
75-7214

KNIAZHY

125 a, Volodymyra Velykoho Street
63-1214

SYKHIV

14, Morozna Street
222-3338, 221-3775

MAKING A RESERVATION

It has been several years since Lviv started attracting flocks of tourists, especially from abroad. The high season in Lviv begins in late April and runs through September. There are a great number of visitors at this time, so it is advisable to reserve accommodation in advance. You can either call the hotel of your choice directly or book the hotel through the Internet. You can also go through a travel agent or real estate agent for rental. An additional fee is charged for this service.

EATING OUT

The peculiarities of the lifestyle in the old town, with houses tightly squeezed along narrow streets and with the balconies facing courtyards, being a fine port view for the curious (from those balconies one can observe not only the neighbor's kitchen but also what is being cooked on the oven), contributes to establishing warm and friendly relationships between Lvivites. More often than not, the neighbors in these old houses will greet each other in a friendly and unobtrusive manner: "I pray to God you stay healthy. Did you sleep well? What did you have for breakfast?" Or an elegant woman will ask a little child: "What did your Mum cook you for lunch?" Or else, two female-friends, whose balconies face the same courtyard, will talk to each other from their balconies. They will inform each other, and all other neighbors for that matter, about the dreams they had last night and their interpretations. Then they will agree to meet, and, sipping coffee and nibbling a cake, they will chatter and gossip about the latest news. Sometimes, two neighbors, Mrs. Stephantsia from the ground floor and her friend Mrs. Stasia from the second floor, will be sharing recipes and cookery advice, not paying attention to anybody or anything else around. Their inexhaustible knowledge in this field allows them to speak about cooking for hours on end, until their beloved husbands call them back home. This being said, one should not forget that here in Lviv all the problems are settled "through a bowl of soup".

The "Tsukernia" confectionary

A large number of new restaurants, bars and coffee shops sprang up in Lviv recently. Even Lviv inhabitants themselves find it difficult to choose a favorite place, and it is only when they are showing their guests around that they can try different establishments and select something to their liking.

Today, Lviv features restaurants of different cuisines. To attract the most demanding customers, restaurants and bar administrations spare no effort to hire the best chef, sometimes inviting cooks from other countries. Every restaurants or café is proud of the "house" dish. In general, restaurants open at 11 a.m. and stay open until midnight, or, "until the last customer leaves". Some establishments operate round the clock.

The catering industry in Lviv now boasts plenty of fine restaurants, offering cuisine, service and prices on a par with other European countries. Here you can impress your business partner by ordering a piquant dish with an in-triguing name. In the middle-range restaurants the cuisine is no less tasty and the staff is no less friendly. However, they will be even more welcoming, if you say a few nice words about the interior and the service and leave a generous tip. Whether you leave a tip or not is completely up to you, however, in some restaurants a service charge is included in the bill, so ask your waiter. The standard tip is about 5-10% of the cost of the meal. In their pursuit to create a unique atmosphere in these establishments the owners decorate their restaurants and cafes in the Baroque or Italian-courtyard style, place antique statues and invite musicians to play the music matching the interior design.

The following signs, indicating services, price ranges and the cuisine served in catering establishments, will help you choose the restaurants, bar or café to your liking.

Three-course lunch per person	🐦 Live music
	💃 Dance hall
① 50-70 UAH	🍸 Bar
② starting from 70 UAH	🍾 Wine menu
	V Vegetarian menu
🌳 Quiet restaurants	🍱 Set menu
📖 Menu in English	🍷 Business lunch
📖 Menu in Polish	🍼 Menu for children
🎀 Business suit required	✑ Facilities for children
VIP VIP-Hall	🐴 Playground
🎋 table booking services	P Parking area
🏠 Summer terrace	🏷 Major credit cards accepted
🔔 Delivery services	

BARS AND RESTAURANTS

ALPAKA
Restaurants
10, Shevchenka Prospect
📞 72-5041
🕐 *11.00 — until the last customer leaves.*

SIMEKS
Restaurants and coffee-shop
17, Kopernika Street
📞 72-6681 🕐 *0.00-23.00*

AMADEI
Restaurants, coffee shop
7, Cathedralna Street
📞 297-8022
🕐 *11.00-23.00*

💳 *Maestro, Master Card, Visa, EuroCard, Visa Elektron.*

European cuisine. House dishes: *"Beef in Mexican Sauce", "Baked Duck" and "Cossacks' Hors d'Oeuvres".*

VYSOKY ZAMOK (HIGH CASTLE)
Up-market restaurants
1, Vysoky Zamok Street
📞 72-4844

💳 *Visa, Master Card, Maestro, Euro Card.*

Ukrainian cuisine, and grill-bar.
The restaurants is located in the Vysoky Zamok Park near the ruins of the old Prince's castle. One of the restaurants halls reflects the atmosphere of the old days and is decorated with portraits, pictures, furniture, plates and dishes of that period. You will feel yourself a dear and welcomed Prince's guest in the cozy and intriguing environment of this establishment.

Summer terrace of the "Amadei" restaurants

VIDENSKA KAVIARNIA (VIENNA COFFEE SHOP)
Restaurants, coffee shop, beer and billiard halls
12, Svobody Prospect
📞 72-2021
www.wienkaffe.lviv.ua
🕐 *9.00-24.00*

💳 *Visa, MasterCard, Maestro, EurpCard, Visa Electron.*

Schweijk is the regular customer of the "Videnska Kviarnia" coffee-shop

European cuisine.
TIt is the domain of a cozy and refined atmosphere. In these beautifully decorated halls any company would seem friendly, especially the company of the brave soldier Schwejk (a character of the humorous story by the Czech writer Hasek). A full-length sculpture of Schwejk is placed seated by the entrance to the café. If you feel like talking to this famous book character, why not get yourself a cup of coffee and sit by him. He, like you, was an ardent admirer of the Indian beverage and a frequent customer of the "Vienna Coffee-Shop".

GRAND RESORT
Top-end restaurants
Basivka Village, Lviv region,
Pustomytivsky rayon,
Basivka village
📞 297-1606, 297-1605
🕐 *24 hours*

💳 *American Express, Master Card, Visa, EuroCard.*

European cuisine.
House dishes: *""Swallow's nest", "Royal chicken fillet", "Salmon steak with crab sauce", "Veal stuffed with cherries, served with cognac;" 10+6 tables and 40+24 seats.*

EXCALIBUR

Bar
1a, Virmenska Street
📞 297-5574
🕐 11.00-23

💳 *Maestro, MasterCard, Visa, Diners Club, EuroCard, American Express.*

European and national cuisine.
House dishes: *House specialty" salad-cocktail; Vienna borsch with mushrooms; meat dishes – "Excalibur", "Black knight" (baked potatoes with meat)*

CACTUS

Restaurants
18, Nyzhankivskoho Street
📞 74-5061, 72-6248
🕐 7.00-23.00,
Fr-Su 7.00-2.00

💳 *Visa, masterCard, Maestro.*

European cuisine.
House dishes: *"Royal steak" (salmon), "Maestro" (veal)*

KILIKIA

Restaurants
13/3, Virmenska Street
📞 72-6201 🕐 11.00-23.00

💳 *Visa, MasterCard.*

European cuisine.
House dishes:
"Kilikia" (veal, pork and liver chops), pancakes with mushrooms, "Kotyhoroshkovy na zub" ("Enough for a kid") (Rib steak, mushrooms, potatoes); dessert – pears in Champaign

KNIAZHY KELUKH

Restaurants, café, night club
16, Svobody Prospect
📞 72-3939
🕐 24 hours

💳 *Visa.*

Old Ukrainian cuisine.
House dish: *"Kniazhy Kelykh" (meat dish)*

KOLYBA

Up-market restaurants
14, Burdenka Street,
Briukhovychy village
📞 59-3141, 293-7082
🕐 24 hours

💳 *Visa, MasterCard, Cirrus.*

National cuisine.
House dishes:
Kulish with meat, "Kolybka" (Meat baked in a pot), "Medovukha" alcohol beverage

NOVARIA -NOVA

Restaurants
Pustomytivsky rayon,
Navaria village
📞 227-2727
🕐 7.00-24.00

💳 *Visa, MasterCard, Maestro, EuroCard.*

European cuisine.

A lunch out-doors. A courtyard of the "Kilikia" restaurants

VERONIKA

*Restaurants, confectionary
and café*
21, Shevchenka Prospect
☎ 297-81-28
e-mail: veronika@lviv.net
🕐 10.00-23.00

Visa, Mastercard.

**European and
national cuisine.**
House dishes: *"Korovai a-la
Alsace" (pork), croussans, Dutch
rolls, home-baked bread, cakes,
ice-cream*

OLMAR

Restaurants
2, Krakiwska Street
☎ 79-8542
🕐 11.00-23.00

*Visa, MasterCard, Maestro,
EuroCard.*

Ukrainian cuisine.
*Even a small artificial fountain
does not disturb the tranquil atmosphere of the restaurants. The
luxurious interior, tasty Ukrainian
cuisine and outstanding service,*

A Saturday night at the "Titanic" café-bar

*all this creates a cozy and com-
fortable environment. Outside is
the busy Rynok Square. Inside the
"Olmar" restaurants it is always
calm and relaxing.*

GRAND HOTEL

Restaurants
13, Svobody Prospect
☎ 72-4091
🕐 7.00-24.00

AT MRS. STEFTSIA'S

10, Svobody Prospect
☎ 79-8435
🕐 10.00-22.00
Ukrainian cuisine.

Delicious cappuccino served in the luxurious "Olmar" restaurants

NOSTALGIA

Café-bar
6, Serbska Street
☎ 72-7750
🕐 11.00-23.00

OZERO

Up-market restaurants
Pustomytivsky rayon,
Navaria village
☎ 227-2598
🕐 24 hours

Ukrainain and Georgian cuisine.

TITANIC

Café-bar
4/6, Teatralna Street
☎ 297-5521
🕐 11.00-23.00

PEKING

Café-bar
8, Hrushevskoho Street
☎ 74-2107
🕐 11.00-23.00

RAFAEL

Café
20, Lesy Ukrainky Street
☎ 79-7033
🕐 10.00-23.00

AT THE BURGER'S

73, Franka Street
📞 75-4954
🕐 24 hours

CONFECTIONARIES

Confectionaries is yet another Lviv's attraction. Although still sparse, they are quickly gaining in popularity. Following the old traditions, confectionaries are decorated in the elegant Secession style with authentic furniture and accessories of that period. But the main lure is definitely in cakes, pliatsyky (pies) and strudels. And, of course, there is fragrant herb tea or coffee. The names of dishes are no less intriguing than the interior: "The Curls of Schiller" or the "Kiss-Kiss" cake. No doubt, that having treated your beloved to a house specialty, you will both remember the date.

CONFECTIONARY

The café serves confectionary, desserts, coffee and tea.
3, Staroevreiska Street
📞 74-0949
🕐 10.00-22.00

VERONIKA

21, Shevchenka Prospect
📞 297-8128
🕐 10.00-23.00

Luscious sweets at the "Tsukernia" confectionary

A pint of beer in "Zoloty Vepr"

ZOLOTY VEPR

Café
17, Rynok Square
📞 72-6794
🕐 10.00-21.00
77, Doroshenka Street
📞 40-3494
🕐 12.00-21.00

OSELIA

Restaurants
11, Hnatiuka
📞 72-1601
🕐 11.00-23.00

CUPOLA

Restaurants
37, Chaikovskoho Street
📞 74-4254, 74-0182
🕐 11.00-23.00

The establishment recreates the atmosphere of ancient Lviv. The interior is decorated with furniture of the late 19th – early 20th centuries and old photographs of that period. Do you think you can recognize Lviv streets and buildings?

COFFEE SHOPS

Coffee-shops and coffee aroma are indispensable Lviv attributes. Here and there you will hear people saying: "Shall we have a cup of coffee?" The phrase is no longer a question, but an affirmative invitation, which you cannot refuse. Here in coffee-shops, people discuss and solve their problems, make appointments, strike up new acquaintances, talk over art projects, it is the place for chattering and gossiping. Some incorrigible coffee-lovers, who made the coffee-drinking ritual their lifestyle, became owners of coffee-shops. Having bought together with some friends a small premise, sometimes too shabby for living, but ideal for a small coffee shop, they will repair it and invite famous artists to decorate the interior. This explains the fact why there are so many authoring establishments, small in size but "free in the spirit". In such coffee shops new artistic circles are formed and art festivals, exhibitions and performances are held. Coffee aroma is the spirit of Lviv. Coffee flavor is the flavor of Lviv. In some coffee shops still cherished is the tradition of making coffee on the hot sand. The coffee absorbs the savor of sand and of a wooden stick, which you use to stir the pitch-black liquid, watching carefully that it does not boil over. And, of course, there is friendly conversation or admiring a pretty female.

ZOLOTY DUCAT (THE GOLD DUCAT)
Coffee shop
20, Fedorova Street
📞 298-6233
🕐 11.00-21.00, Su 22.00

The establishment features a bar, menu for children, and "house" coffee: "Zoloty Ducat" and "Potsilunok Pryvyda" (A Ghost's Kiss), 3 tables, 15 seats.

NOAH'S ARK
Coffee shop
9, Stavropihijska Street
📞 72-6521
🕐 11.00-23.00

"PAGE" COFFEE HOUSE
Store and coffee shop
23, Shevchenka Prospect
📞 72-6840
🕐 9.00-20.00

💳 Visa, MasterCard, Maestro.

The establishment features different kinds of coffee, coffee-making appliances, coffee-ware, menu for children, and cappuccino for children. At your request the coffee of your choice will be ground and a small cup of beverage will be made for you to taste.10 tables, 40 seats.

PID SYNOJU PLIASHKOJU (BY THE BLUE BOTTLE)
Coffee shop
4, Russka Street
📞 294-9152
🕐 10.00-22.00

"By the blue bottle"

🀄🛋🍷🍾⚱🍨🍧

The establishment features a bar, wine card, vegetarian menu, set menu, menu for children, menu in English, and a wide choice of sandwiches, cheeses, and sweets. Advance booking is advisable. House dishes: "Fondue" (meat, cheese and chocolate), "Kosher". Beverages: coffee with pepper, the "Fire" coffee (with the fire), the Mak Khmilny" (Heady Poppy Seeds), "Kmynivka", "Kalhanivka". The "Fire" ice-cream. 7 tables, 26 seats.

The dim light and scarce sun-rays penetrating through small windows and reflecting on jest portraits and on the old newspapers, which cover the walls, create the artistic atmosphere. The "Fire" ice-cream will only add to the romantic ambiance.

PID KLEPSYPDROYU (BY CLEPSYDRA)
Artistic coffee-shop
35, Virmenska Street
📞 *297-5612*
🕙 *10.00-22.00*

The café is imbued with the artistic spirit. Sipping Lviv coffee with cream and chocolate, and smoking a cigarette, you can admire the works of art on the ancient walls and contemplate life. The coffee shop houses an antique store, where one can buy pictures, sculptures, furniture and jewelry, or purchase paints, brushes and other tools for creating your own master-piece.

HALKA
Coffee shop
4, Kovzhyna Street
📞 *297-8104*
🕙 *10.00-22.00*

VIRMENKA
Coffee shop
19, Virmentska Street
📞 *297-5637*
🕙 *9.00-20.00*

The famous coffee brewed on sand

Lviv's inhabitants enjoy small cafes, for it is the venue where they can bare their soul to a friend or solve acute problems, while slowly

Summer terrace of the "Pid kleipsidroyu" artistic coffe-shop

*Details of the
"Smachna Plitka" interior*

drinking coffee or cognac (by the way, in the Soviet times a visit to a café cost less than 1 ruble, so you could have even treated your girl-friend to a cake). Some ten years ago cafes were scarce and the customers were many. Always overcrowded, filled with smoke and, above all, imbued with coffee fragrances, the establishments, not necessarily attractive on the façade, had something indefinable about them, which draw customers like magnets. The "Virmenka" coffee-shop is one of the legendary cafes. Once, it was popular with artists, hippies, punks, with those who smoke dope, and those who were after them. It has always been permeated with the spirit of liberty. Even now, through the thick layer of modern whitewashing one still can read the old inscriptions. It is one of the few coffee-shops where the beverage is made on the hot sand.

Restaurants and coffee-shops abound in Lviv, with reasonable prices and tasty food. So, fast-food chains are only for those who are short of time and want to have a quick snack. But even in a fast-food restaurants you will be surprised by the level of service and quality of food.

ITALIJSKE PODVIRYA (ITALIAN COURTYARD)
Café
6, Rynok Square

📞 72-0671 🕐 10.00-20.00

Antique sculptors, Renaissance architecture and saxophone music, all create an unforgettable atmosphere.

SVIT KAVY (THE WORLD OF COFFEE)

6, Kathedralna Square
📞 297-5675
100, Vyhovskoho Street,
"VAM" supermarket
🕐 9.00-22.00

Here you can choose between more than 40 kinds of coffee.

"Svit Kavy" coffee-shop on Cathedral Square

PIZZAS:

Kartopliana Khata (Potato Hut)
16, Slovatskoho Street
tel. 74-1825, 74-4657
10.00-23.00
20, Kyivska Street
tel. 237-8304
47 a, Vyhovskoho Street
tel. 41-7260
65, Chornovola Prospect
tel. 41-7260, 52-1975
9.00-22.00, in the summer time the
establishment is open until 23.00

New-York Street
36, Chuprynky Street
tel. 35-2236
4, Stefanyka Street
tel. 74-1147
2, Sviatoho Theodora Square
10.00-23.00

"OMO" Pizza
Pizza bar
1, Zamarstynivska Street
tel. 72-8028
11.00-23.00

"Pepperoni" Pizza
75, Franka Street
tel. 76-2791
11.00-23.00

"Chelentano" Pizza
7, Kniazia Romana Street
tel. 72-5942
24, Svobody Prospect
tel. 74-1135
10.00-23.00

Toronto
20, Lepkoho Street
tel. 74-06-71
11.00-23.00

Kasteliary
6, Vynnychenka Street
tel. 76-5832
10.00-22.00
Ice-cream, varenyky (ravioli),
pizza, salads

Pizza-Jazz
16 a, Pekarska Street
10.00-23.00

FAST FOOD

Restaurants and coffee-shops abound in Lviv, with reasonable prices and tasty food. So, fast-food chains are only for those who are short of time and want to have a quick snack. But even in a fast-food restaurants you will be surprised by the level of service and quality of food.

DE MADGARO
19, Doroshenka Street
📞 74-3221

Halytska Street, 10
📞 75-7029
🕐 Mo-Fr 9.00-22.00,
Su 12.00-22.00

The establishment offers pizzas, steaks, shish kebab, sausages, salads, soups, and ice cream, cocktails, coffee or tea for dessert. Air-conditioned.

B-317
6, Kostiushka Street
📞 72-8747

PYRAMID
74, Horodotska Street
📞 296-5092

40, Doroshenka Street
📞 296-6837
2, Levytskoho Street
📞 76-2253

Fast food chain. Hot lunches, steaks, pizzas, pancakes, salads, desserts, juices and beverages. Just like your Mum cooks!

McDONALDS
7, Shevchenka Prospect
📞 297-4191

12, Chornovola Prospect
📞 297-4192, 297-4193

24 a, Volodymyra Velykoho Street
📞 65-9276, 65-9277
🕐 8.00-23.00

ENTERTAINMENT

THEATERS

▦ *Lviv offers theaters of various genres with the repertoire to satisfy all tastes. Famous musicians and theater companies come to Lviv on tour, as do celebrated directors and actors with their productions.*

Tickets are sold at theatre box offices, and prices vary. Famous pop-stars frequent Lviv, although not all of them are necessarily in their prime of glory.

Academic theaters perform classical music concerts or stage classical plays. Some theaters offer "alternative" performances. Children have not been disregarded either. There are two children's theaters, where kids can enjoy the theatrical productions and their parents can take a trip back to the world of childhood.

The pride of Lviv is the two annual international festivals, the theater festival of "Zolotyi Lev" (Golden Lion), and the music festival of "Virtuosi".

Stanislav Liudkevych Lviv Regional Philharmonic Hall

7, Chaikovskoho Street
☏ *72-1042, 74-1086*
🕐 *Theater box offices 11.00-18.00;*
   The Philarmonic Hall also features the "Za Kulisamy" (Bihind the Curtains) artistic coffee-shop

Les Kurbas Lviv Youth Theater

3, Kurbasa Street
☏ *79-8657, 72-9204*
e-mail: kurbas@litech.lviv.ua, kurbas@aol.com
🕐 *Performances: o 18.00; Tickets are purchased in ticket boxes on the day of the performance from 12.00 to 18.00.*
🖼 *10 UAH*

Lviv House of Organ and Chamber Music

8, Bandery Street
☏ *39-8842, 39-8842*
🖼 *5 UAH*

A scene from "Marco the Cursed, or an Oriental Legend" by the Les Kurbas Youth Theater

"Voskresinnia" (Resurrection) Lviv Religious Theater

5, General Hryhorenka Square
☏ *74-1300, 74-1160*
e-mail: goldenlion@litech. lviv.ua
🕐 *Performances: 18.00, 19.00.*
🖼 *for students — 5 UAH, for adults —10 UAH*
   The organizer of the "Zoloty Lev" (Golden Lion) Theater Festival.

Lviv Regional Puppet Theater

1, Danyly Halytskoho Street
☏ *72-0832, 72-0773*
🕐 *Performances: 11.00, 13.00, 15.00.* 🖼 *3,50 UAH*
   The theater also features the "Lialka" (Puppet) artistic coffee-shop

Scenes from "UBN" and "Kaidash's family" by the Maria Zankovetska Theater

Maria Zankovetska National Academic Drama Theater

1, Lesy Ukrainky Street
📞 72-0760, 72-0762
Theater box office 72-0583, open: 11.00-14.00, 17.00-19.00.
www.zankovetska.lviv.ua
🕐 *Performances: 12.00, 19.00, у зимовий час — 18.00.*
🎫 *10 UAH;*

   The theater also features the"Komaryk" coffee-shop

Theater of the Western Operation Command

36, Horodotska Street
📞 233-3185, 233-3188

First Ukrainian Theater for Children and Youth

11, Hnatiuka Street
📞 72-6855
🕐 *Performances: 11.00, 14.00. Ticket box offices open 11.00 to 17.00.*
🎫 *3 to 5 UAH*

Lviv State Circus

83, Horodotska Street
📞 72-4048
Theater box office 72-4048 (advance booking is avalable).

"People and Puppets" Theater

6, Fedra Street
📞 74-0025

Solomia Krushelnytska State Academic Opera and Ballet Theater

Decorative details of the Lviv Opera House façade

28, Svobody Prospect
📞 72-8672
www.operalviv.org
📞 *Theater box offices 72-8672*
🕐 *11.00 to 19.00, advance booking is avalable).*
🕐 *Performances: Matinees — o 12.00, Evening — o 18.00.*
🎫 *10-100 UAH*

Artistic decorations of the yard in front of the First Ukrainian Theater for Children and Youth

FESTIVALS

"Zoloty Lev" (Golden Lion) Theater Festival

74-1300,
fax 74-1160
e-mail:
goldenlion@litech.
lviv.ua

The annual international theater festival was first organized in 1989 as a festival for artistic youth. The festival is run by the "Voskresinnia" (Resurrection) Lviv Theater. The festival, featuring famous directors, actors and producers, is held in the fall, when yellowish leaves, shed by trees, "gild" the ground.

Poster of the "Zoloty Lev" theater festival

"Virtuosi" Music Festival

72-1042

Conducted in spring, the "Virtuosi" annual festival attracts world-famous participants. It is a marked event in the cultural life of the city. Free from any restrictions by genres (the festival features modern, folk and pop music) or participants' age, the festival does not set any mercenary aims. Its credo is to promote the High Art, world-acclaimed music schools as well as young and talented performers. The festival is held in the Liudkevych Lviv Regional Philharmonic Hall.

Solomia Kryshelnytska Festival of Opera Art

72-8672
www.operalviv.org

The festival is held in November in the premises of the Krushelnytska Lviv State Academic Theater of Opera and Ballet. Celebrated singers as well as young and talented actors perform operas, which the world-famous singer Solomia Krushelnytska once sang.

Contrasts

72-5847, 74-2349
e-mail: spilka@mail.
lviv.ua

The international music festival presents classical, modern, postmodern and avant-garde music.

Zoloty Telesyk (Golden Telesyk – a character of a Ukrainian fairy-tale)

72-0832

The international puppet-theater festival is held in May by the Lviv Regional Puppet Theater. The event creates a warm, friendly and benevolent environment.

Publishing Houses Forum

76-4694, 76-4152
e-mail: forum@snail.lviv.ua
www.snail.lviv.ua

The Publishing Houses Forum is a National Publications Trade Exhibition, which attracts publishing houses, book trade organizations, libraries, bookstores and private entrepreneurs from all over Ukraine. For many years Forum has been featured by the Ukrainian mass media.

CINEMAS

■ Due to limited financing, most cinemas in Lviv are in a deplorable state and look miserable, especially in the wintertime, if the heating is off. Perhaps, beauty salons too suffer from lack of clients in winter, as it is common knowledge, that frost is good for your skin, yet, watching an interesting film, the viewer forgets all the inconveniences. Thus, if you are traveling in winter and feel like visiting a Lviv cinema, do not leave your coat in the cloakroom – it will keep you warm while watching the film.

However, in the "Lviv" and "Kinopalace" cinemas you will always feel comfortable. These two modern cinemas are equipped with all modern facilities and services to make your stay pleasant.

Regardless of all the inconveniences, Lviv cinemas feature the latest films from all over the world and run film festivals showing the best movies of different countries. You can book and reserve tickets in advance or purchase them right before the performance at the cinema cash desks. Some cinemas have snack bars, where you can buy something to munch on during the performance. Just make sure you do not disturb other visitors while champing loudly. Tickets are more expensive for evening and weekend performances, as well as premiers, than for daytime showings.

Oleksadr Dovzhenko Cinema

1, Dovzhenka Street
☎ *221-6131*

The cinema has the largest Halychyna screen, 150 m².

Kyiv

8, Shevchenko Prospect
☎ *72-6773*

Lviv

12, Samchuka Street
☎ *70-4480*

Halychyna Cinema Art Center

3, Shevchenko Prospect
☎ *72-3630*
🎞 *children — 5 UAH, adults — 7-10 UAH.*

Kinopalace

22, Teatralna Street
☎ *297-5050*
297-5005

MUSEUMS

Lviv, as any other city with rich history and traditions, has a lot to reveal to visitors as well as to the local population. A large number of museums and galleries unfold mysteries of the city's past and present. In the History Museum, roam the former Royal quarters. Having paid a small additional fee, take a picture of yourself sitting in the splendid armchair for spiritualistic séances or ask the attendant to play the old gramophone. The Lviv National Museum is well-known far beyond Ukraine for its rich art collections, with the icon collection being, perhaps, the most important in the country. Many celebrated composers, artists, singers and writers who lived and worked in Lviv, are immortalized in small memorial museums. The Art Gallery holds a collection of art-works by famous masters. In Lviv's oldest pharmacy-museum you can not only buy medicine, but also walk down into the museum basement and see the alchemist's workshop. Lviv Galleries of Contemporary Art exhibit exquisite works by modern artists.

Museum of Ethnography and Crafts

Following the gods example. Henrih Semiradsky, 1879
Lviv Art Gallery

Lviv Art Gallery

3, Stefanyka Street
📞 72-3948
🕐 Tu-Su 11.00-17-00
🎫 for children and students — 1 UAH, for adults — 3 UAH.

Lviv History Museum

6, Rynok Square
📞 74-3304
The department of the history of the 20th century
4, Rynok Square

📞 72-0671
The department of feudalism
24, Rynok Square
📞 72-0874
🕐 Th-Tu 10.00-17.30
🎫 for children and students — 0.50 UAH, for adults — 1 UAH.

Museum of Ethnography and Crafts

15, Svobody Prospect
📞 72-7012
🕐 We-Su 9.00-17.30
🎫 for children and students – 0.50 UAH, for adults – 1 UAH.

Lviv National Museum

20, Svobody Prospect
☏ 74-2280
🕐 Sa-Th 10.00-18.00
42, Drahomanova Street
☏ 72-8063
🕐 Sa-We 10.00-18.00
🎟 for children and students
– 0.50 UAH,
for adults – 2 UAH.

Furniture and Porcelain Museum

10, Rynok Square
☏ 74-3388
🕐 We-Su 9.00-16.30
🎟 for children and students
– 0.50 UAH,
for adults – 1 UAH.

A Girl Carrying Breakfast on a Tray. Martin Yablonsky, 1837
Lviv Art Gallery

A Girl with a Puppy. Oleksandr Murashko, 1901
Lviv National Museum

Lviv Museum of the History of Religion

1, Museina Square
☏ 72-91-00
🕐 Tu-Su 10.00-17.00
🎟 for children and students
– 0.50 UAH,
for adults – 1 UAH.

"By the Black Eagle" Pharmacy-Museum

2, Drukarska Street
☏ 72-00-41
🕐 10.00-17.00
🎟 for children and students
– 0.50 UAH,
for adults – 1 UAH.

Open-Air Museum of Folk Architecture and Rural Life

1, Chernecha Hora
☏ 71-2360
🕐 Tu-Su 9.00-16.30
🎟 for children and students
– 75 коп.,
for adults – 1,50 UAH.

The "Arsenal" Museum of Weaponry

5, Pidvalna Street
☏ 72-7060
🕐 Th-Tu 10.00-18.00
🎟 for children and students
– 0.50 UAH,
for adults – 3 UAH.

An ancient warrior's armor, "Arsenal"
Museum of Weaponry

Museum of Lviv Antiquities

1, Uzhorodka Street
☎ 72-2886
🕐 *Tu-Su 10.00-17.00*
🎫 *for children and students – 0.50 UAH, for adults – 1 UAH.*

Museum of Ancient Ukrainian Books (Art Gallery Branch)

15 a, Kopernyka Street
☎ 72-2536
🕐 *Tu-Su 10.00-18.00*
🎫 *for children – 0.50 UAH, for adults – 2 UAH.*

Deisis. From an iconostas in Bohorodchansk. Job kondzelevych, 1698-1705
Lviv National Museum

Pinzel Museum of Sacral Baroque Sculpture of the 18th century

2, Mytna Street
☎ 75-6966
🕐 *Tu-Su 10.00-17.00*
🎫 *for children and students – 1 UAH, for adults – 2 UAH.*

Lviv Art Palace

17, Kopernika Street
☎ 297-0010
🕐 *Tu-Su 9.00-17.00*

National Scientific and Research Restoration Center

10, Lesy Ukrainky Street
☎ 72-8970
🕐 *Mo-Fr 9.00-18.00*

ART GALLERIES:

"Dzhuha" Art And Cultural Center

35, Virmenska Street
☎ 297-5612, 76-7420
🕐 *10.00-21.00*

"Ramar" Art Show-Room

11, Lystopadovoho Chynu Street
☎ 79-8632
🕐 *Mo-Fr 9.00-18.00*

A romantic entrance to the "Dzyha" gallery

"Ravlyk" gallery

Basement in the Jesuit Church
☎ 298-2595
🕐 *Mo-Fr 17.00, Sa-Su 15.00, 17.00*
🎫 *for children – 2 UAH, for adults – 3,5 UAH.*

Tea Set. A. Ivchenko.
"Ravlyk" art showroom

Photography Gallery of Vasyl Pylypchuk

14, Shevchenka Prospect
☎ 72-9181
🕐 *9.00-23.00*

"Herdan" Gallery

4, Russka Street
☎ 72-5046, 72-4695
🕐 *Mo-Fr 14.00-17.00*

A relief over the entrance door to the "Herdan" gallery

PARKS AND GARDENS

■ *Lviv's parks are the best hiding place from the "vanity of vanities" of the modern city. Lviv offers more than twenty parks, where anyone can enjoy a peaceful walk admiring exotic trees, bushes and flowers. Each park is unique in itself.*

In a cozy shady corner one can have a picnic with family and friends. However, before you lay your traveling rug carefully examine the ground. It could be that a pack of dogs has already had their picnic there. Despite the prohibitions to walk dogs in public places, pet owners disregard the law. In addition, you should watch out for huge dogs, which, although walked by their owners, might bite people. Owners rarely muzzle their pets, neglecting the desperate pleas of mothers walking with their children and senior citizens. Such a situation might occur in small parks in the downtown area

The most popular and the safest recreation area is the Kaiserwalt or the Open-Air Museum of Folk Architecture and Rural Life. The forested area lends itself to peaceful walks. Maybe only a crow's cry will disturb the tranquil atmosphere. But you cannot blame the bird; it also wants to be noticed. Roaming among the architectural monuments of the past and admiring the mastery and aesthetic taste of the ancestors, have a rest on an old wooden bench by an old thatched cottage. Children can visit the improvised small zoo.

The Khmelnytsky Park offers a wide variety of attractions, from safe children's swings to Ferris Wheels for the bravest. Tickets are surprisingly cheap on weekdays and are twice as expensive on weekends and holidays. Beware of pickpockets. Watching you kids swinging high in the air, you will hardly notice when you are relieved of your purse, camera, or some other valuable belongings.

The Sryisky Park is popular with sweethearts. The small pond with swans is the newlyweds' favorite background for wedding pictures. However, the swans, frightened by cheerful exclamations of the wedding party, are reluctant to swim close to the newlyweds. Yet, with a lump of sweet wedding pie, the elegant birds can be tempted close to the shore.

The "Zalisna Woda" (Iron Water) park features an open-air swimming pool, "Trudovy Reservy", open all year round.

"Vysoky Zamok" Park
Uzhorodska Street
📞 *74-3269*

Popular both with tourists and the locals, the park is located on the highest hill in Lviv and preserves the remains of the old Prince's Palace, once home of the founder of the city, Prince Danylo of Halychyna.

"Znesinnya" Regional Landscape Park
32, Novoznesenska Street
📞 *59-2735*

The first settlements, which gave rise to the city, were located on the territory of the present-day "Znesinnya" Park. Here you can indulge in cycling in summer, or dog-sledging in winter, or even practice foot-racing. The park houses ecological and educational summer camps, as well as the annual ecological festival "Clean Ukraine – the Clean Earth".

Khmelnytsky Central Park
4, Bolharska Street
📞 *72-7931*

Being one of the youngest parks in Lviv, it is also an entertainment area and one of the best planned forested spaces. The park features the "Romantic" concert and dance hall, the "Yunist" (Youth) stadium, an amusement area, a summer theater and several cafes and restaurants. It is here that all the all-city festivals are held, as well as popular beer festivals.

Stryisky Park
15, Styiska Street
📞 *76-3202*

The Stryisky Park is considered one of the most picturesque parks in Ukraine. The exhibition pavilions were constructed to house the 1894 Regional Trade Exhibition. The park, famous for its amount of valuable trees, contains more than 200 species of trees and plants.

Franko Park
2, Lystopadovoho Chynu Street
📞 *74-4287*

One of the oldest parks in Lviv, it was laid out in the landscape style. The park boasts three hundred year-old oaks and maple-trees.

"Zalizna Woda"
(Iron Water) Park
Stusa Street

"Snopkivsky" Park
Zelena Street

"Pohulianka" Park
Vakhnianyna Street

The Open-Air Museum of Folk
Architecture and Rural Life
Chernecha Hora Street

Lychakivsky Park
Lychakivska Street, Pasichna Street

Briukhovytsky Woods
Shevchenka Street, Zamastynivska Street

Franko Botanical Garden
Cheremshyny Street

Kortumova Hill
Tunnelna Street

NIGHT CLUBS

■ *After long walks in the daytime and all the coffee you have drunk in various coffee-shops, you will hardly feel like going to bed early. Intrigued by what you have encountered during the day, there is no doubt you will want to see the city by night. The city offers a wide range of night entertainment. It is up to you to choose, be it an expensive nightclub or casino, or a cheerful artistic disco with all sorts of competitions going on until dawn. For the risky lot there are casinos, roulette and Black-Jack. The entrance charges differ and depend on the entertainment on offer. Women are offered discounts or, in some cases, free entrance. For the shows featuring famous singers it is advisable to purchase tickets in advance. Most of the night establishments offer striptease shows. Clubs run concerts and theme parties with different competitions. Those who love dancing can go to a disco club. For billiard-players there are numerous billiard halls.*

The following signs will help you choose the entertainment establishment to your liking

▶◀	business suit	⚫	Billiard hall
🐦	live music	⚙	Casino
🍴	restaurants	🂠	Card games
🥂	bar	▤	Slot-machines
♨	Menu in English	$	Currency exchange
⊓	Table booking service	P	Parking area
💃	Dance hall	⬭	Major credit cards accepted
🕺	Strip-tease		

"Sofia" Grand Club

10, Shevchenka Prospect

📞 *72-9000*

🕐 *20.00–6.00*

💳 *MasterCard, Visa, American Express*

"Grand Club" Casino

10, Shevchenka Prospect
Interior of the "Sofia"
Grand Club

📞 *72-9000*

🕐 *21.00–6.00*

💳 *MasterCard, Visa, American Express, Maestro, Eurocard*

Picasso

Nightclub
88, Zelena Street

📞 *75-3272*

We-Mo 20.00–3.00,
Sa 20.00-4.00

e-mail:picasso_club@ukr.net

Split

Nightclub
6/7, Mickiewicha Street

📞 *298-7133*

🕐 *24 hours*

💳 *MasterCard, Visa, Visa Elektron, EuroCard*

The establishment features a parking area, live music, striptease show, casino, bar, currency exchange office, and menu in English. It is advisable to book tables in advance.

One of the elite entertainment establishments in Lviv. Casino: American

roulette, Poker, Black Jack. VIP-hall

Split-Carpathy

59, Chornovola Prospect

📞 *52-9160* 🕐 *24 hours*

On Thursdays – male striptease programs, on Saturdays – entertainment shows.

Millennium

Nightclub
2, Chornovola Prospect

📞 *240-3591*

🕐 *Tu-Su 20.30 – until the last customer leaves*

The establishment features parking, live music, striptease programs, bar, billiard hall, casino, laser show, narghile bar.

"Ostrava" Bowling Club

103, Konovaltsa Street

📞 *295-3886*

🕐 *10.00-24.00*

SLOT MACHINES HALLS:

"Royal"
www.royal-ltd.com.ua

- 4, Shevchenka Street
- 2, Vynnychenka Street
- 18, Kniazia Romana Street
- 44-46, Franka Street
- 15, Torhova Street
- 12, Doroshenka Street
- 5, Svobody Prospect

"Lialka" Club

1, Danyly Halytskoho
Square, , the Puppet Theatre
📞 *298-0809*
🕐 *Mo-Su 11.00 — until the*
last customer leaves

Assol

Night disco club
106 a, Tarnavskoho Street
📞 *298-1515*
🕐 *19.00–5.00*

Beat

Disco club
3, Petrushevycha Street
📞 *78-1758*
🕐 *Mo-Fr 22.00-6.00,*

Sa-Su 20.00-8.00
e-mail:
beatclub@inclub.com.ua
www.bt.lviv.ua

Cosmo

Nightclub
2, Petrushevycha Square
📞 *296-5445*
🕐 *21.00–6.00*

Platinum

Disco bar
10, Shevchenka Prospect
📞 *72-9000*
🕐 *21.00–6.00*

Romantic

Night disco
4, Bolharska Street
(in the park);
📞 *76-9185, 221-3759*
🕐 *Tu-Su 20.00–6.00*

Safari

Nightclub

186, Zelena Street
📞 *70-4066*
🕐 *21.00–5.00*

Cassiopeia

Billiard
and slot machines hall
129, Kulparkivska Street
📞 *65-9375*
🕐 *24 hours*

BILLIARD HALLS:

Bristol
19, Svobody Prospect
tel. 297-0139

"Videnska Kaviarnia"
(Vienna Coffee-Shop)
12, Svobody Prospect
tel. 72-2021

Carpathy-Sofia Grand Club
10, Shevchenka Prospect
tel. 72-9000

Romantic
4, Bolharska Street **tel. 76-9185**

Split-Carpathy
59, Chornovola Prospect
tel. 52-9160

CASINOS:

"George" Casino
2, Voronoho Street
tel. 79-9011

"Grand Club" Casino
10, Shevchenka Prospect
tel. 72-9000

Split Club
6/7, Mickiewicz Square
tel. 298-7126

The establishment features American roulette, Poker and Black Jack; VIP-hall.

In the "Videnska Kaviarnia"
coffee-shop

SHOPPING

Trading has always been an active part of the life of Lviv. Since ancient times Lviv has been at the crossroads of the trade routes between West and East, and South and North. Numerous trading points in town were owned by peoples from all over the world: Greeks, Armenians, Jews, Poles, etc. Honoring the old traditions, the owner of any shop, outlet or roadside-stand extends a hearty welcome to all the customers. To a friendly "Can I help you?" You will hear: "Yes, please. You look wonderful today, Miss. Do you think you have anything for me?"

SHOPS

Most shops in Lviv open at 8.00 or 9.00 and close at 19.00 or 20.00. Recently, some smaller shops, known as mini-markets, appeared in Lviv. Some of them work round the clock. They are located by almost all apartment blocks, which is very convenient when you run short of bread or some unexpected visitors drop in. There are also larger supermarkets, "Arsen" and "Barvinok", which offer a wider assortment of foodstuffs. Qualified staff is available to help you make your choice. Here you can buy not only food, but also household and stationary goods. In a supermarket's coffee-shop you can have a rest and ponder about what else you wanted to buy. These shops are air-conditioned, and some of them accept credit cards.

The supermarket chain "Ecolan" is popular with the locals for the wide assortment of freshly baked bread, as is "Barkom" for the "Rodynna Kovbaska" sausage department.

Department stores, like other shops, open at 10.00 and close at 18.00 or 19.00. The largest of them is the recently reconstructed TSUM (abbreviation for "Tsentralny Univermag" or Central Department Store) at 1, Shpytalna Street right behind the Opera House. Lately, the store has recovered its old name of "Magnus". Here, aside from shopping, you can derive pleasure from wandering along beautifully decorated windows with furniture, live or artificial flowers and mannequins. On the top floor there is a coffee shop where you can have a cup of coffee and enjoy the magnificent city panorama. In addition to this, you can have a ride in a glass elevator, especially popular with kids.

Well-liked is the new department store, "Lviv", at 106, Kniahyny Olhy Street. The store offers a wide selection of goods, which might cost different amounts on each floor. Thus, it is advisable to first study carefully the assort-

Art Opening in Lviv

ment and only then make the decision. If you are tired of meandering along the departments have a cup of coffee and a cake in one of the numerous coffee-shops.

Most of the expensive boutiques, called "museums" for the high-priced and luxurious goods they sell, are located in the downtown area. As a rule, there are not too many

customers inside, so the curious can have a good look at the interior. Svobody Prospect and the neighboring streets abound with expensive shops. During Christmas holidays boutiques hold competitions for the best window decoration.

If you want to buy some trifles as a souvenir – have a look in the Lviv's main artistic venue, known colloquially as "Kitschok" (a derivative from "Kitsch style"). Here you can buy antique icons, coins, clothes or a piece of silverwork (ask the vendor whether he can assist with obtaining the documents allowing you to take the articles abroad), as well as pieces of contemporary art – pictures, tapestries, decorations, embroideries and ceramics. Here you can acquire a real masterpiece for a reason-

A piece of folk kitchen-ware or embroidery makes a fine souvenir from Lviv

**SUPERMARKETS
AND STORES:**

Arsen
www.intermarket.ua
60, Chervonoi Kalyny
Prospect
tel. 297-6321
Mo-Sa 8.00-22.00,
Su 9.00-21.00
93, Chornovola Prospect
tel. 41-6452
The supermarkets accept: Visa, Maestro, Master Card, Visa Elektron.
The supermarkets feature currency exchange offices, ATM machines, free parking space, a coffee-shop and toilet facilities.

Barvinok
Supermarket chain
5, Dovzhenka Street
tel. 221-1292
3, Boichuka Street
tel. 63-0009
105, Stryiska Street
tel. 64-5295
40, Velychkovskoho
Street
tel. 291-5998
70 a, Shyroka Street
tel. 67-7574
113, Volodymyra
Velykoho Street
tel. 63-1596
11 a, Chyhyrynska Street
tel. 293-9607
Mo-Sa 8.00-21.00,
Su 9.00-20.00

VAM
110, Vyhovskoho Street
tel. 295-2893
Mo-Fr 9.00-22.00

Hyper-Market
93, Kulparkivska Street
tel. 292-0591
Mo-Sa 9.00-21.00,
Su 9.00-19.00

Intermarket
Cash & carry
147, Zelena Street
tel. 70-0052
359, Horodotska Street
tel. 297-6166
e-mail:
office@intermarket.
lviv.ua,
www.intermarket.lviv.ua
Mo-Fr 8.00-20.00,

Sa 9.00-20.00,
Su 10.00-17.00
2, Patona Street
tel. 62-2167
Mo-Sa 8.00-23.00,
Su 9.00-22.00

**"Lviv"
Department Store**
106, Kniahyny Olhy Street
**tel. 63-2388,
63-7265**
Mo-Fr 9.00-20.00,
Sa 9.00-18.00,
Su 11.00-17.00

**"Na Rynky"
Department Store**
32, Rynok Square
**tel. 72-0930,
72-6639**
Mo-Fr 10.00-19.00,
Sa 10.00-17.00

**"Magnus"
Shopping Center**
1, Shpytalna Street
tel. 297-0745
10.00-21.00
"Tarko" bistro is on the top
floor, open: (10.00-23.00)

BRAND STORES:

Suit-store
of Mikhail Voronin
4, Aleksandra
Nevskoho Street
tel. 72-3485
6, Cathedralna Square
tel. 297-5674

GERRY WEBER HOUSE
11, Rynok Square
tel. 297-5532

Roksolana
5, Mickiewicz Square
tel. 79-7093

**PERFUMES
AND SOUVENIRS:**

"Basel"
Swiss boutique
22, Svobody Prospect
tel. 297-5090
Mo-Su 10.00-20.00

Brocard
7/1, Kopernik Street
tel. 297-9170
Mo-Fr 11.00-19.00,
Sa 12.00-18.00

"Zapakh Rossy"
14, Krakiwska Street
tel. 74-2152
Mo-Sa 10.00-19.00,
Su 12.00-17.00
8a, Franka Street
tel. 298-1969
Mo-Fr 10.00-19.00,
Sa 11.00-18.00

L'Escale
35, Svobody Prospect
tel. 74-2087
Mo-Fr 10.00-19.00,
Sa 10.00-18.00,
Su 10.00-17.00

Chetar
Stationary goods, brief
cases, suitcases and
purses
11, Fedorova Street
42, Sakharova Street
tel. 298-1809
e-mail: artchetar@lviv.net

MARKETS

**Halytske
Perekhrestia**
2, Poliska Street
tel. 52-3580, 59-1622

**Pryvokzalny
Market**
2, Horskoi Street
tel. 35-4113, 35-2580

**Vynnykivsky
Market**
4, Solodova Street
tel. 75-3457

**Stryisky
Market**
81, Franka Streett
tel. 76-1156

**Central
Market**
11, Bazarna Streett
**tel. 233-8052,
233-8056**

**Pivdenny
Market**
Schyretska Street
tel. 64-9428

**Shuvar
Market**
tel. 221-0069

BOOKSTORES:

Budynok Knyhy
8, Mickiewicz Square
tel. 74-4164

Druzhba
8, Mickiewicz Square
tel. 72-2729

Bookva
6, Shevska Street
tel. 294-8208
10.00-21.00
daily "Bookva Punkt"
café 9.00-22.00

Mistetstvo
8, Mickiewicz Square
tel. 72-6004

COFFEE, TEE, SWEETS:

HALKA
brand-store
coffee, tea
4, Kovzuna Street
tel. 74-2883

Svit Kavu (Coffee World)
coffe from all over the world
6, Cathedralna Shuare
tel. 297-5675

Svitoch
Confectionary and sweets
10, Sevchenka Prospect
tel. 72-6741

Interior of the "Svitoch"
cofectionary

able price. However, vendors will charge you two to three times more if they find out you are a foreigner, so it is advisable to first talk

Searching for a masterpiece

to your guide or a local acquaintance. Remember, it is a market place, so do not hesitate to bargain for a better price. Prices rocket in high tourist season. Outstanding art-works are sold at the "Khudoznik" (Artist) art gallery at 8, Svobody Prospect. Although prices are set and much higher than in the market, the gallery guarantees top quality goods.

Lvivites read a lot, so bookstores are extremely popular here. Bookshops are mainly located in the center. The largest bookstore complex is in the "Budynok Knyhy" (The

House of Books) store at 8, Mickiewicz Square. The outlet offers a large assortment of printed matter: books on medicine, art, economy, children's and foreign literature, etc. A wide selection of books

is offered in the "Bookva" (Letter) bookstore at 6, Shevska Street, right next to Rynok Square. The store was opened in the recently restored 17th century edifice. It should be admitted, that prices are much higher in this outlet. Next-door is a coffee-shop, where you can have a cup of coffee or indulge in a piece of cake while thumbing through a book or a magazine. If a particular book cannot be found in the shops, try the organized book market by the monument to Ivan Fedorov.

MARKETS

Lvivites' favorite shopping and promenade venue is the "Europe" shopping center, colloquially known as the Pivdenny (South) Market. It is a gigantic shopping city inside the city. Here in expensive and beautifully decorated shops and stalls all manufactured items are traded: clothing, shoes, tableware, perfumes, and many more. In some stalls prices are exorbitant. For customers with moderate demands there are booths, offering goods at more attractive prices and not always of a poorer quality. Apart from extensive selection of manufactured and household goods the center features pharmacies, a dentist's office, hotel, photo laboratory, dry-cleaner's, bars, cafes, etc. There is even a small chapel where the sellers come to pray to have better trading and customers – to buy better goods. It is customary to bargain at the Pivdenny Market. Here you can often hear a seller saying

that he "cannot back down on price" and he is taking a big chance on this personally. However, if your patience and persistence hold out a little longer, you might save a couple of hryvnia for a marshrutka or a cup of coffee. The market is in the southern part of the city and takes its name from its location. Getting to the market is easy, marshrutka's run here from all corners of the city. Catch the number 71 marshrutka (the fare is 1 UAH) at the Opera House, or the number 21 trolleybus by the Franko University. You can also get to the market by car, which can be parked at a guarded parking area by the shopping center. For a trip to the shopping center you will need at least four or five hours to study all the goods on offer and finally decide what you really need.

There is a smaller market for manufactured goods – "Halytske Perekhrestia" (Halychyna Crossroads). It is located within the city limits in the eastern region. Its numerous shops, stalls and booths offer clothing, shoes, carpets,

SOUVENIRS:

"Elite" Gallery
26, Rynok Square
tel. 72-5053
10.00-19.00
It is the largest Ukraine souvenir shop. The store features furniture, plates and dishes from all over the world as well as toys, pictures and a wide assortment of decorative weapons.

"Gothic Hall" Art Gallery
6, Rynok Square
tel. 72-6091
10.00-18.00

Porokhova Vezha (Gun-Powder Tower)
4, Pidvalna Street

RAVLUK
Art Salon
15, Svobody Prospect (inside the Museum of Ethnography)
tel. 298-2595 *10.00-18.00*

Chess-board. V. Prysiazhniuk

Sugar-pot and a tea-cup. Yu. Moravsky

Born, but not created. E. Bilinska

From the art collection of the "Ravlyk" art showroom

furniture, and many other items to suit all tastes. This shopping center is less impressive, but is always overcrowded. To get to "Halytske Perekhrestia" catch a marshrutka. If you travel by car, you can leave it at a guarded parking area.

There are small, improvised markets everywhere, consisting of half a dozen booths and trading in ba-

Fancy cakes in the "Tsukernia" confectionary at 3, Staroevreiska Street

"Korolivstvo Vyn – Vyna Koroliv" (The Kingdom of Wines – Wines of Kings)
12, Rynok Square
tel. 297-5054
10.00-22.00

The store feature wines from countries all over the world, including Ukraine and France, as well as a wide assortment of coffee and tea. The store is housed in the 17th century mansion; the interior stonewalls are lined with shelves for wine-bottles. Major credit cards are accepted.

sic household items. These markets operate from early in the morning until late at night, daily. Food markets are located in nearly all of the districts of Lviv, the cheapest of them being the Pryvokzalny (By the Train Station) market. For sellers who travel here from the neighboring villages the location of the market is convenient – just across the road from the train station.

Another famous Lviv's market is the Central market, also known as Krwakiwsky, which rivals the Pivdenny. New shops and stalls are being built one upon another, as space is scarce and expensive. The market offers not only an extensive selection of food products, but also a wide assortment of clothing. Here you can buy practically everything, including pets – birds, mice, dogs, cats and fish as well as pets' trinkets.

The market is located within walking distance from the downtown area, close to the "Magnus" shopping center. People say, that despite all the guards, the market is often hit by a group of pickpockets, so watch your bags and purses. If you want to surprise someone with a lovely bouquet, go to the Halytsky market by the monument to Danyla of Halychyna. The market offers a wide assortment of flowers, from small bouquets to huge flower compositions. In the covered part of the market there is a phyto-design service, where qualified designers will make a beautiful bouquet in your presence and according to your tastes. However, this service is not necessarily cheap. But money is "nothing", compared to the joys a beautiful present will bring to your beloved.

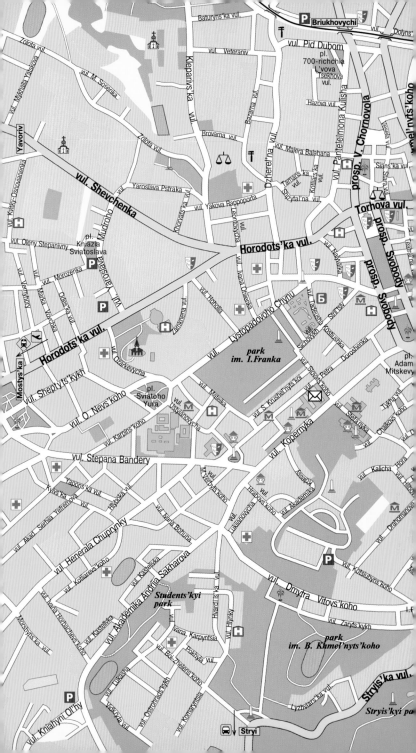

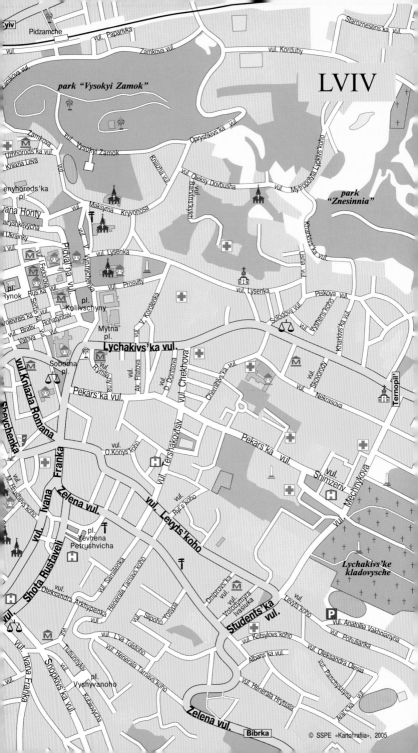

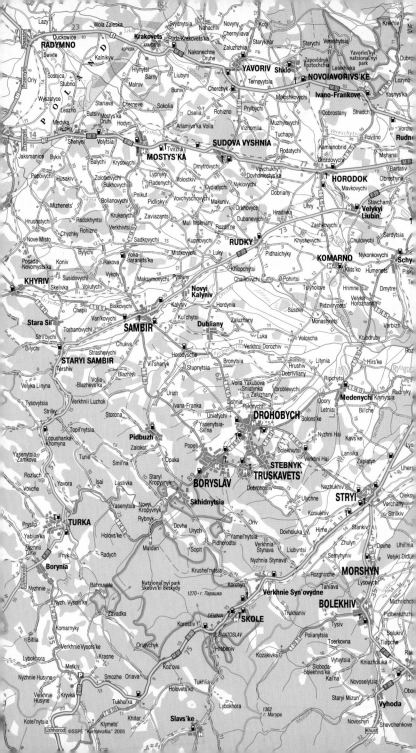